ABORTION AND THE LAW

ABORTION
and the LAW

EDITED BY DAVID T. SMITH
Associate Professor of Law
Western Reserve University

ESSAYS BY
    B. James George, Jr.
    Kenneth R. Niswander
    Kenneth J. Ryan
    Harold Rosen
    Robert F. Drinan
    Immanuel Jakobovits
    Vera Skalts and
      Magna Norgaard
    Henrik Hoffmeyer
    Leopold Breitenecker and
      Rudiger Breitenecker
    Robert E. Hall

Cleveland
THE PRESS OF WESTERN RESERVE UNIVERSITY
1967

Preface

There is perhaps no greater quandary presently facing society than determining the conditions, if in fact there are any such conditions, under which the human fetus may be destroyed within the womb, and preventing and perhaps punishing its destruction under any other conditions. Nature only is responsible for the spontaneous abortion, and nature needs no justification. Society, however, is still in the process of deciding whether therapeutic abortion exists (except as a phrase of those practicing it) and, if so, defining its boundaries. Consideration must also be given to measuring the complementary area of criminal abortion, discouraging its occurrence, and exacting penalty when it does occur.

These problems (for they are problems, rather than one, single, simple problem) do not belong to any solitary discipline. Although the medical profession is, of course, most directly concerned with therapeutic abortion, which, it may be noted, is the one variety over which organized society seems to be able to exert something approaching control, religion and law have significant roles in dealing with all aspects of abortion as arbiters of presumed or real standards of conduct. It is law, particularly, as the executor of the firmest standards society has, that has the ultimate concern with the rightness and wrongness of abortion. Law is the arena for the conflicting religious, medical, and philosophical values on the subject. Law hopefully will be the agency that determines priority between the religious and philosophical claims of the inviolability of the right to be born and the absolute proscription of the destruction of life, and the medical and sociological claims of the primacy of the mother's life and the necessity of preventing the birth of the defective individual or the individual whom circumstances of environment can only compel to lead a defective life.

It is under the aegis of law, then, that the discussion in these pages is presented. *Abortion and the Law* is a collection of essays presenting representative ideas from the three learned professions involved with the "abortion problem": religion, medicine and law. The objective of this volume is modest. These essays are published with the hope that through enlightened discussion and debate a higher level of understanding of some perplexing problems may be achieved, as a step toward their eventual resolution.

Without doubt criminal statutes and administrative sanctions regulating abortion practices have a direct relation to the attitudes of society in the matter. In the first section of the book, Professor B. James George, Jr., of the University of Michigan Law School, presents an analysis of the effect of current state abortion statutes. Professor George, a highly regarded American legal scholar, demonstrates their inadequacy in meeting present-day problems. He considers present law unnecessarily strict and is of the opinion that any enforcement of criminal statutes in their present form would be detrimental to the medical profession, although likely affording all the protection possible against untrained abortionists. Professor George believes that the scope of justifiable therapeutic abortion must be expanded. His conclusions are threefold. There must be: (1) procedural changes to minimize prosecutions in therapeutic abortion cases; (2) liberalized scope for therapeutic abortion as defined in the criminal code; and (3) liberalized abortion authorized by medical licensing statutes.

Following Professor George's legal views are the views of several American doctors. Doctors Kenneth R. Niswander and Kenneth J. Ryan are in agreement with the law professor that present abortion legislation ought to be liberalized to allow for termination of pregnancy if this is necessary to preserve the life or health of the mother. They are in disagreement, however, as to whether abortion ought to be allowed if the mother's life is not endangered but there is a chance that the child may be born abnormal. Dr. Niswander, Associate Professor of Obstetrics and Gynecology at the State University of New York at Buffalo, would extend therapeutic abortion further than would Dr. Ryan, Arthur H. Bill Professor of Obstetrics and Gynecology and Chairman of the Department of Obstetrics and Gynecology at Western Reserve University.

Dr. Harold Rosen, Associate Professor of Psychiatry at The Johns Hopkins University, believes that "current abortion practices and current abortion laws in the United States are incompatible with concepts of human dignity." In his opinion, women should be given the right to decide whether or not they will abort their own pregnancies. Yet he realizes that such a solution is not possible in today's social climate. As the best possible present alternative, he suggests higher standards of sexual conduct through education, establishment of consultation centers, extension of facilities providing advice on contraception, and a liberalization of present abortion laws.

Religious principles are discussed by the Reverend Robert F. Drinan, S.J., Dean and Professor of Family Law at the Boston College Law School, and Rabbi Dr. Immanuel Jakobovits, Rabbi of the Fifth Avenue Synagogue in New York City.

Father Drinan, Chairman of the Family Law Section of the American Bar Association, discusses the Roman Catholic position on abortion, "that an abortion is the taking of the life of an unborn but, nevertheless, a real human being." If one accepts the premise that a human fetus is, in effect, a human being, or at least is to be treated as such for legal purposes, then it follows that the fetus has concomitant rights, and the precept concerning the inviolability of the right of a human being to life has long been embedded in Anglo-American law. Father Drinan points out that the fetus has many legal rights akin to those of a human being. It is his conclusion that the fetus is a human being and that any laws designed to permit unrestrained abortion would necessitate a change in basic Anglo-American law which, at present, precludes the destruction of an innocent human being by other human beings to serve their own ends.

"Jewish Views on Abortion" is the title of Rabbi Jakobovits' discussion of the Orthodox Jewish position in contrast to the more liberal Conservative and Reform views. He indicates that the traditional stand is somewhere between the more rigid Catholic view and the more permissive Protestant approach. Rabbi Jakobovits, formerly Chief Rabbi of Ireland, explains that Jewish law permits an abortion only when the mother's life is placed in danger, apparently on a "self-defense theory" justification. Yet, with the exception of this one situation, Jewish law gives priority to the individual's claim to life. He concludes: "A classic statue by a supreme master is no less priceless for being made defective, even with an arm or a leg missing. The destruction of such a treasure can be warranted only by the superior worth of preserving a living human being."

The last section of the book is designed to provide insight into the experiences of other countries in attempting to solve their own abortion problems. This survey of such foreign law experience reveals that law in many foreign countries has responded more rapidly and more broadly than has American law to the conflicts the question of abortion has generated.

Vera Skalts and Magna Norgaard, officials at the Mothers Aid Center in Copenhagen, begin this section with a discussion of Danish abortion legislation, tracing its development in that country over the last three decades and documenting its present functioning. Danish abortion legislation emphasizes programs of help and guidance for pregnant women and has established Mothers Aid Centers for the fulfillment of a remedial program. Adding to the discussion of the Danish system is Dr. Henrik Hoffmeyer, until recently the chief of the psychiatric staff of the Mothers Aid Center in Copenhagen, and now Assistant Superintendent of the State Psychiatric Hospital there. Dr. Hoffmeyer discusses the medical practices that have developed under the Danish legislation, paying particular attention to the various types of medical indications which are considered in evaluating applications for abortions.

In an essay on the abortion laws and practices of the German-speaking countries of Europe, Dr. Leopold Breitenecker, Professor and Chairman of the Institute for Legal Medicine at the University of Vienna, and his son, Dr. Rudiger Breitenecker, Assistant Medical Examiner of the State of Maryland, trace the current and proposed code provisions concerning abortion in Austria, Germany, and Switzerland. The Breiteneckers observe that one basic attitude toward therapeutic abortion may be discerned in all of the German-speaking countries, and that is that abortion should be performed only as a last resort, after therapy has been unsuccessfully attempted.

This collection concludes with a Commentary by Dr. Robert E. Hall, Associate Professor of Obstetrics and Gynecology at the College of Physicians and Surgeons of Columbia University, and President of the Association for the Study of Abortion. He discusses the papers that precede his and presents his own views. He writes from a distinct perspective and with as much conviction as the general contributors. His evaluation, valuable in itself, also indicates that it is impossible to discuss a complex social issue such as abortion without finding strongly divergent opinions in educated men.

All essays except the Commentary were originally published in substantially the same form in Volume 17 of the *Western Reserve Law Review* under the auspices of the Western Reserve University School of Law. I specifically wish to acknowledge that the primary editorial responsibility for this book belongs to the Editorial Staff of the *Review* for the academic year 1965-66: David A. Basinski, Richard C. Binzley, Philip J. Campanella, Leslie J. Crocker, James D. Kendis, Associate Editors; Dale C. LaPorte, Managing Editor; and Robert L. Matia, Editor-in-Chief. Beyond all others at this institution, they made this book possible, and they are entitled to full co-editorship. I act for them only in a representative capacity.

I wish to thank the individual authors whose essays appear in this volume for their kind consent to the publication of their work in book form. Of course, the opinions expressed herein are theirs and do not necessarily represent the views of the editors.

DAVID T. SMITH

Western Reserve University
Cleveland, Ohio
October 1, 1966

Contents

ABORTION AND THE LAW

1

Current Abortion Laws: Proposals
and Movements for Reform

B. James George, Jr.

Laws regulating sexual behavior have no peer at stirring up intense emotional reaction; and when the element of life itself is involved, the reaction is compounded. Abortion is perhaps the only problem in which attitudes toward sexual activity itself and toward life and being are in seething turmoil. This turmoil is reflected in existing legislation and constitutes the controlling element whenever legislative or judicial changes in existing law are proposed. Although the specifics of the conflict are usually the details of statutory language, the real disagreement arises over which interests are of primary importance and how these interests are to be protected by law.

I. CONFLICTING INTERESTS AFFECTED BY ABORTION LEGISLATION

There appear to be four focal points for a discussion of the interests affected by abortion. The first of these is the fetus itself. Concern for the fetus is generally based upon one of two theories. One is that there is life in being from the time of fertilization of the ovum, and that this life, as any other life, is inviolate. The strongest adherence to this view is of course within the Roman Catholic faith, which condemns abortion under all circumstances;[1] but there

---

[1] Canon 2350, § 1. See 8 AUGUSTINE, COMMENTARY ON CANON LAW 397-402 (1931); 3 BOUSCAREN, CANON LAW DIGEST 669-70 (1954); 2 WOYWOD, PRACTI-

is also strong Protestant support for the idea.[2] The second theory is that the fate of the fetus, if it goes to term, should be taken into account. If the child will be born deformed, mentally defective, or otherwise incapable of living a normal life, or if it will be born into a highly detrimental environment, which cannot be reasonably compensated for,[3] it is preferable that its incipient life be nipped in the bud. This premise is likely to be an incidental argument to advocacy of liberalized abortion based on social need. Adoption of the first view of fetal life means rejection of all abortion, or any abortion unnecessary to save the life of the mother;[4] to adopt the second is usually to favor abortion in at least some situations.

The second focus is the pregnant woman. Most of the propositions advanced on this point are basically favorable to her position. The only exception is the argument that pregnancy is the result of intercourse, which itself is licit only within marriage and for procreation.[5] Therefore, if the woman becomes pregnant it is both her misfortune and her fulfillment of Divine mandate, and she must carry the child, whatever the consequences. This exception aside, most statements of policy are sympathetically inclined toward the pregnant woman, although these do not necessarily favor abortion. The most obvious point of concern is for her life, because there are medical indications that she may not survive a pregnancy,[6] because

---

CAL COMMENTARY ON THE CODE OF CANON LAW 545-46 (Smith rev. 1948). Also important is the Papal Encyclical of Pius XI, CASTI CONUBII (ON CHRISTIAN MARRIAGE) (Dec. 31, 1930), particularly the portion reprinted in ASSOCIATION OF AMERICAN LAW SCHOOLS, SELECTED ESSAYS ON FAMILY LAW 132, 149-51 (Sayre ed. 1950).

2 *E.g.*, THIELICKE, THE ETHICS OF SEX 226-47 (Doberstein trans. 1964).

3 Dahlberg, *Abortion*, in SEXUAL BEHAVIOR AND THE LAW 379, 389 (Slovenko ed. 1965).

4 THIELICKE, *op. cit. supra* note 2.

5 For an interpretation of Saint Augustine's view of sexual relations not too far from this, see BROMLEY, CATHOLICS AND BIRTH CONTROL 9-15 (1965).

6 With advances in medical knowledge, there are probably fewer instances now than formerly in which the woman is not likely to survive pregnancy. See Guttmacher, *Abortion Laws Make Hypocrites of Us All*, 4 NEW MEDICAL MATERIA 56 (1962); Hall, *Therapeutic Abortion, Sterilization, and Contraception*, 91 AMERICAN J. OBSTETRICS & GYNECOLOGY 518 (1965); Russell, *Therapeutic Abortions in California in 1950*, 60 WESTERN J. SURGERY 497 (1952). The hypothetical cases used in the survey reported in Packer & Gampell, *Therapeutic Abortion: A Problem in Law and Medi-*

she may commit suicide if she is not permitted to have an abortion,[7] or because she may die at the hands of an untrained abortionist if she is denied the facilities of a reputable hospital or clinic.[8] All of these factors tend to favor liberalized abortion laws. A further concern is for the pregnant woman's health, either physical or mental.[9] Most of these arguments support a broadening of abortion laws, except perhaps the one which asserts that the abortion works irreparable psychological harm to the woman,[10] and therefore should be restricted or prohibited.

A third focus is the family unit of which the pregnant woman is a part and into which the new baby will be born. At times the concern is for the freedom of the sexual partners to decide whether and when they will have children.[11] At other times the emphasis is placed on the economic well-being of the whole family, which may be adversely affected if the same resources must be stretched to care for another member, or on the mother's care of the living siblings, which might be detrimentally affected.[12] A person who

---

cine, 11 STAN. L. REV. 417, 431-44 (1959), include several in which the life of the mother might well be shortened if the pregnancy is carried to completion.

[7] This is not a particularly high statistical probability. Bolter, *The Psychiatrist's Role in Therapeutic Abortion: The Unwitting Accomplice*, 119 AMERICAN J. PSYCHIATRY 312 (1962); Rosenberg & Silver, *Suicide, Psychiatrists and Therapeutic Abortion*, 102 CALIF. MEDICINE 407 (1965).

[8] Calderone, *Illegal Abortion as a Public Health Problem*, 50 AMERICAN J. PUBLIC HEALTH 948 (1960); Culiner, *Some Medical Aspects of Abortion*, 10 J. FORENSIC MEDICINE 9, 12 (1963).

[9] In addition to the sources cited *supra* notes 6 and 7, see Kummer, *Post-Abortion Psychiatric Illiness — A Myth?*, 119 AMERICAN J. PSYCHIATRY 980 (1963); Moore & Randall, *Trends in Therapeutic Abortion: A Review of 137 Cases*, 63 AMERICAN J. OBSTETRICS & GYNECOLOGY 28, 38-40 (1952).

[10] The Kinsey study does not particularly bear this out. GEBHARD, POMEROY, MARTIN & CHRISTENSON, PREGNANCY, BIRTH AND ABORTION 208-11 (1958).

[11] "Is it not time . . . that we matured sufficiently as a people to assert once and for all that the sexual purposes of human beings and their reproductive consequences are not the business of the state, but rather free decisions to be made by husband and wife?" Rabbi Israel Margolies, quoted in Hall, *Thalidomide and Our Abortion Laws*, 6 COLUMBIA UNIVERSITY FORUM 10, 13 (1963). See also FLETCHER, MORALS AND MEDICINE 92-99 (Beacon Press ed. 1960).

[12] Only Japan appears to embody this specifically in its statute. Art. 3(5) of the Eugenic Protection Law (Law No. 156 of 1948; ROPPO ZENSHO 1778 [1965 ed.]) permits a discretionary abortion "if there are several children and the mother's health will be seriously impaired if she again delivers." Art. 14 permits a doctor empowered

emphasizes these factors is almost certain to favor liberal abortion, particularly that which is approved and administered through medical channels.

The final focus is on the needs of the community. Any of the concerns already listed can of course be restated in terms of social interests (*e.g.*, protection of the life of fetus or mother, protection of the health of the mother, or protection of the viable family unit), and all of them certainly have this dimension. But there are at least two other concerns evident. One is the factor of population control. Abortion is clearly one means of birth control, albeit a much less satisfactory method than mechanical or chemical means of contraception. In only one country, Japan, does the primary function of the statutes which liberalize abortion appear to be population limitation, and that is because of the traditional belief in Japan that contraceptives are not used by proper married couples;[13] the same attitudes do not apply to the practice of abortion. As contraception becomes more generally accepted among younger couples, as seems to be happening,[14] the population-control function of abortion in Japan will probably decline to about the same level as in Western countries. Some writers suggest that there may be an impermissible exercise of state power inherent in any legal use of abortion as a means of population control,[15] or that there may be too serious a decline in population to permit the state to survive.[16] In general, however, population control is only incidental to the practice of abortion and

by a district medical association to terminate a pregnancy, in his discretion and with the consent of both husband and wife, for several reasons, including the likelihood of substantial injury to the mother's health for either physical or economic reasons if the pregnancy continues to term. (Author's translation and paraphrase.) Some Scandinavian laws go almost this far. Clemmesen, *State of Legal Abortion in Denmark*, 112 AMERICAN J. PSYCHIATRY 662 (1956); Klintskog, *Survey of Legislation on Legal Abortion in Europe and North America*, 21 MEDICO-LEGAL J. 79 (1953).

13 See BEARDSLEY, HALL & WARD, VILLAGE JAPAN 335-36 (1959).

14 DORE, CITY LIFE IN JAPAN 205, 451 n.196 (1958).

15 See THIELICKE, *op. cit. supra* note 2, at 215-25.

16 This factor may account for the rescission of the law permitting easy abortion in the U.S.S.R. See WILLIAMS, THE SANCTITY OF LIFE AND THE CRIMINAL LAW 219-20, 224 (1957). This rescission in turn seems to have been modified, however. See GEBHARD, POMEROY, MARTIN & CHRISTENSON, *op. cit. supra* note 10, at 218.

is not a primary objective;[17] thus abortion poses no major threat either to private liberties or to population.

The other social factor is the freedom of the medical profession to handle the abortion problem as it would any other medical problem — free from arbitrary legal controls.[18] This argument is usually advanced in support of relaxed abortion laws.

While not necessarily providing a complete list of the various policy interests which are affected by and affect the coverage of the abortion statutes, this discussion summarizes the major policy arguments advanced in the debate over abortion legislation. How they are reflected in current legislation is another matter.

II. LEGAL REGULATION OF ABORTION PRACTICES

A. Criminal Statutes

(1) *Statutes Penalizing Abortion.*—Criminal statutes outlawing abortion are of relatively recent vintage;[19] there is so little common law authority covering abortion that it plays no significant role in evaluating the legality of abortion.[20] The statutes may be roughly classified as those which, in form, prohibit all abortions and those which permit some abortions under carefully limited circumstances.

The statutes in four states — Louisiana,[21] Massachusetts,[22] New

---

17 Sulloway, *The Legal and Political Aspects of Population Control in the United States*, 25 LAW & CONTEMP. PROB. 593, 597-98 (1960); Tietze, *The Current Status of Fertility Control*, 25 LAW & CONTEMP. PROB. 426, 442-44 (1960).

18 *Cf.* Hall, *supra* note 6, at 518, 522; Leavy & Kummer, *Criminal Abortion: Human Hardship and Unyielding Laws*, 35 SO. CAL. L. REV. 123, 138-39 (1962).

19 Quay, *Justifiable Abortion — Medical and Legal Foundations*, 49 GEO. L.J. 395, 431-38 (1961); WILLIAMS, *op. cit. supra* note 16, at 152-56.

20 Most common law cases reach only conduct which causes a miscarriage of a pregnant woman after the fetus has quickened. PERKINS, CRIMINAL LAW 101 (1957). This rules out most abortions, which must be performed within the first trimester of pregnancy if there is to be no serious danger to the pregnant woman.

21 LA. REV. STAT. § 14:87 (Supp. 1964). The only intent required is the intent to procure premature delivery of the embryo or fetus. There is internal inconsistency in Louisiana statutes, however, in that the statement of causes for revocation of a medical license, in LA. REV. STAT. § 37:1285 (1964), includes:

Procuring, aiding or abetting in procuring an abortion unless done for the relief of a woman whose life appears in peril after due consultation with another licensed physician. . . .

Jersey,[23] and Pennsylvania[24] — provide no specific exceptions to the general prohibition against abortion. In Massachusetts, however, the Supreme Judicial Court by judicial construction has added a limitation in favor of a physician who acts in the honest belief that the operation is necessary to save the woman from great peril to her life or health, if his judgement corresponds "with the average judgment of the doctors in the community in which he practices."[25] In New Jersey the Supreme Court apparently agreed that a doctor can act to save the life of the mother, although it did not agree that he could act merely to protect her health.[26] In New Hampshire and South Carolina, the statutes prohibiting attempted abortion[27] provide no exception, although the statutes penalizing actual abortion[28] do justify acts necessary to save the mother's life.[29] In North Carolina there is a similar discrepancy between the sections on abortion and those on using drugs or instruments with intent to produce a miscarriage.[30]

In all the other states, the legislatures have specifically provided for certain instances in which abortions may be legally performed.

If both are considered *in pari materia*, Louisiana law is in accord with the majority of states, as listed in note 31 *infra*.

[22] MASS. GEN. LAWS ANN. ch. 272, § 19 (1956).

[23] N.J. REV. STAT. § 2A:87-1 (1953). The statute reads "without lawful justification"; nothing in the license revocation statute, N.J. REV. STAT. § 45:9-16 (1963), provides any clue to what may be lawful justification. See, however, the case cited *infra* note 26.

[24] PA. STAT. ANN. tit. 18, § 4718 (1963). The only qualification is "unlawfully"; there is no elaboration in the licensing statute, PA. STAT. ANN. tit. 63, § 271 (1959). On Pennsylvania law, see Trout, *Therapeutic Abortion Laws Need Therapy*, 37 TEMP. L.Q. 172, 184-86 (1964).

[25] Commonwealth v. Brunelle, 341 Mass. 675, 677, 171 N.E.2d 850, 852 (1961). Apparently some consultation is required.

[26] State v. Brandenburg, 137 N.J.L. 124, 58 A.2d 709 (Sup. Ct. 1948).

[27] N.H. REV. STAT. ANN. § 585:12 (1955) (attempts to procure miscarriage); S.C. CODE § 16-83 (1962) (attempted abortion; the catchline "abortion or attempted abortion not resulting in death" is a misnomer).

[28] N.H. STAT. ANN. § 585:13 (1955) ("unless, by reason of some malformation or of difficult or protracted labor, it shall have been necessary, to preserve the life of the woman. . . ."); S.C. CODE § 16-82 (1962).

[29] The South Carolina statute justifies acts necessary to save the child's life as well.

[30] N.C. GEN. STAT. §§ 14.44, 14.45 (1953).

In forty-six states[31] and the District of Columbia,[32] an abortion is permissible if it is necessary to save the life of the mother. However, there is a wide variation in the details of how the permitted abortion is to be performed.

One difference is in the matter of who is to be allowed to perform an abortion done to save the pregnant woman's life. Thirty-one states[33] appear to permit anyone to perform the operation, but eleven require that it be done by a physician or surgeon.[34] The Missouri statute seems to favor the unlicensed person. There, an abortion is unlawful unless necessary to preserve the woman's life or that of her unborn child. However, if the person who performs the abor-

---

[31] ALA. CODE tit. 14, § 9 (1959); ALASKA STAT. § 11.15.060 (1962); ARIZ. REV. STAT. ANN. § 13-211 (1956); ARK. STAT. ANN. § 41-301 (1964); CAL. PEN. CODE § 274; COLO. REV. STAT. ANN. § 40-2-23 (1964); CONN. GEN. STAT. ANN. § 53-29 (1960); DEL. CODE ANN. tit. 11, § 301 (1953); FLA. STAT. ANN. §§ 782.10, 797.01 (1965); GA. CODE ANN. §§ 26-1101, -1103 (1953); HAWAII REV. LAWS §§ 309-3, -4 (1955); IDAHO CODE ANN. § 18-601 (1948); ILL. ANN. STAT. ch. 38, § 23-1 (Smith-Hurd 1964); IND. ANN. STAT. § 10-105 (1956); IOWA CODE ANN. § 701.1 (1950); KAN. GEN. STAT. ANN. § 31-410 (Supp. 1963) (this is a manslaughter statute; there is no abortion statute as such unless it be § 31-409); KY. REV. STAT. § 436.020 (1959); ME. REV. STAT. ANN. ch. 17, § 51 (1965); MD. ANN. CODE art. 27, § 3 (1957); MICH. STAT. ANN. § 28.204 (1962); MINN. STAT. ANN. § 617.18 (1964); MISS. CODE ANN. § 2223 (1957); MO. ANN. STAT. § 559.100 (1953); MONT. REV. CODES ANN. § 94-401 (1949); NEB. REV. STAT. §§ 28-404, -405 (1965); NEV. REV. STAT. § 201.120 (1963); N.H. REV. STAT. ANN. § 585:13 (1955) (abortion of quick child); N.M. STAT. ANN. §§ 40A-5-1, -3 (1964); N.Y. PEN. LAW §§ 80-81, N.Y. REV. PEN. LAW §§ 125.05, 125.40-.55; N.C. GEN. STAT. §§ 14-44 (1953) (and see the text accompanying note 30 supra); N.D. CENT. CODE § 12-25-01 (1943); OHIO REV. CODE § 2901.16; OKLA. STAT. ANN. tit. 21, § 861 (Supp. 1964); ORE. REV. STAT. § 163.060 (1964) (but see text accompanying notes 46 and 85 infra); R.I. GEN. LAWS ANN. § 11-3-1 (1957); S.C. CODE ANN. § 16-82 (1962) (see text accompanying notes 27-29 supra); S.D. CODE § 13.3101 (1939); TENN. CODE ANN. § 39-301 (1955); TEX. PEN. CODE ANN. art. 1191 (1961); UTAH CODE ANN. § 76-2-1 (1953); VT. STAT. ANN. tit. 13, § 101 (1959); VA. CODE ANN. § 18.1-62 (1960); WASH. REV. CODE § 9.02.010 (1956); W. VA. CODE ANN. § 5923 (1961); WIS. STAT. ANN. § 940.04 (1958); WYO. STAT. ANN. § 6-77 (1959).

[32] D.C. CODE ANN. § 22-201 (1961).

[33] Ala. (but see the license revocation statute, ALA. CODE tit. 46, § 270 (1959)), Alaska, Ariz., Conn., Del., Hawaii ("surgeon or other person"), Idaho, Ind., Iowa, Ky., Me., Mich., Minn., Mont., Neb., Nev., N.C., N.D., Ohio, Okla., R.I., S.C., S.D., Tenn., Tex., Utah, Vt., Va., Wash., W. Va., Wyo. The statutes are cited note 31 supra.

[34] D.C., Ark., Colo., Ill., Md., Miss., Mo., N.M., N.Y. (Revised Penal Law; the present statute, in effect through Aug. 31, 1967, is not so limited), Ore. (though the statutes are internally inconsistent; see the text accompanying notes 41-42 infra), Wis. The statutes are cited notes 31-32 supra.

tion "is not a duly licensed physician," the abortion is lawful if "the said act has been advised by a duly licensed physician to be necessary for such a purpose."[35]   Thus, while the licensed physician is held to a standard of "objective necessity" for abortions he performs, the unlicensed person apparently is justified in acting upon the advice of a licensed physician, whether or not the abortion is objectively necessary.

A second point of difference turns on whether necessity is to be determined on an objective, or strict liability, basis or whether the important thing is the good faith belief that necessity exists.   Thirty statutes, in form, support an interpretation that necessity is an objective element of the crime,[36] although five of them have been interpreted to include, as a defense, good faith belief of necessity despite their strict wording to the contrary.[37]   The harshness of these statutes is also modified to a degree if, as in some of these jurisdictions, the burden is on the state to prove the lack of necessity.[38]   In ten states and the District of Columbia,[39] however, the statutes make it clear that it is the motivation and not the objective necessity which constitutes the basis for the exception from coverage.   The new New York Revised Penal Law takes an intermediate position by requiring that the belief be "reasonable" when a duly licensed physician performs the abortion.[40]

---

35 MO. ANN. STAT. § 559.100 (1953).

36 Ala., Alaska, Ariz., Cal., Conn., Del., Idaho, Ill., Ind., Iowa, Ky., Md. (good faith belief no defense: Adams v. State, 200 Md. 133, 88 A.2d 556 (1951)), Me. (good faith belief no defense: State v. Rudman, 126 Me. 177, 136 Atl. 817 (1927)), Mich., Minn., Mo. (*but see* the text accompanying note 35 *supra*), Mont., Nev., N.Y. (*but see* Revised Penal Law), N.C., N.D. (good faith belief no defense: State v. Shortridge, 54 N.D. 779, 211 N.W. 336 (1926)), Okla., Ore., R.I., S.C., S.D., Utah, Vt., Wash., Wyo.   The statutes are cited note 31 *supra*.

37 Steed v. State, 27 Ala. App. 263, 170 So. 489 (1936) (*semble*) (a woman who consents to an abortion is an accomplice, unless she does so under an honest belief that the abortion is necessary to save her own life); People v. Ballard, 167 Cal. App. 2d 803, 335 P.2d 204 (1959); State v. Dunklebarger, 206 Iowa 971, 221 N.W. 592 (1928); Honnard v. People, 77 Ill. 481 (1875); State v. Elliott, 234 Ore. 522, 383 P.2d 382 (1963): "From the statute it is clear that there is to be established for conviction a specific intent to destroy the unborn child, and no intent to preserve the life of the mother." *Id.* at 528, 383 P.2d at 385.

38 See the text accompanying notes 123-28 *infra*.

39 Ark., Colo., Hawaii, Miss., N.M., Tenn., Tex., Va., W. Va.   The statutes are cited notes 31, 32 *supra*.

40 N.Y. REV. PEN. LAW § 125.05 (3).

A final point of difference is whether prior consultation with one or more physicians is necessary before a claim of justification can be made. In thirteen states[41] the abortion statute itself requires advice or consultation, while in three others[42] the same thing is accomplished through statutes governing revocation of licenses to practice medicine. In other states, the fact of consultation presumably has no legal relevance, although it probably determines whether any criminal prosecution is ever brought against a doctor who performs an abortion after regular hospital consultation.

A few states provide broader statements of justification. Seven states[43] permit abortions to preserve the life of the unborn child. This qualification probably has no functional effect other than to make it clear that induced labor is not a violation of the criminal law. Since a fetus has little chance of survival if it is born before the seventh month of gestation, and since most medically justified abortions are performed within the first trimester of pregnancy, the limitation has no very great impact on the abortion problem as such, and serves only to remove any hypothetical bars to legitimate obstetrics practice. A few statutes grant an even broader license to perform abortions when they are necessary to prevent serious and permanent bodily injury[44] or to protect the health of the mother.[45] Massachusetts, as indicated above,[46] has accomplished the same thing by judicial decision. This permits a more normal medical determi-

---

41 Ark. (§ 41-2224 only), Fla., Ga., Kan., Md., Miss., Mo. (non-physician only), Neb., Nev., N.M., Ohio, Tex., Wis. The statutes are cited note 31 *supra*. See also the consultation element in Commonwealth v. Brunelle, 341 Mass. 675, 171 N.E.2d 850 (1961).

42 ALA. CODE tit. 46, § 270 (Supp. 1963); LA. REV. STAT. ANN. § 37:1285 (1964); ORE. REV. STAT. §§ 677.190 (medical doctor), 681.140 (osteopath) (1963), and see State v. Buck, 200 Ore. 87, 262 P.2d 435 (1953).

43 Conn., Minn., Mo., Nev., N.Y. (but not under the *Revised Penal Law*), S.C., Wash. The statutes are cited note 31 *supra*.

44 Colo., N.M. The statutes are cited note 31 *supra*.

45 D.C., Ala. The statutes are cited notes 31, 32 *supra*. The Oregon licensing statute, note 42 *supra*, uses the phrase "health in peril." Whether the Maryland statute, cited note 31 *supra*, belongs in this category depends on what interpretation is placed on the clause "satisfied . . . that no other method will secure the safety of the mother." No Maryland decision provides an answer.

46 See text accompanying note 25 *supra*.

nation to be made than is the case when necessity to preserve the *life* of the woman is the requirement.

The old common law requirement that the child be quick before the abortion could be criminal has disappeared from the statute law. This is most commonly achieved by referring to pregnancy; thirty-two states utilize this approach.[47]   Five other states[48] specify that quickening does not matter, usually through the phrase "whether quick or not."   In the remaining states, this matter is resolved by the statutory provisions dealing with the attempt problem, discussed immediately below.   Whether the child is quick, however, determines the severity of the punishment in ten states.[49]

Additional problems arise when, despite the effort to abort the woman, no miscarriage is in fact brought about. This may be either because the abortion operation is bungled or because the woman is not pregnant.   Forty-one states eliminate the first problem by penalizing the use of instruments, the administration of drugs, or the use of any other means intended to produce an abortion;[50] Texas has a special attempt statute.[51]   If the woman is not pregnant, however, it might be argued that the crime was "impossible" to attempt.[52]   Several states eliminate this as a possibility either by covering the doing

---

[47] Ala., Alaska, Ariz., Colo. ("then being with child"), Del., Ga., Hawaii ("with child"), Idaho, Ill., Ind., Kan., Ky. ("at any time during the period of gestation"), La. (LA. REV. STAT. ANN. § 14:87 (1964), Md. ("at any period of pregnancy"), Mich., Miss., Mont., Neb., Nev., N.H., N.J., N.M., N.C., N.D., Okla., Ore., S.C. ("with child"), S.D., Tenn., Tex., Utah, Wyo. Except as otherwise indicated, the statutes are cited note 31 *supra.*

[48] Ark., Ky., Me., Neb., Tenn. The statutes are cited note 31 *supra.*

[49] Fla., Hawaii, Kan., N.H., N.Y., N.D., Okla., Pa. (PA. STAT. ANN. tit. 18, § 4719 (1963)), S.C., Wis. Except as otherwise indicated, the statutes are cited note 31 *supra.*

[50] D.C., Ala., Alaska, Ariz., Ark., Cal., Conn., Del., Fla. (FLA. STAT. ANN. § 797.01 (1965)), Ga., Idaho, Ill., Ind., Iowa (under an "attempt" catchline), Kan., Ky., La. (LA. REV. STAT. § 14:87 (1950)), Me., Mass. (MASS. GEN. LAWS ANN. ch. 272, § 19 (1956)) Mich., Miss., Mo., Mont., Neb., Nev., N.H. ("attempt" catchline), N.J. (N.J. REV. STAT. § 2A:87-1 (1951)), N.Y., N.C., N.D., Ohio, Ore., S.C., S.D., Tenn. ("attempt" catchline), Utah, Va., Wash., W. Va., Wyo. Except as otherwise indicated, the statutes are cited notes 31, 32 *supra.*

[51] TEX. PEN. CODE art. 1193 (1961) ("provided it be shown that such means were calculated to produce that result. . . .").

[52] See PERKINS, CRIMINAL LAW 489-94 (1957). *Cf.* Dupuy v. State, 204 Tenn. 624, 325 S.W.2d 238 (1959).

of the prohibited acts to "any woman,"[53] to a woman "whether pregnant or not,"[54] or to a woman believed by the defendant to be pregnant.[55] Several decisions support the idea that under statutes like these the victim need not be pregnant.[56] In two states, however, punishment varies according to whether or not a miscarriage is actually produced.[57]

(2) Statutes Prohibiting Killing an Unborn Quick Child.— Eight states make it a separate offense wilfully to kill an unborn quick child under circumstances in which, if the mother and not the fetus had been killed, it would have been murder.[58] The aim of these statutes is not entirely clear from either the language or the interpreting cases, but their target is probably the person who intends to cause a pregnant woman to abort without her consent and who uses physical violence against her body to achieve the purpose. Conceptually these statutes clearly accord independent personality to the fetus, for the killing of the fetus under these circumstances is called manslaughter, and the sections themselves are usually found with the other homicide sections.

(3) Statutes Penalizing Death of the Pregnant Woman Result-

---

[53] Ten jurisdictions use this language: D.C., Cal., Fla., Iowa, Mass. (MASS. GEN. LAWS ANN. ch. 272, § 19 (1956)), Ohio, Pa. (PA. STAT. ANN. tit. 18, § 4719 (1963)), Va., Wash., W. Va. Except as otherwise indicated, the statutes are cited notes 31, 32 *supra.* There is some internal inconsistency in the Virginia and West Virginia statutes which speak of "intent to destroy her unborn child," and the woman was pregnant in the reported cases, *e.g.*, Anderson v. Commonwealth, 190 Va. 665, 58 S.E.2d 72 (1950); Coffman v. Commonwealth, 188 Va. 553, 50 S.E.2d 431 (1948); but the exact question has not apparently been presented for decision.

[54] Ill. ("it shall not be necessary in order to commit abortion that such woman be pregnant . . ."), Mo., N.Y. (in both N.Y. Penal Law and N.Y. Rev. Penal Law). The statutes are cited note 31 *supra.*

[55] Ind. ("whom he supposes to be pregnant"), Ky. ("has reason to believe pregnant"), R.I. ("woman supposed by such person to be pregnant"), Vt. (same), Wyo. ("whom he supposes to be pregnant"). The statutes are cited note 31 *supra.*

[56] *E.g.*, People v. Kutz, 187 Cal. App. 2d 431, 9 Cal. Rep. 626 (1960); Urga v. State, 155 So. 2d 719 (Fla. App. 1963), *cert. denied*, 379 U.S. 829 (1964); Wyatt v. State, 77 Nev. 490, 367 P.2d 104 (1961).

[57] Ky., Me. The statutes are cited note 31 *supra.*

[58] ARK. STAT. ANN. § 41-2223 (1964); FLA. STAT. ANN. § 782.09 (1965); KAN. GEN. STAT. ANN. § 21-409 (1964); MICH. STAT. ANN. § 28.554 (1962); MISS. CODE ANN. § 2223 (1957); N.Y. PEN. LAW § 1050(2) (this is not carried as such into the Revised Penal Law); N.D. REV. CODE § 12-25-06 (1960) (*semble*); OKLA. STAT. tit. 21, § 713 (1961).

ing from Abortion.—If a pregnant woman dies as the result of an abortion, there should be little difficulty in establishing either (a) second degree murder, based either on felony murder in the context of commission of a felony not enumerated in the first-degree murder statute, the intentional infliction of great bodily injury, or the performance of an act with known dangerous consequences, or (b) manslaughter, based on gross criminal negligence.[59] Several states, however, meet the problem directly in the context of the abortion statutes by providing for increased punishment for abortion if the woman dies as a result of the abortion,[60] or by characterizing the death as either murder,[61] manslaughter,[62] or assault with intent to murder.[63]

(4) Statutes Penalizing the Woman Who Seeks an Abortion.— Where there is no specific statute governing this matter, a woman who seeks or submits to an abortion is usually not considered to be an accomplice to the abortion.[64] Rhode Island[65] and Vermont[66]

---

[59] Wechsler & Michael, *A Rationale of the Law of Homicide*, 37 COLUM. L. REV. 701, 702-23 (1937).

[60] Mass. (MASS. GEN. LAWS ANN. ch. 272, § 19 (1956)), N.J. (N.J. REV. STAT. § 2A:87-1 (1951)), N.M., R.I., S.C., (S.C. CODE § 16-82 (1962)), Vt. Except as otherwise indicated, the statutes are cited note 31 *supra.*

[61] D.C. (second-degree murder), Colo., Ky. (KY. REV. STAT. § 435.040 (1962)) ("murder or voluntary manslaughter, as the facts may justify"), Miss., N.H. (N.H. REV. STAT. ANN. § 585.14 (1955)) (second-degree murder), Tex. (TEX. PEN. CODE ANN. art. 1194 (1961)), W. Va. Except as otherwise cited, the statutory references are found at notes 31, 32 *supra.*

[62] Alaska, Fla., Kan. (KAN. GEN. STAT. ANN. § 21-410 (1964)) (manslaughter in the first degree), Mich., Mo., N.Y. (N.Y. REV. PEN. LAW § 125.20) (manslaughter in the first degree), N.D. (N.D. CENT. CODE § 12-25-02 (1960) (manslaughter in the first degree), Ore. Statutes not cited here are found in note 31 *supra.*

[63] GA. CODE ANN. § 26-1403 (1953).

[64] See, *e.g.*, Commonwealth v. Follansbee, 155 Mass. 274, 29 N.E. 471 (1892); Petition of Vickers, 371 Mich. 114, 123 N.W.2d 253 (1963) (woman cannot claim self-incrimination); *In re* Vince, 2 N.J. 443, 67 A.2d 141 (1949) (issue of self-incrimination; the woman is not incriminated unless the fetus has quickened, in which case the offense is against the fetus and not the mother); State v. Shaft, 166 N.C. 407, 81 S.E. 932 (1914); Smartt v. State, 112 Tenn. 539, 80 S.W. 586 (1904); Willingham v. State, 33 Tex. Crim. 98, 25 S.W. 424 (1894). *Contra*, Steed v. State, 27 Ala. App. 263, 170 So. 489 (1936); State v. McCoy, 52 Ohio St. 157, 39 N.E. 316 (1894). Iowa has held that even though she is not an accomplice, she can become guilty of a conspiracy by agreeing to have the operation performed upon herself. State v. Crofford, 133 Iowa 478, 110 N.W. 921 (1907). In that case she was not charged (she had died as a result of the abortion) and the theory was used to make her statements admis-

preserve this doctrine by statute, and the Reporter's Comment to the Louisiana statute[67] indicates that there is no intent to change the earlier Louisiana case law to the same effect.

In several states, however, the legislature has decreed that the woman commits a criminal act by soliciting or submitting to an abortion.[68]

These statutes seem to have two significant legal effects, and probably one practical effect as well. First, they are often accompanied by statutes requiring the woman's testimony to be corroborated,[69] or are held by judicial construction to require corroboration.[70] Second, the fact that the woman is deemed to have committed a criminal act means that the woman may claim privilege when she is summoned to testify for the state.[71] However, because of the importance, in many instances, of the woman's testimony in establishing the abortionist's guilt, legislatures have had to provide either that the privilege against self-incrimination does not apply[72] or that immunity against prosecution is conferred upon the

---

sible as a declaration in promotion of the common enterprise. The Pennsylvania Supreme Court has said that the woman cannot be guilty of conspiracy, since she is the victim. Commonwealth v. Fisher, 398 Pa. 237, 246, 157 A.2d 207, 212 (1960).

[65] R.I. GEN. LAWS ANN. § 11-3-1 (1957).

[66] VT. STAT. ANN. tit. 13, § 101 (1959).

[67] LA. REV. STAT. ANN. 14:87 (1964).

[68] ARIZ. REV. STAT. ANN. § 13-212 (1956); CAL. PEN. CODE § 275; CONN. GEN. STAT. ANN. § 53-30 (1960); IDAHO CODE ANN. § 18-602 (1948); IND. ANN. STAT. § 10-106 (1956); MINN. STAT. ANN. § 617.19 (1964); N.Y. PEN. LAW § 81, N. Y. REV. PEN. LAW §§ 125.50, .55; N.D. CENT. CODE § 12-25-04 (1960); OKLA. STAT. ANN. tit. 21, § 862 (1958); S.C. CODE ANN. § 16-84 (1962); S.D. CODE § 13.3102 (1939) (but see State v. Burlingame, 47 S.D. 332, 198 N.W. 824 (1924), which held the woman not to be an accomplice under the abortion statute itself, § 13.3101); UTAH CODE ANN. § 76-2-2 (1953) (but see State v. Cragun, 85 Utah 149, 38 P.2d 1071 (1934), in which it was held that this statute did not make her an accomplice under the main abortion statute, § 76-2-1); WASH. REV. CODE § 9.02.020 (1956); WIS. STAT. ANN. § 940.04 (1958); WYO. STAT. ANN. § 6-78 (1959).

[69] CAL. PEN. CODE § 1108; IDAHO CODE ANN. § 19-2115 (1948); MONT. REV. CODES ANN. § 94-7216 (1949); N.D. CENT. CODE § 12-25-07 (1960); S.C. CODE §§ 16-82, 16-83 (1962).

[70] People v. Peyser, 380 Ill. 404, 44 N.E.2d 58 (1942); State v. McCoy, 52 Ohio St. 157, 39 N.E. 316 (1894).

[71] See Commonwealth v. Fisher, 398 Pa. 237, 157 A.2d 207 (1960).

[72] MINN. STAT. ANN. § 617.21 (1964); WASH. REV. CODE § 9.02.040 (1956). Whether or not these statutes are consistent with the privilege against self-incrimination embodied in the respective state constitutions, they appear clearly to be unconstitutional

woman when she testifies for the state.[73] This brings the matter
around full circle to about where it would be if the woman were not
considered a criminal in the first place.[74]

In addition to these two legal problems created by criminal sanctions against the woman, there may be some slight practical advantage to the prosecution in being able to coerce cooperation from the
woman by threatening to prosecute her if she does not cooperate,
while promising her immunity from prosecution if she cooperates.

(5) *Statutes Penalizing Activity Which Facilitates Performance of Abortions.*—A medical doctor who performs an abortion
utilizes instruments which are part of the regular equipment of any
gynecologist or obstetrician.[75] It is not realistic to try to control
traffic in these instruments; in any event the very nature of the
channels which supply equipment to physicians and hospitals makes
it unlikely that a layman can casually purchase them. But self-in-
duced abortion is a major medical problem;[76] and the devices or
chemical substances used for "do-it-yourself" abortion are sufficiently
identified, and probably with few other modern uses, that some effort at controlling them can be made. In any event, legislatures
have fairly consistently tried to regulate their availability.

Advertising abortifacients is penalized in twenty-seven jurisdictions. In twenty-two of them there is a special statute covering the
abortifacient either alone or in the context of medicines preventing
conception, curing venereal disease, and the like,[77] while in six juris-

---

as a matter of fourteenth amendment due process under Malloy v. Hogan, 378 U. S. 1
(1964).

[73] NEV. REV. STAT. § 201.140 (1955); N.J. REV. STAT. § 2A:87-2 (1953); N.Y.
PEN. LAW § 81-a; OHIO REV. CODE § 2901.17; S.C. CODE ANN. 16-85 (1962).

[74] See, *e.g.,* Petition of Vickers, 371 Mich. 114, 123 N.W.2d 253 (1963); *In re*
Vince, 2 N.J. 443, 67 A.2d 141 (1949).

[75] BATES & ZAWADSKI, CRIMINAL ABORTION 38-39 (1964).

[76] *Id.* at 85-91.

[77] ARIZ. REV. STAT. ANN. § 13-213 (1956); CAL. BUS. & PROF. CODE § 601;
CONN. GEN. STAT. ANN. § 53-31 (1960); DEL. CODE ANN. tit. 11, § 302 (1953);
FLA. STAT. § 797.02 (1965); HAWAII REV. LAWS § 155-73 (1955) (outdoor advertising only); IDAHO CODE ANN. § 18-603 (1948); ILL. ANN. STAT. ch. 38, § 23-3
(Smith-Hurd 1964); IND. ANN. STAT. § 10-2806 (1956); LA. REV. STAT. ANN. §
14:88 (1964); ME. REV. STAT. ANN. ch. 17, § 53 (1965); MD. ANN. CODE art. 27, §
3 (1957); MASS. GEN. LAWS ANN. ch. 272, § 20 (1956); MICH. STAT. ANN. §

dictions this sort of advertising is prohibited in the context of obscenity.[78] Whether these statutes are in fact invoked at the local level is uncertain; there is a dearth of appellate opinion construing them.[79]

State legislation also frequently seeks to regulate the actual traffic in abortifacients by prohibiting their manufacture,[80] transportation,[81] distribution,[82] furnishing,[83] sale or keeping or exposing for sale,[84] giving away,[85] or lending.[86] Two states require that all sales

28.223 (1962); Mo. REV. STAT. § 563.300 (1953); PA. STAT. ANN. tit. 18, § 4525 (1963); R.I. GEN. LAWS ANN. § 11-3-4 (1957); S.D. CODE § 13.1508 (1939); VT. STAT. ANN. tit. 13, § 104 (1959); VA. CODE ANN. § 18.1-63 (1960); WIS. STAT. § 143.075 (1963); WYO. STAT. ANN. § 6-105 (1959).

[78] D.C. CODE ANN. § 22-2001 (1961); COLO. REV. STAT. ANN. § 40-9-17 (1964); IND. ANN. STAT. § 10-2804 (1956); MASS. GEN. LAWS ANN. ch. 272, § 21 (1956); MISS. CODE ANN. § 2289 (1957); N.Y. PEN. LAW § 1142. (The Revised Penal Law does not continue this and does not transfer it to N.Y. PUB. HEALTH LAW § 12-d.)

[79] The author has found only two cases: People v. McKean, 76 Cal. App. 114, 243 Pac. 898 (Dist. Ct. App. 1925); Commonwealth v. Hartford, 193 Mass. 464, 79 N.E. 784 (1907). See also Shapiro v. Board of Regents, 22 App. Div. 2d 243, 254 N.Y.S.2d 906 (1964), a license suspension case, which appears to stress the physician's misrepresentation or fraud rather than his offering to produce an abortion.

[80] MASS. GEN. LAWS ANN. ch. 272, § 21 (1956); MINN. STAT. ANN. § 617.20 (1964); NEV. REV. STAT. § 201.130 (1955); N.Y. REV. PEN. LAW § 125.60; WASH. REV. CODE § 9.02.030 (1956).

[81] IND. ANN. STAT. § 10-2804 (1956).

[82] ILL. ANN. STAT. ch. 38, § 23-2 (Smith-Hurd 1964) (other than to a licensed physician); LA. REV. STAT. ANN. § 14:88 (1951).

[83] TEX. PEN. CODE ANN. art. 1192 (1961) (treated as accomplice).

[84] D.C. CODE § 22-2001 (1961); COLO. REV. STAT. ANN. §§ 40-9-17 (obscenity statute), 66-3-65 (1964); ILL. REV. STAT. ANN. ch. 38, § 23-2 (Smith-Hurd 1964); IOWA CODE ANN. § 205.51 (1949) (other than on prescription); MD. ANN. CODE art. 27, § 3 (1957); MASS. GEN. LAWS ANN. ch. 272, § 21 (1956); MICH. STAT. ANN. § 28.205 (1962) (except on prescription); MINN. STAT. ANN. § 617.20 (1964); MISS. CODE ANN. § 2289 (1957); MO. REV. STAT. § 563.300 (1959); NEV. REV. STAT. § 201.130 (1955); R.I. GEN. LAWS ANN. § 11-3-4 (1957); VT. STAT. ANN. tit. 13, § 104 (1959); WASH. REV. CODE § 9.02.030 (1956).

[85] D.C. CODE § 22-2001 (1961) (obscenity statute); COLO. REV. STAT. ANN. § 40-9-17 (1964) (obscenity statute); IOWA CODE ANN. § 205.1 (1949); MASS. GEN. LAWS ANN. ch. 272, § 21 (1956); MINN. STAT. ANN. § 617.20 (1964); MISS. CODE ANN. § 2289 (1957) (obscenity statute); MO. REV. STAT. § 563.300 (1959); NEV. REV. STAT. § 201.130 (1955); VT. STAT. ANN. tit. 13, § 104 (1959); WASH. REV. CODE § 9.02.030 (1956).

[86] COLO. REV. STAT. ANN. § 40-9-17 (1964) (obscenity statute); MASS. GEN. LAWS ANN. ch. 272, § 21 (1956); MISS. CODE ANN. § 2289 (1957) (obscenity statute).

be on prescriptions which are then registered.[87]   Oregon penalizes
one who furnishes a place knowing that abortions, other than those
performed as therapeutic under the medical licensing statutes,[88] are
to be performed there.[89]   These statutes have produced no appellate litigation, but their fate may well be that of the federal
statutes which prohibit mailing, importing, and transporting various
kinds of "obscene" matter, including articles for "producing abortion."[90]   The limited case law interpreting these sections in the context of traffic in abortifacients[91] suggests that so long as the substance sold or transported has a legitimate medical or commercial
use it will not in fact be effectively covered by the legislation.

B.   Administrative Sanctions

Criminal penalties are blunt instruments with which to regulate
human conduct.   More efficient control can often be maintained
through granting and revoking special licenses to engage in a business or profession, or by imposing administrative fines or penalties;
many aspects of prostitution are controlled primarily in this way.[92]
In the context of abortion, however, only licensed medical personnel
and hospitals are subject to control through administrative action; a
layman or a person with medical training whose license to practice
has been revoked can be reached only through criminal prosecution.
This does not mean, however, that licensing statutes and license revocation proceedings are unimportant in the context of abortion control.   The claim that an abortion is justified because it is necessary
to preserve the life, or the life or health, of the pregnant woman on
whom it is performed is either limited in law to, or asserted in fact
by, licensed medical personnel.   Loss of a license to practice is such a
fearsome thing to a professional person that medical licensing

---

87 COLO. REV. STAT. ANN. 66-3-66 (1964); MICH. STAT. ANN. § 28.205 (1962).

88 ORE. REV. STAT. §§ 677.190 (physicians and surgeons), 681.140 (osteopaths)
(1961).

89 ORE. REV. STAT. § 465.110 (1961).

90 18 U.S.C. §§ 1461, 1462 (1964).

91 Youngs Rubber Corp. v. C. I. Lee & Co., 45 F.2d 103 (2d Cir. 1930) (dictum).

92 George, *Legal, Medical and Psychiatric Considerations in the Control of Prostitution,* 60 MICH. L. REV. 717, 736-42 (1962).

and license-revocation standards and procedures must be considered as prime controls on the availability of therapeutic abortions.

The overwhelming majority of jurisdictions authorize revocation of a medical doctor's license when he has committed or participated in the commission of a criminal abortion.[93] Two states provide for revocation of the license in the criminal provision itself.[94] In most of these states the reference is to "criminal abortion" or "unlawful abortion," which seems to mean that the administration of the criminal law determines the administration of the medical licensing law. But in three jurisdictions the licensing statute provides for therapeutic abortion procedures not referred to in the criminal statutes themselves.[95] There is no case law reconciling the possible inconsistency between the sections; but where the legislature has carefully spelled out in the licensing statute procedures for performing a therapeutic abortion, it appears unlikely that a court would hold that a doctor is guilty of a crime when he has complied with specific statutory requirements. The specific should still control the general.

Performance of a criminal abortion is not mentioned as a ground for revocation of a license in the laws of the remaining jurisdictions.

---

[93] ALA. CODE tit. 46, § 270 (Supp. 1963); ALASKA STAT. §§ 08.64.330, .380 (1962); ARIZ. REV. STAT. ANN. § 32-1401 (1956); ARK. STAT. ANN. § 72-613 (1957); CAL. BUS. & PROF. CODE § 2377; COLO. REV. STAT. ANN. § 91-1-17 (1964); DEL. CODE ANN. tit. 24, § 1741 (Supp. 1964); FLA. STAT. ANN. § 458.12 (1965); GA. CODE ANN. § 84-916 (Supp. 1963); IDAHO CODE ANN. § 54-1810 (1957); ILL. ANN. STAT. ch. 38, § 23-2 (Smith-Hurd 1964); IOWA CODE ANN. §§ 147.55, .56 (1949); KY. REV. STAT. § 311.595 (1963); LA. REV. STAT. ANN. § 37:1285 (1964); MD. ANN. CODE art. 43, § 145 (1957); MICH. COMP. LAWS § 338.53 (Supp. 1963); MINN. STAT. ANN. § 147.02 (1946); MISS. CODE ANN. § 8893.1 (Supp. 1964); NEB. REV. STAT. § 71-148 (1960); NEV. REV. STAT. §§ 630.030, .300 (1963); N.J. REV. STAT. § 45:9-16 (1963); N.M. STAT. ANN. § 67-5-9 (1961); N.Y. EDUC. LAW § 6514; N.C. GEN. STAT. § 90-14 (1965); N.D. CENT. CODE § 43-17-31 (1960); OKLA. STAT. ANN. tit. 59, § 509 (1963); ORE. REV. STAT. § 677.190 (1963); PA. STAT. ANN. tit. 63, § 410 (Supp. 1964); R.I. GEN. LAWS ANN. § 5-37-4 (Supp. 1964); S.D. CODE § 27.0311 (1939); TENN. CODE ANN. §§ 63-618, -619 (1955); TEX. REV. CIV. STAT., arts. 4505, 06 (1960); UTAH CODE ANN. § 58-12-18 (1963); VT. STAT. ANN. tit. 26, § 1398 (1959); VA. CODE ANN. §§ 54-316, -317 (1958); WASH. REV. CODE §§ 18.71.120, .140, 18.72.030 (1959); WIS. STAT. § 147.20 (1963); WYO. STAT. ANN. § 33-340 (1959).

[94] MISS. CODE ANN. § 2223 (1957) ("The license of any physician or nurse shall be automatically revoked upon conviction under the provisions of this act."); MO. REV. STAT. § 559.100 (1959).

[95] Ala., La., Ore., cited note 42 *supra*.

However, in these states there is statutory authorization for revocation based on conviction of a felony[96] or unprofessional conduct in general.[97] Since abortion has been declared a form of unprofessional conduct,[98] it is clear that there is no state in which a proven abortionist can continue to practice without his license being subject to revocation.

Many of the statutes cited above also list practitioners of the healing arts other than medical doctors. Some jurisdictions, however, have enacted special statutes covering osteopaths,[99] nurses,[100] midwives,[101] and other practitioners specially regulated by law.[102]

Most revocation proceedings are carried on as a purely administrative matter, and are subject to review as are administrative proceedings in general. Reviewing decisions usually examine only whether the administrative agency stayed within the proper limits of discretion in determining that charges were properly laid and substantiated and that disciplinary penalties were properly assessed.[103]

There are, however, two questionable aspects of the use of license revocation procedures against professional persons who are alleged to have committed criminal abortions. It has been held that license

---

[96] D.C. CODE ANN. § 2-131 (1961); CONN. GEN. STAT. ANN. § 20-45 (1960); IND. ANN. STAT. § 63-1306 (1962); ME. REV. STAT. ANN. ch. 32, § 3203 (1964); N.H. REV. STAT. ANN. § 329:17 (Supp. 1963); OHIO REV. CODE § 4731.22; S.C. CODE ANN. § 56-1368 (1962) (conviction of "illegal practice" is also included; this may well include abortion).

[97] MASS. GEN. LAWS ANN. ch. 112, § 61 (1965); MONT. REV. CODES ANN. § 66-1004 (1947). This phrase is also included in the various statutes cited notes 93, 96 *supra*.

[98] Lawrence v. Board of Registration, 239 Mass. 424, 132 N.E. 174 (1921); State *ex rel.* Sorenson v. Lake, 121 Neb. 331, 236 N.W. 762 (1931); *cf.* Moormeister v. Department of Registration, 76 Utah 146, 288 Pac. 900 (1930).

[99] ARIZ. REV. STAT. ANN. § 32-1854 (1956); ORE. REV. STAT. § 681.140 (1963).

[100] ARIZ. REV. STAT. ANN. § 32-1663 (1956); ILL. ANN. STAT. ch. 91, § 35-46 (Smith-Hurd 1956); CAL. BUS. & PROF. CODE §§ 2761 (nursing), 2878 (vocational nursing).

[101] COLO. REV. STAT. ANN. § 91-4-6 (1964); GA. CODE ANN. § 84-3312 (1955); ILL. ANN. STAT. ch. 91, § 16a (Smith-Hurd 1956).

[102] FLA. STAT. ANN. §§ 460.13 (chiropractor), 462.14 (naturopath) (1965); NEV. REV. STAT. § 634.010 (1963) (chiropractor); N.Y. EDUC. LAW § 6514 (physiotherapy); ORE. REV. STAT. §§ 684.100 (chiropractor), 685.110 (naturopath) (1963).

[103] See, *e.g.*, Application of Jones, 4 App. Div. 2d 994, 168 N.Y.S.2d 42 (1957).

revocation proceedings may be begun even though the statute of limitations has run on a criminal prosecution[104] or the defendant has been acquitted earlier in a criminal prosecution based on the same act.[105] Although, as a general matter, agencies which regulate professions should be able to remove the unfit from practice whatever may happen in specific criminal prosecutions or civil actions against them, it is doubtful that a properly performed abortion creates any medical problem as such or reflects adversely in any way on the level of professional skill of the person who performs it. Therefore, to revive an outlawed transaction or to proceed despite an acquittal looks as if the state is seeking again to exact retribution rather than that the medical profession is endeavoring to protect the public against an inept medical practitioner. In this context, it is interesting to note that at least two states have held that revocation of a license is a penalty which is outlawed by a statute conferring immunity in return for incriminating testimony.[106]

The other questionable aspect is that it has been held that disciplinary proceedings may be carried through even though a pending prosecution based on the same act of abortion has not reached final disposition.[107] This places the respondent in the disciplinary proceedings in a difficult position. He may assert, in good faith, the privilege against self-incrimination in the disciplinary proceeding[108] without being disciplined for his refusal to testify, but this may well mean that he will have his license revoked because he does not controvert the testimony adduced by the grievance committee. On the other hand, if he testifies in the license revocation matter, he may find that, in fact, he provides useful information to the state which can

---

104 Blumberg v. State Bd. of Medical Examiners, 96 N.J.L. 331, 115 Atl. 439 (Sup. Ct. 1922).

105 State v. Lewis, 164 Wis. 363, 159 N.W. 746 (1916); FLA. OPS. ATT'Y GEN. 505, 509 (1962).

106 Florida State Bd. of Architecture v. Seymour, 62 So. 2d 1 (Fla. Sup. Ct. 1952) (architect's license); Malouf v. Gully, 187 Miss. 331, 192 So. 2 (1939) (liquor license).

107 Florida State Bd. of Medical Examiners v. James, 158 So. 2d 574 (Fla. App. 1964).

108 *In re* Vaughan, 189 Cal. 491, 209 Pac. 353 (1922); Matter of Grae, 282 N.Y. 428, 26 N.E.2d 963 (1940); Matter of Levy, 255 N.Y. 223, 174 N.E. 461 (1931).

be used against him in the criminal prosecution as a party admission. Under circumstances like these, the revocation proceedings have little claim to priority over the criminal prosecution, and probably ought to be suspended until the outcome of the criminal case is clear.

C. Civil Responsibility

From time to time the question has arisen as to whether the woman on whom an abortion has been performed, or her representative if she is dead as a result of the operation, can sue civilly to recover damages. If a court were disposed to deny recovery, it might invoke the traditional concept that one cannot recover for injuries arising from activities in which he voluntarily engaged (*volenti non fit injuria*) or from activities which are by their nature "highly offensive and injurious to society,"[109] and are thus both immoral and illegal. If, on the other hand, it were predisposed toward permitting recovery, the court might hold that the state is wronged and, therefore, permit the recovery in indirect enforcement of its policies[110] or that consent to the abortion is not consent to bungled aftercare.[111]

As one might expect, the cases are not in agreement, although something of a consistent pattern develops if one ascertains (1) whether the action is against the doctor himself or the male friend of the woman plaintiff who both made her pregnant and put her in contact with the abortionist, (2) whether the woman is alive or dead, and (3) whether death, if it occurred, stemmed from the abortion itself or can be attributed to failure to provide adequate aftercare when the woman was in a position of peril in which emergency treatment by the physician might have been expected.

It seems unlikely that a woman will be permitted to maintain an action against someone who cooperated with her in making contact with the abortionist who performed the bungled operation.[112] This

---

109 Martin v. Morris, 163 Tenn. 186, 188, 42 S.W.2d 207 (1931).

110 Milliken v. Heddesheimer, 110 Ohio St. 381, 388, 390, 144 N.E. 264, 267 (1924).

111 See the cases cited note 117 *infra*.

112 Sayadoff v. Warda, 125 Cal. App. 2d 626, 271 P.2d 140 (1954); Goldnamer v. O'Brien, 98 Ky. 569, 33 S.W. 831 (1896); Bowlan v. Lunsford, 176 Okla. 115, 54 P.2d 666 (1936).

holding appears fair enough, since in fact the woman and her paramour were in trouble together and equally motivated to have the abortion performed. There is, therefore, no good legal or practical reason why he, rather than she, should bear the economic burden of the aftermath of the abortion (at least as long as joint tortfeasors in general cannot distribute losses among themselves) or why courts should lend their aid to support a subsequent falling out between the couple.

When the action is by the woman against the doctor, there is a split of authority over whether any suit may be maintained. Two cases deny the possibility of an inter vivos action no matter how careless the doctor may have been;[113] but other courts have permitted the woman to recover,[114] at least to the extent of the injuries actually suffered.[115]

If the woman has died from the abortion operation itself (as in a case in which an embolism results from the insertion of instruments into the uterus) or because of complications arising thereafter (like septicemia), it is possible that her survivors may commence a wrongful death action, chiefly against the doctor. Only two cases refuse to permit this action under these circumstances;[116] the rest of the cases permit recovery.[117] In these latter decisions it is evident that if the courts can point to wilful or negligent failure of the defendant doctor to provide adequate medical aftercare for the aborted woman whom he knows to be in need of qualified medical attention they find it easier to justify a recovery of damages than

---

[113] Nash v. Meyer, 54 Idaho 283, 31 P.2d 273 (1934); Martin v. Morris, 163 Tenn. 186, 42 S.W.2d 207 (1931).

[114] Richey v. Darling, 183 Kan. 642, 331 P.2d 281 (1958).

[115] Lembo v. Donnell, 117 Me. 143, 103 Atl. 11 (1918); Miller v. Bayer, 94 Wis. 123, 68 N.W. 869 (1896).

[116] Szadiwicz v. Cantor, 257 Mass. 518, 154 N.E. 251 (1926) (there is no indication in the report that the defendant was in fact a doctor; the negligence consisted of using "non-sterile instruments"); Miller v. Bennett, 190 Va. 162, 56 S.E.2d 217 (1949).

[117] Martin v. Hardesty, 91 Ind. App. 239, 163 N.E. 610 (1928); True v. Older, 227 Minn. 154, 34 N.W.2d 700 (1948); Milliken v. Heddesheimer, 110 Ohio St. 381, 144 N.E. 264 (1924); Henrie v. Griffith, 395 P.2d 809 (Okla. Sup. Ct. 1964); Androws v. Coulter, 163 Wash. 429, 1 P.2d 320 (1931) (only for negligent aftercare, not for the abortion itself).

they do if they must base recovery on the fact of the abortion itself. This showing of subsequent neglect can probably be made in many instances and is something which the plaintiff's attorney should keep in mind as he presents his medical evidence.

Though some reservation has been expressed about permitting civil recovery based on a bungled abortion under any circumstances whatever,[118] there seems to be no special reason to treat this situation any differently from any other malpractice situation.[119] If a doctor fails to provide the sort of aftercare which is expected according to generally accepted medical standards, he ought to be liable in damages whether or not the original operation or technique is an abortion. Holdings in line with the majority position not only promote higher standards of medical care in general, but serve also to support any efforts which may be made to put control over therapeutic abortions primarily in the hands of the medical profession itself.[120]

III. Trends and Techniques toward Liberalization

Whether one stops at this point and rests content with a description of present statutes and case law, or proceeds to suggest changes in the present law, depends on his basic attitude toward abortion and on the policy considerations which he chooses to stress. For some, the majority position, which permits abortion only to save the life of the mother, is the most liberal that one can safely take; no change is either needed or proper. For certain others, even an exception in favor of saving the mother's life is intolerable; there should be absolute prohibition of all abortions, whatever the circumstances. Roman Catholic writings come close to advocating this position.[121] However, for many in law, medicine, and society in general, the present law is unnecessarily strict and must be liberalized.

---

118 40 Ky. L.J. 410, 414-15 (1952).

119 *Cf.* Shartel & Plant, The Law of Medical Practice §§ 1-17, -18 (1959).

120 See the text accompanying notes 152-64 *infra.*

121 Quay, *Justifiable Abortion — Medical and Legal Foundations,* 49 Geo. L.J. 173, 233-35 (1960); 39 Notre Dame Law. 310, 313-14 (1964).

The author stands with the latter group; this, of course, dictates in large measure the form and content of what follows, and slants it considerably. The author prefers to make this clear, however, rather than hiding behind a façade of objective legal scholarship. Briefly stated, then, his premises are these: women cannot be deterred from having sexual relations, nor their partners motivated to join them in abstinence, by the fear that if they become pregnant they will have to carry a child to term, any more than they will be deterred by being denied contraceptives or anaesthesia during childbirth.[122] If they intend sexual relations, they will have them despite legal controls or unpleasant but remote physical consequences. To put it another way, proscribing abortion does not promote celibacy, and liberalizing abortion does not promote promiscuity. Among women, married and unmarried, who become pregnant, a certain number will wish to be aborted. Those with money and connections will either find a compliant practitioner who will terminate the pregnancy safely, though not cheaply, or purchase a ticket to a country in which an abortion can be performed legally. For those without the means or the connections necessary to secure an abortion in that way, the choice is less satisfactory. The mother may have to carry the child to term; if so, it may not be born into a satisfactory home or may not be adoptable. She may have to find an unqualified quack who butchers his patients, or she may have to try to induce an abortion herself. Either of the latter routes poses an abnormally high statistical possibility of serious bodily injury, sterility, or death. Though the community may encourage exhaustion of all other alternatives before allowing abortion, it should facilitate performance of abortions on women in aseptic clinics rather than in motels or filthy tenement rooms if it is in fact concerned about the life and health of women who do not want to carry their pregnancies to term. To accomplish this the present criminal law must be modified. There are three ways in which this might be achieved: (1) adoption of procedural changes which make it difficult to convict doctors who perform, in a hospital or clinic, dilitation and curettage or other acceptable medical techniques to terminate a preg-

---

[122] WILLIAMS, THE SANCTITY OF LIFE AND THE CRIMINAL LAW 61-63 (1957).

nancy; (2) embodiment in the criminal code provisions of much broadened categories of therapeutic abortions, the performance of which is exempted from criminal penalties; or (3) complete elimination of criminal law regulation of therapeutic abortions and, in its place, establishment of regulation by the medical profession itself.

A.   Procedural Changes to Minimize Prosecutions
   in Therapeutic Abortion Cases

It is easy to equate the fact of legislation with the fact of control or, to state it somewhat differently, to assume that by the act of legislating the problem is solved.   But in many circumstances it is not so much the content of the statute which concludes the case as it is the matter of who has the burden of proof. Therefore, enforcement of inherited legal standards to prevent the gradual development of medical and hospital practice can either be promoted or retarded by the rules, in effect in the jurisdiction, establishing burden of proof or requiring a special quantum of proof.

Whether the burden of disproving medical necessity, as defined in the particular state statute, is on the state depends upon whether that element is considered an exception to the statute or a proviso. One state, Michigan,[123] relieves the prosecution by statute from any obligation to disprove necessity, and Illinois uses the terminology of affirmative defense concerning the issue of necessity.[124] Otherwise the matter has been left to judicial interpretation. Only two courts have stated clearly and directly that the burden of proving necessity is on the defendant;[125] these cases are overbalanced by decisions in fifteen other states which require the state to plead and prove the want of necessity.[126]

---

[123] MICH. STAT. ANN. § 28.204 (1962).

[124] ILL. ANN. STAT. ch. 38, § 23-1(b) (Smith-Hurd 1963).

[125] Williams v. United States, 138 F.2d 81 (D.C. Cir. 1943); Fitch v. People, 45 Colo. 298, 100 Pac. 1132 (1909).

[126] People v. Gallardo, 41 Cal. 2d 57, 257 P.2d 29 (1953); State v. Lee, 69 Conn. 186, 37 Atl. 75 (1897); State v. Brown, 26 Del. 499, 85 Atl. 797 (1912); Holloway v. State, 90 Ga. App. 86, 82 S.E.2d 235 (1954); State v. Dunklebarger, 206 Iowa 971, 221 N.W. 592 (1928); Commonwealth v. Stone, 300 Mass. 160, 14 N.E.2d 158 (1938); Ladnier v. State, 155 Miss. 348, 124 So. 432 (1929); State v. DeGroat, 259 Mo. 364, 168 S.W. 702 (1914); People v. Harrison, 40 Misc. 2d 601, 243 N.Y.S.2d

If one's purpose is to encourage medical personnel in licensed hospitals and clinics to develop their own concepts of what "life" or "life and health" mean, the burden of proving non-necessity must remain with the state. A zealous prosecuting attorney would then have to assume the obligation of establishing that the collective medical judgment of those who authorized the abortion to be performed in the hospital or clinic was itself not medically sound, an almost impossible burden for him to discharge. Several medical journals contain descriptions of abortions which might not have met the statutory tests for legality if they were tested in the courtroom but which were approved openly in hospitals;[127] no prosecutions were brought, which suggests that prosecutors are not anxious to lock horns with the organized medical profession. Conversely, if one's aim is to discourage activity by the medical profession, one should place the burden of proving necessity on the doctor. He could probably do so in many instances, but the fear of being called upon to prove medical necessity (which contrasts strongly with the attitude of "let the prosecuting attorney impeach the validity of our medical judgment if he wishes") is likely to encourage the timid to shun all abortions.[128] Liberalization requires that the burden of proving non-necessity remain with the state.

Mention has already been made of statutes and cases which require corroboration of the aborted woman's testimony in order for

432 (Sup. Ct. 1963); Moody v. State, 17 Ohio St. 110 (1866); State v. Elliott, 206 Ore. 82, 289 P.2d 1075 (1955); State v. St. Angelo, 72 R.I. 412, 52 A.2d 513 (1947); State v. Wells, 35 Utah 400, 100 Pac. 681 (1909); State v. Montifoire, 95 Vt. 508, 116 Atl. 77 (1921); State v. Bates, 52 Wash. 2d 207, 324 P.2d 810 (1958). The Connecticut, Oregon, and Washington decisions, however, hold that the state carries the burden by proving that the woman was healthy immediately prior to the time the abortion was performed.

127 Henker, *Abortion and Sterilization From Psychiatric and Medico-Legal Viewpoints*, 57 ARK. MEDICAL SOC'Y J. 368 (1961); May, *Therapeutic Abortion in North Carolina*, 23 N.C. MEDICAL J. 547 (1962); Moore & Randall, *Trends in Therapeutic Abortion*, 63 AMERICAN J. OBSTETRICS & GYNEOLOGY 28 (1952); Russell, *Therapeutic Abortions in California in 1950*, 60 WESTERN J. OF SURGERY, OBSTETRICS & GYNECOLOGY 497 (1952).

128 *Cf.* the cowed attitude of the medical profession toward administering narcotics to hold an addict at the level of his addiction while he is being treated. LINDESMITH, THE ADDICT AND THE LAW 246-52, 254-66 (1965); RUBIN, PSYCHIATRY AND CRIMINAL LAW 122-31 (1965). The reason is primarily the vigorous crusading and browbeating attitude of federal narcotics authorities.

there to be a conviction. It might be contended that this requirement be extended in order to encourage the performance of abortions by licensed doctors in hospitals. This is not likely to be the
result achieved, however. If an abortion is performed after due consultation, hospital records are almost certain to contain corroborating
documentation. It is also doubtful that the doctors who were consulted in advance of the abortion could refuse to testify, unless possibly on the basis of the privilege against self-incrimination, by
asserting that they might be charged as conspirators with the doctor
who in fact performed the abortion. The only type of defendant
who is likely to profit from the corroboration requirement is the
clandestine abortionist, and it is doubtful that anyone particularly
wants to encourage him in his practice.

B.   Liberalized Scope for Therapeutic Abortion as Defined in the Criminal Code

A second means of liberalizing the abortion law is to broaden
the scope of justifiable abortions in the criminal code itself. Mention has already been made[129] of a few statutes which permit abortions intended to preserve the health of the mother. To include this
alternative is certainly to encourage the performance of therapeutic
abortions in hospitals by licensed physicians; all hospital abortions
are in fact performed for health reasons. Whether the term "health"
includes psychic health is partly a medical and partly a legal issue.
It seems clear that many therapeutic abortions now performed are
motivated more by mental health considerations than by strictly
physiological considerations, although, of course, the two cannot be
totally separated.[130] Whether, however, a court will construe the
statutory term "health" to include mental health is somewhat less
clear. About all one can cite in favor of a broad interpretation is a
portion of the charge in the famous case of *Rex v. Bourne*[131] and one

---

129 See text accompanying notes 44-46 *supra*.

130 See Bolter, *The Psychiatrist's Role in Therapeutic Abortion: The Unwitting
Accomplice*, 119 AMERICAN J. OF PSYCHIATRY 312 (1962); Rosenberg & Silver, *supra*
note 7 at 407; Rosenberg & Silver, *Psychiatric Therapeutic Abortion* (abstract), 33
MODERN MEDICINE 256 (1965).

131 [1939] 1 K.B. 687, 694; Hudson v. Foster, [1939] 3 All E.R. 615, 619 ("that
the probable consequences of the continuance will be to make the woman a physical or
mental wreck").

Iowa decision[132] in which the court described the aborted woman as being in a distraught condition, although in fact it decided the case on a point of statutory construction. Unless the statute refers specifically to mental health, it is not at all clear that the word "health" will be extended by judicial construction beyond "physical health."[133]

No American statute authorizes an abortion to be performed on eugenic grounds, *i.e.*, based on the possibility that the fetus may be born in a mentally or physically abnormal condition. No lawful relief is, therefore, available to a woman who has contracted rubella[134] during the first trimester of pregnancy or who has taken thalidomide or other drugs which may produce deformed offspring.[135]

Nor do American statutes take into account either the psychological damage which may result to a woman if she is forced to carry to term a child conceived through an act of rape (and the possible non-adoptibility of the resulting child) or the fairly high possibility that a child born of an incestuous relationship may be mentally retarded.[136] If no relief is authorized in cases like these, it follows, of course, that there is no authorization of abortions intended to prevent either economic hardship to the family unit into which the child will be born or diminution in the level of maternal care to be given all of the children in the family. And there is not the slightest legal sanction for an abortion based on the convenience of the mother, whatever the personal considerations may be.

The drafters of the American Law Institute Model Penal Code moved strongly to expand the scope of justifiable abortion beyond its common form in the United States. Section 230.3[137] defines

---

[132] State v. Dunklebarger, 206 Iowa 971, 221 N.W. 592 (1928). The doctor apparently acted because the woman "was in a highly nervous condition, and was threatening to kill herself, and was complaining of much pain." *Id.* at 972, 221 N.W. at 593.

[133] If, however, the abortion is performed in a hospital after appropriate consultations, the chances of a prosecution are minimal. See the materials cited note 127 *supra*.

[134] Commonly known as German measles.

[135] The statutes cited at note 43 *supra* do not cover this situation, since abortion in eugenic cases is intended to destroy, not preserve, the fetal life.

[136] *Taboos Against Incest Prove Well-Founded*, 6 MEDICAL WORLD NEWS 94 (1965) reporting double the normal incidence of mental retardation anticipated on the basis of classical genetic theory.

[137] MODEL PENAL CODE (Proposed Official Draft 1962).

justifiable abortion to be termination of a pregnancy by a licensed physician on any of three grounds: (1) that continuance of the pregnancy would gravely impair the physical and mental health of the mother (this builds on the exception in the present Alabama and District of Columbia statutes, and makes it clear that psychic considerations can justify an abortion); (2) that the child would be born with a grave physical or mental defect (this embodies eugenic considerations not hitherto known in American law); and (3) that the pregnancy resulted from rape, incest, or felonious intercourse, defined to include illicit intercourse with a girl below the age of sixteen. (This exception combines considerations of mental and physical welfare of the pregnant woman with humanitarian considerations. It is intended to embody considerations set out in the *Bourne* case, and to prevent repetition of a case in which the housewife victim of a rapist conceived and was forced to carry the child to term because she could not obtain a lawful abortion.)[138]

However persuasive the arguments in support of the Model Penal Code provisions may be to those who are pre-disposed to favor liberalized abortion, they have so far been repudiated by state legislatures to which they have been submitted. The drafters of the proposed Illinois Criminal Code advocated, like the proponents of the Model Penal Code, that justifiable abortion include abortions "medically advisable because continuance of the pregnancy would endanger the life or gravely impair the health of the pregnant woman" or because the fetus would be born with a "grave and irremediable physical or mental defect" and abortions of women pregnant through "forcible rape or aggravated incest."[139] The legislature, however, rejected the draft and limited the exception for justifiable abortion to operations necessary to preserve the woman's life.[140] The authors of the Minnesota Criminal Code proposed that rape victims be permitted an abortion if a complaint has been filed with prosecut-

---

[138] MODEL PENAL CODE § 207.11, comment pp. 154-55 (Tent. Draft No. 9, 1959).

[139] PROPOSED ILL. REV. CRIM. CODE § 32-1 (Burdette-Smith Co. ed. 1961).

[140] *Ibid.* The revised Committee Comments state: "Due to the opposition, and criticism of the entire Code, encountered because of the inclusion of these affirmative defenses to abortion, the Joint Committee agreed to their deletion and to the draft of the section in its present adopted form."

ing authorities, and that therapeutic abortions be permitted, if performed on the advice of two licensed physicians, "to save the life of the mother, or to avoid grave impairment of the physical or mental condition of the mother or to prevent the birth of a child with grave physical or mental defects."[141] The legislature struck out the whole chapter on sex crimes, including abortion, and preserved the existing statute which limits lawful abortions to those necessary to preserve the life of the mother.[142] In New York the matter did not progress even this far. The proposed penal law was drawn to include as justification only the necessity "to preserve the life of the female or of an unborn child with which she is pregnant,"[143] though the revision commission suggested that it still had the question of a more liberal provision under advisement.[144] When the Revised Penal Code was adopted, however, the only justifying factor retained was necessity to save the life of the mother.[145] Efforts at liberalization in New Hampshire are also reported to have failed in the legislature.[146]

There are, however, two other ways in which the lot of the medical profession may be improved even though no liberalization of grounds for abortion is achieved. One is to make it explicit that the doctor's belief in the necessity for the abortion is sufficient to legitimize the abortion, even though after the fact it might appear that from an objective point of view there was no necessity. This is now the position taken in some of the states[147]—a position embodied in the Model Penal Code as well.[148] Mention has already been made of the qualification in the New York Revised Penal Law that the belief be reasonable;[149] the Model Penal Code requires certificates

---

[141] PROPOSED MINN. STAT. ANN. § 609.345 (West ed. 1963).

[142] MINN. STAT. ANN. § 617.18 (1964).

[143] PROPOSED N.Y. PENAL LAW § 130.05 (Thompson ed. 1964).

[144] PROPOSED N.Y. PENAL LAW § 130.05 (Thompson ed. 1964) (Commission Staff Notes).

[145] N.Y. REV. PENAL LAW § 125.05 (McKinney 1965) (effective Sept. 1, 1967).

[146] Ridgeway, *One Million Abortions*, New Republic, Feb. 9, 1963, p. 14.

[147] See the text accompanying notes 36-42 *supra*.

[148] MODEL PENAL CODE § 230.3(2) (Proposed Official Draft 1962).

[149] N.Y. REV. PENAL LAW § 125.05(3) (McKinney 1965) (effective Sept. 1, 1967).

from two physicians and creates a presumption that the abortion was unjustified unless the certificates are produced.[150] Either device is preferable to a strict liability concept based on objective necessity.

The other method to improve the lot of the medical profession is to set out, in the criminal code itself, procedures which a doctor may follow to gain legal standing to commit a therapeutic abortion. Some states now permit abortions to be performed if there is advice or certification by physicians that an abortion is necessary.[151] These provisions, however, do not give much assistance to doctors in determining what procedures are appropriate in giving advice to the physician or other person who performs the abortion; the qualifying term "reputable" in the Mississippi statute adds another complicating factor. A more detailed provision establishing basic procedural norms is desirable. The chief question is whether detailed procedural provisions belong in the criminal code[152] or whether they should be placed among the statutes regulating the medical profession and hospitals. The author believes the latter preferable, in part because it is better not to clutter up the criminal code with details which can just as easily be incorporated by reference from other statutes, and in part because changes in regulations are more easily made when the legislature is asked by the profession or group affected by a proposed change to amend the laws relating to that profession or group than when it is the criminal code itself which is sought to be changed. However, any of the detailed provisions discussed in the section which follows can as well be included in the criminal code as in regulatory statutes.

---

150 MODEL PENAL CODE § 230.3(3) (Proposed Official Draft 1962).

151 FLA. STAT. ANN. § 782.10 (1965) ("advised by two physicians to be necessary"); GA. CODE ANN. § 26-1101 (1953) ("advised by two physicians to be necessary"); KAN. GEN. STAT. ANN. § 21-410 (Supp. 1963) ("advised by a physician to be necessary"); MISS. CODE ANN. § 2223 (1957) ("upon the prior advice, in writing, of two reputable licensed physicians"); MO. REV. STAT. § 559.100 (1953) ("advised by a duly licensed physician to be necessary for such a purpose" if defendant not a physician; see the text accompanying note 35 *supra*); NEB. REV. STAT. §§ 28-404, 28-405 (1965) ("advised by two physicians to be necessary"); N.H. REV. STAT. ANN. § 585:13 (1955) (quick child only; "advised by two physicians to be necessary"); N.M. STAT. ANN. § 40A-5-3 (1964) ("two [2] physicians who are licensed to practice in this state, in consultation, deem it necessary"); OHIO REV. CODE § 2901.16 ("advised by two physicians to be necessary").

152 An illustration is the legislation proposed in Leavy & Kummer, *Criminal Abortion: Human Hardship and Unyielding Laws*, 35 SO. CAL. L. REV. 123, 146-48 (1962).

C. Liberalized Abortion Authorized by Medical Licensing Statutes

If in fact it is the medical profession, or segments of it, that wishes liberalization of abortion laws, so that decisions to perform dilatation and curettage or other medical operations can be made as any other medical determination might be, it seems appropriate to make the primary legal context within which those decisions are to be made that of the statutes regulating doctors and hospitals. On the face of it, this has certain advantages. Interpretation of statutory terms can be made within the framework of civil provisions affecting the medical profession rather than the penal concepts of the criminal code; this might lead to primacy of medical considerations rather than penal. Furthermore, pressures from within the medical profession for change can be exerted along familiar channels to reach officials who are themselves members of that profession. In theory, this should work changes more efficiently than if the same energies are directed through non-existent or unfamiliar paths toward laymen in the legislature. And, perhaps, it makes it crystal clear that claims of medical necessity cannot be advanced in criminal prosecutions by those who are not in the licensed group.

There are at least two ways in which this change of context can be accomplished — one which has been tried and one which has not. The first is to incorporate, either in the provisions governing revocation of medical licenses or as a part of the statutes regulating hospital practices in general, specific requirements for the performance of therapeutic abortions. There are three states which have experimented with this first alternative by setting up standards for consultation which can be asserted as a defense to license revocation. Two of them, Alabama and Louisiana, require only consultation, without providing any further procedural details.[153] Oregon is the one state which to date has sought to provide further guidelines. Medi-

---

153 ALA. CODE tit. 46, § 270 (Supp. 1963) ("before resorting to any of said methods of saving a woman's life the attending physician shall use diligence to obtain the advice and help of one or more consulting physicians"; there is internal inconsistency with the abortion statute itself, ALA. CODE tit. 14, § 9 (1959), which legitimates abortion done to preserve the woman's "life or health." Piecemeal amendment may be the practical cause.) LA. REV. STAT. ANN. § 37:1285 (1964) ("after due consultation with another licensed physician").

cal doctors[154] and osteopaths[155] are given a standard — "health . . . in peril because of her pregnant condition" — by which to make their determinations and are also given procedures of consultation and recording by which the basis for their decision can be ascertained and perpetuated.[156] In confirmation of the monopoly of lawful abortions by medical doctors and osteopaths, chiropractors[157] and naturopaths[158] are specifically forbidden to perform abortions under any circumstances.

No state has yet tried the second alternative, which is to place the requirements for performance of a therapeutic abortion in the affirmative context of statutes regulating hospitals rather than in the negative context of license regulation. One state, California, has experienced attempts to do this, though so far without success. An ambitious regulatory statute, based on recommendations of two law school professors,[159] was introduced in the California legislature to establish minimum procedural requirements for the performance of therapeutic abortions.[160] The bill sought to permit hospital "therapeutic abortion committees" of five members or more, to include at least two specialists in obstetrics, one in internal medicine and one in psychiatry. Each committee was to be certified by the

---

154 ORE. REV. STAT. § 677.190 (1963).

155 ORE. REV. STAT. § 681.140 (1963).

156 ORE. REV. STAT. § 677.190 (1963). A medical doctor is required to have "due consultation" with "another duly licensed medical physician and surgeon who is not an associate or relative of the physician or surgeon and who agrees that an abortion is necessary." ORE. REV. STAT. § 681.140 (1963). An osteopath is permitted consultation with "another duly licensed osteopathic or medical physician and surgeon who is not an associate or relative." In either case, "the record of this consultation shall be in writing and shall be maintained in the hospital where the consultation occurred or in the offices of all the physicians and surgeons participating in the consultation for a period of at least three years after the date of the abortion."

157 ORE. REV. STAT. § 684.100 (1963).

158 ORE. REV. STAT. § 685.110 (1963).

159 Packer & Gampell, *Therapeutic Abortions: A Problem in Law and Medicine*, 11 STAN. L. REV. 417, 449-55 (1959).

160 It also proposed elimination from Penal Code coverage of any abortion performed under the therapeutic abortion statute, and expansion of the grounds for abortion to include pregnancy resulting from rape or incest or which created substantial risk that the mother, or the child if born, would suffer grave and irremediable impairment of physical or mental health. This corresponds closely to the Model Penal Code recommendations described in the text accompanying notes 137-38 *supra*.

State Department of Public Health. A physician wishing to perform a therapeutic abortion was to file a written request supported by written opinions of not less than two medical practitioners, one of whom was to be a specialist in the field of medicine within the ambit of which the stated basis for the abortion fell; these practitioners could not be members of the committee. Written consent by the woman and either her husband, if she were married, or her parent or guardian, if she were not, also was to be submitted to the committee. If the committee approved, the abortion could then be performed in the hospital.[161] The bill died in committee in both the 1961 and 1963 sessions; it was reported out of committee in the 1965 session, although it was thereafter referred to another committee, from which it was withdrawn by its sponsor for want of sufficient support.[162]

A second approach to the problem — that of delegating the decision-making to an appropriate administrative agency — has not been attempted directly in the context of abortion, although it is well established in other areas. To achieve this, the criminal code provision would be amended to exempt from its coverage (1) any abortion necessary, or believed to be necessary by a licensed physician, to preserve the life, or life or health if that is the existing statutory phrase, of the pregnant woman, and (2) any therapeutic abortion performed under duly promulgated regulations of the state commissioner of hospitals, department of health, or whatever (depending on the state), embodying (a) medical grounds for therapeutic abortion and (b) general hospital procedures governing performance of therapeutic abortions. The first part of the proposal is necessary to prevent construction of the amended statute as retroactive in coverage; abortions lawful prior to amendment of the penal code section would continue to be lawful afterwards. The

---

161 Two states, incidentally, now require that lawful abortions be performed in a medical facility, though this requirement is in the criminal code provision. ILL. ANN. STAT. ch. 38, § 23-1 (Smith-Hurd 1964) ("in a licensed hospital or other licensed medical facility"); WIS. STAT. § 940.04 (1963) ("unless an emergency prevents, is [to be] performed in a licensed maternity hospital").

162 Information supplied through the courtesy of Assemblyman John T. Knox, the sponsor of the original bill. See also Kummer & Leavy, *Therapeutic Abortion Law Confusion*, 195 A.M.A.J. 140, 143 (1966).

second part would leave extension of the concept of therapeutic abortions to administrative regulation.

If there are constitutional problems inherent in this scheme, they are within the field of administrative law and not criminal law. There is no delegation of power to determine affirmative criminal norms; any regulations promulgated by the specified state agency would inure to the benefit of a defendant doctor and not to his detriment. Most case law appears to support the power of the legislature to delegate norm-creating functions to administrative bodies.[163] Regulation of the professions has been consistently upheld in the face of claims of denial of equal protection or due process;[164] only if regulation of medical practice is delegated to a private agency is there any major problem.[165] Accordingly, it would appear that experimentation along these lines could readily survive constitutional attack.

Would delegating legislation make any practical difference in the availability of safe therapeutic abortion through medical channels? In the abstract it has advantages. It gives members of the medical profession the opportunity of making gradual alterations in hospital practices based on expanded medical knowledge; specifics are not encysted in statutes. Changes would be promulgated by an agency largely composed of members of the medical profession, and thus in one sense answerable to it. Amendments of norms are more quickly and easily accomplished by administrative agencies than by the legislature itself. There is not the same likelihood of campaigns in the press about the morality of abortions, campaigns which have occurred each time liberalization of the abortion provisions in state criminal codes has been attempted. The total impact ought to be a transition toward exercise of considered medical opinion in place of gladiatorial combat.

---

163 DAVIS, ADMINISTRATIVE LAW §§ 2.04-2.15 (1959).

164 Hawker v. New York, 170 U.S. 189 (1898); Dent v. West Virginia, 129 U.S. 114 (1889); State ex rel. Bond v. State Bd. of Medical Examiners, 209 Ala. 9, 95 So. 295 (1923).

165 See Group Health Ins. v. Howell, 40 N.J. 436, 193 A.2d 103 (1963), modified on other grounds, 43 N.J. 104, 202 A.2d 689 (1964). See also 67 HARV. L. REV. 1398 (1954).

In fact, however, this legislation or any other legislation which ties issues of therapeutic abortion to the regulation of the medical profession in general is likely to be of little immediate effect. One reason is the extreme conservatism of the medical doctors who staff state agencies, hospital boards, and committees of state and local medical societies. Breezes of reform chill these leaders even more, if that is possible, than their counterparts in the legal profession. It might well be two generations before any impact could be made on their armor of conservatism.

But there is probably a more basic reason. For generations much of the medical profession has been able to avoid coming to grips with the problem of abortion because it has had the ready excuse that discussion of liberalized therapeutic abortion is moot as long as the penal law of the state forbids it. At the same time, however, it has apparently tolerated the marginal practitioners who perform the abortions which its more prestigious members shun out of fear or distaste; the medical profession, as well as the legal, has its prostitutes.[166] The primary reason why most doctors shun abortions is because of their view of themselves as preservers of life; abortion creates, although perhaps to a somewhat lesser degree than the related problem of euthanasia, a real tension between the physician's desire to preserve life and his awareness that by performing an abortion he is terminating life. When he practices in a field of medicine in which he sees the hardships which refusal to perform an abortion works on his pregnant patients, he probably arrives by stages at a satisfactory accommodation between his abstract image of himself as a healer and preserver of life and his feelings as to what the best interests of his patients require. Certainly, the strongest advocates of liberalized abortion are specialists in gynecology, obstetrics, and psychiatry, who encounter pregnant women as persons and not as a non-specific class. To make the medical profession face the fact that it has its own responsibility to determine where it stands on the issue of therapeutic abortions, which is what results

---

[166] Dr. George L. Timanus was a defendant in the case of Adams v. State, 200 Md. 133, 88 A.2d 556 (1951). See his complaint that doctors who had referred patients to him were unwilling to come forward and testify at his trial. ABORTION IN THE UNITED STATES 62-63 (Calderone ed. 1958). This looks very much like the "status dilemma" described in CARLIN, LAWYERS ON THEIR OWN 173-84 (1962).

from elimination of the problem from the coverage of the criminal code, is to place it in a position of stress and trauma. One might expect no very great increase in the number of therapeutic abortions actually performed, and a very great effort to defer the problem to some other segment of the community, like welfare agencies or the legal profession, so that the medical profession can avoid these internal and external pressures. These efforts ought to be resisted; for if the problem rests with medicine for solution, the medical profession will be forced to recognize that the abortion dilemma is as much its own responsibility to resolve as it is that of any other group in society. In that event, perhaps it will begin to reconsider its attitudes toward abortion in the same way the legal profession has begun to reconsider its attitudes with respect to the practice of criminal law.

IV. CONCLUSION

To continue the present restrictive laws on abortion is to purchase the illusion of security at the cost of considerable human loss. Enforcement of criminal statutes in their present form may accomplish about all the protection possible against untrained abortionists, but with corresponding disadvantages which perhaps more than offset the gains. These disadvantages are the harassment of the medical profession by zealous prosecutors, and the creation of intolerable tension in the doctor who is torn between his desire to perform an abortion, which he believes to be necessary on humanitarian grounds, and his fear of performing it because it is illegal. In the long run the best way to salvage pregnant women from the hands of unqualified abortionists is to make it possible for them to receive proper treatment, openly, in licensed hospitals. This can be achieved by liberalizing the definition of justifiable therapeutic abortion in the criminal code or by incorporating by reference similar expanded provisions in statutes or regulations affecting the medical profession directly. Doctors will face considerable emotional crisis if the second avenue is followed; ingrained emotional expectations and traditions in society make the former difficult to accomplish. If neither alternative is attempted, however, doctors and lawyers must bear on their own consciences the injustices inherent in the present law.

2

Medical Abortion Practices
in the United States

Kenneth R. Niswander, M.D.

Criminal abortion has become a major cause of maternal death. A recent survey of maternal deaths in California found that almost one-third of the deaths studied were related to illegal abortion.[1] In 1961, according to the records of the New York Department of Health, 47 per cent of the maternal deaths occurring in metropolitan New York were due to illegal abortion.[2] A review of therapeutic abortions during the past two decades in New York City has shown that criminal abortion has accounted for an increasing percentage of puerperal deaths.[3] More alarmingly, the increased number of puerperal deaths seemed inversely proportional to the decreasing number of therapeutic abortions performed in New York.[4] Although it is impossible to verify the figure, it has been estimated that between 300,000 and a million or more criminal abortions are performed each year in the United States.[5] Kinsey found that 22 per

---

[1] Montgomery & Hammersly, *Maternal Deaths in California, 1957-1962*, 100 CALIF. MEDICINE 412, 415 (1964).

[2] Guttmacher, *Induced Abortion*, 63 N.Y.J. MEDICINE 2334 (1963) (editorial).

[3] Gold, Erhardt, Jacobziner & Nelson, *Therapeutic Abortions in New York City: A 20-year Review*, 55 AMERICAN J. PUBLIC HEALTH 964, 965 (1965).

[4] Can one speculate that if therapeutic abortion were more readily available there would be fewer deaths from illegal abortion?

[5] Fisher, *Criminal Abortion*, in THERAPEUTIC ABORTION: MEDICAL, PSYCHIATRIC, LEGAL, ANTHROPOLOGICAL AND RELIGIOUS CONSIDERATIONS 3, 6 (Rosen ed. 1954).

cent of the married women interviewed had had one or more abortions in marriage by the age of forty-five.[6]   Between 88 and 95 per cent of the premarital pregnancies in his sample were resolved by abortion.[7]   Obviously, modern society, like earlier ones, finds a frequent need for interruption of pregnancy.   Existing laws prevent legal recourse for this need, and criminal abortion results.   Guttmacher has stated that "illegal or criminal abortion is the only great pandemic disease which remains unrecognized and untreated by modern medicine."[8]   It should be recognized that criminal abortion not only terminates many pregnancies, but is in itself the direct cause of many maternal injuries and deaths.   An estimated five to ten thousand women who choose illegal abortion die each year.[9]   In all probability, liberalizing the laws on therapeutic abortion would significantly decrease this major medical hazard.

What are the present practices of reputable hospitals in the United States with regard to therapeutic abortion?   Is there variation in the interpretation of state laws by different hospitals and by different doctors?   Is there prevalent disregard for the state laws governing therapeutic abortion?   Is there a substantial medical opinion that restrictive state laws should be liberalized?   If there is, to what extent should the present laws be changed?   These questions seem to warrant more attention at this time.

I.   HISTORY

Abortion is undoubtedly an ancient practice.   The records of almost every civilization indicate knowledge of abortifacient agents and abortive techniques.   Among primitive people, the more extreme methods were gruesome and remain so among certain groups today.   One tribe encouraged large ants to bite the woman's body, and occasionally the insects were taken internally.[10]   Gross trauma-

---

[6] ABORTION IN THE UNITED STATES 50, 54 (Calderone ed. 1958) (see remarks of Dr. Kinsey).

[7] *Ibid.*

[8] Guttmacher, *supra* note 2.

[9] TAUSSIG, ABORTION, SPONTANEOUS AND INDUCED: MEDICAL AND SOCIAL ASPECTS 28 (1936); Fisher, *supra* note 5, at 9.

[10] Devereux, *A Typological Study of Abortion in 350 Primitive, Ancient, and*

tization of the pregnant abdomen was a popular method of attempting to induce abortion and is still used by some primitive groups. The early Hebrews knew abortive techniques although they strongly disapproved of the practice. The Greeks, on the other hand, advocated abortion in order to control population size and insure good social and economic conditions among the people. Hippocrates advised abortion in certain situations but, as a general rule, condemned the practice because it so often resulted in the mother's injury or death. Christian belief in the immortality of the viable fetus' soul has been largely responsible for the Church's condemnation of abortion. Doctrine has placed abortion in the same category as infanticide, and the unbaptized soul of the fetus, like that of the infant, was considered in danger of hellfire. It is interesting to note, however, that many early canonists did not feel that the soul entered the fetus at the time of conception; rather, the belief was prevalent that the soul entered the body of a female fetus at eighty days gestation, and the soul of the male fetus was present after the fortieth day of gestation. This belief accounted for the fact that interruption of the pregnancy before the fortieth day was punished only by a fine, whereas abortion when the soul was present was regarded as murder and was punished accordingly. In 1869 this distinction became unimportant since abortion before the soul entered the fetus became "anticipated homicide."[11] In spite of the Church's opposition, abortion *was* practiced and not infrequently resulted in the mother's death.

The Renaissance woman who was poor was liable to the death penalty by crucifixion if she induced abortion, whereas her rich sister might buy her way out of such punishment. Today, the indigent patient may still have a more difficult time than the wealthy in obtaining legal sanction for even a medically indicated abortion, with the result that criminal abortion still accounts for a disproportionately higher number of deaths among the underprivileged. A report on abortions in New York City covering the past two decades pointed out that 90 per cent of the therapeutic abortions were per-

---

Pre-Industrial Societies, in THERAPEUTIC ABORTION: MEDICAL, PSYCHIATRIC, LEGAL, ANTHROPOLOGICAL AND RELIGIOUS CONSIDERATIONS 97, 125 (Rosen ed. 1954).

11 WILLIAMS, THE SANCTITY OF LIFE AND THE CRIMINAL LAW *passim* (1957).

formed on white women.[12]   In a recent review of the abortions in
Buffalo hospitals, it was evident that therapeutic abortion seemed
rarely indicated among non-white patients.[13]   The indications for
abortion may have changed over the centuries, but discrimination
against the lower socioeconomic classes and the very real dangers of
criminal abortion are both still present today.

Taussig, in his classical book on abortion, gives a good historical
account of the medical indications for abortion and cites references
to this practice in the oldest writings.[14]   Plato and Aristotle clearly
encouraged abortion on social or economic grounds.   Hippocrates
practiced abortion but wanted only physicians to abort patients.
In Rome, especially in the Empire period, abortion was approved
for social considerations.   The influence of Christianity, although
not actually diminishing the practice of abortion, did make it socially
unacceptable.   Therefore, with the dawn of Christianity, writings
about therapeutic abortion almost disappeared.   Early in the Christian era, Priscianus, a physician, recommended abortion to save the
life of the mother, but the ramifications of the abortion issue do not
seem to have been reconsidered until 1772.   At that time William
Cooper suggested therapeutic abortion in cases of contracted pelvis
in order to prevent the horrors of attempted delivery through a malformed bony structure.   Dewees, Velpeau, Hodge, and other prominent physicians continued to encourage abortion in cases of contracted pelvis.   This suggestion was accepted by many obstetricians
in Europe, and during the latter half of the nineteenth century "the
indications, especially in Germany, were extended to include tuberculosis, heart disease, nephritis, and certain forms of psychoses."[15]
These indications became more prevalent, and in recent years there
has been a growing tendency to abort for fetal reasons.   There seems
little doubt that psychogenic and socioeconomic factors have also
exerted increasing influence in the decision to abort.

---

[12] Gold, Erhardt, Jacobziner & Nelson, *supra* note 3, at 966.

[13] Niswander, Klein & Randall, *Changing Attitudes Toward Therapeutic Abortion*
(unpublished paper presented at Annual Convention of the American Medical Association, New York, N.Y., 1965 and reported in the N.Y. Times, June 22, 1965, p. 92,
col. 4).

[14] TAUSSIG, *op. cit. supra* note 9, at 31.

[15] *Id.* at 278.

II. CONTEMPORARY INDICATIONS FOR THERAPEUTIC ABORTION

Present-day indications for therapeutic abortion can be conveniently divided into four categories: (a) medical, (b) fetal, (c) psychiatric, and (d) socioeconomic. Invariably, these categories overlap, for the gravida[16] with rubella[17] in the first trimester of pregnancy is likely to be psychiatrically, or at least emotionally, disturbed. Extreme poverty may be an important adjuvant reason to terminate pregnancy when organic disease decreases the mother's ability to care for a larger family.

A. Medical Indications

The medical indications for therapeutic abortion are so numerous that it is impossible to consider them all, or to mention those which were considered to indicate abortion in the past. The majority of them, however, can be included in one of the following types of disease: cardiovascular, gastrointestinal, renal, neurologic, pulmonary, diabetic, and malignant. Each will be briefly considered.

(1) Cardiovascular Disease.[18]—Cardiovascular disease has long been thought to increase the risk of maternal death during pregnancy, and indeed, it has accounted for a significant percentage of maternal deaths. Patients with rheumatic heart disease, congenital heart disorders, or chronic hypertensive disease must be watched closely by their physicians for signs of impending heart failure. In instances where the cardiac disease is severe, digitalis or other cardiac supporting drugs are often used. Labor is often terminated earlier than in the normal pregnant patient. With improved prenatal care (including the significant advances recently provided by cardiac surgery), the number of women with cardiovascular disease whose life is actually in danger during pregnancy has decreased substantially. Certain reports state that with adequate medical

---

16 A woman in her first pregnancy is referred to as *Gravida I*; in the second pregnancy *Gravida II*; etc. [medical definitions are from SCHMIDT, ATTORNEYS' DICTIONARY OF MEDICINE AND WORD FINDER (1965)].

17 Commonly known as German measles.

18 Disease involving the heart and the blood vessels, *i.e.*, the arteries and the veins.

attention practically every pregnancy of a cardiac patient can be completed successfully with little risk of maternal death.[19] As with some of the other medical indications, consultations suggesting interruption of pregnancy in a cardiac patient are not infrequently influenced by appreciation of the difficult situation that will eventually face the disabled cardiac patient who must try to take care of her new baby.

(2)   Gastrointestinal Diseases.—Ulcerative colitis,[20] either active or quiescent, is perhaps the most common gastrointestinal disease which has been thought to indicate therapeutic abortion. There is general agreement that emotional factors affect the medical course of the patient with ulcerative colitis.   Since pregnancy regularly and sometimes severely affects the emotional stability of women, it has been felt that pregnancy may adversely affect the outcome of this hazardous disease.   Fortunately, the disease is not a common one.

(3)   Renal Disease.[21]—Patients in this category are likely to be the victims of chronic glomerulonephritis,[22] hypertension of renal origin,[23] or, less commonly, they may have only one functioning kidney, or a history of nephrolithiasis.[24]   Since therapy in chronic nephritis[25] is still neither definitive nor effective, there seem to be

---

[19] Gorenberg & Chesley, *Rheumatic Heart Disease in Pregnancy: The Remote Prognosis in Patients with "Functionally Severe" Disease,* 68 AMERICAN J. OBSTETRICS & GYNECOLOGY 1151, 1159 (1954).

[20] An inflammation of the colon (the large bowel) characterized by ulceration of its lining membrane.

[21] A disease pertaining to, or involving the kidneys.

[22] A variety of kidney disease in mild form in which the tufts formed by the tiny blood vessels are inflammed.   It leads to hypertension (high blood pressure) and, eventually, to uremia, a poisoning of the body due to failure of the kidneys to eliminate the toxic substances.

[23] See note 22 *supra.*

[24] An abnormal condition marked by the presence of concretions or calculi (*i.e.,* "stones") in the kidney or kidneys.   Also, the various disorders resulting from the presence of the concretions.

[25] The prolonged and progressive form of nephritis (inflammation of the kidney or a deterioration of the tissue forming its delicate structure) which may follow an acute attack or may result from other diseases of the body, from poisons, alcohol, germs, etc.   The fine and delicate structure of the kidney becomes distorted.   The fine blood vessels become thicker; the supporting tissue (the non-functional part) begins to overgrow the functional parts; even the heart is affected.

nephritis patients whose lives will actually be shortened by the effects of pregnancy. Heroic measures, such as the use of the artificial kidney, may see these women through severe life-threatening episodes; but all therapy will, in certain instances, eventually prove ineffective.[26] Some of the renal conditions which might seem to indicate therapeutic abortion, however, do not so significantly affect the risk of maternal death. Often if one kidney has been removed, there appears to be little increased risk for the pregnant patient so long as her remaining kidney functions well. The risk of nephrolithiasis cannot be minimized, but the instances when it might actually increase the risk of death in a pregnant patient seem remote.

(4) Neurologic Disease.—Diseases such as multiple sclerosis,[27] post poliomyelitis paralysis, epilepsy, and various congenital neurologic diseases form the bulk of the neurologic diseases indicating therapeutic abortion. The patient with multiple sclerosis sometimes is made worse by pregnancy, but the effect of pregnancy on the disease is unpredictable.[28] Riva, Carpenter, and O'Grady have found no justifiable indication for pregnancy interruption in patients with multiple sclerosis.[29] There appears to be little evidence that the disease actually increases the risk of death during pregnancy. Much the same can be said about epilepsy in a pregnant patient. About one-third of pregnant epileptics seem worse during pregnancy, but the effect of the pregnancy is unpredictable. Epilepsy, in itself, does not seem to increase the risk of death for the pregnant woman.[30] As with cardiovascular disease, however, it is evident that a woman with

---

[26] Herwig, Merrill, Jackson & Oken, *Chronic Renal Disease and Pregnancy*, 92 AMERICAN J. OBSTETRICS & GYNECOLOGY 1117, 1120 (1965).

[27] A disease of the brain and spinal cord. The spinal cord is the "cable" of nerves in the spinal column. In this condition, various parts of the brain and spinal cord are subjected to a type of deterioration called sclerosis. Sclerosis in this instance is a sort of hardening of the nerve tissue and its displacement by overgrowing connective (supporting) tissue. In other words, functional nerve tissue gives way to supporting, nonfunctional tissue. The disease is slow in progress but incurable.

[28] Cohen & Krueger, *Multiple Sclerosis and Pregnancy; Report of a Case*, 6 OBSTETRICS & GYNECOLOGY 144, 145 (1955).

[29] Riva, Carpenter & O'Grady, *Pregnancy Associated with Multiple Sclerosis*, 66 AMERICAN J. OBSTETRICS & GYNECOLOGY 403, 407 (1953).

[30] Sabin & Oxorn, *Epilepsy and Pregnancy*, 7 OBSTETRICS & GYNECOLOGY 175, 179 (1956).

a severe paralysis or a disabling sensory disorder will find it difficult, if not impossible, to care for a newly born child once she leaves the hospital.

(5) *Pulmonary Disease.*—Tuberculosis accounts for nearly all of the pulmonary conditions thought to indicate therapeutic abortion. In former years, pregnancy was felt to adversely affect the tubercular patient and, in some instances, actually to increase the risk of death from tuberculosis. With the advent of drug therapy, tuberculosis has practically disappeared as an indication for therapeutic abortion. In addition to a possibly increased risk of maternal death, consultants often feel, as with some of the other diseases indicating abortion, that the tubercular patient cannot properly care for her newborn child; and this consideration undoubtedly enters into the decision to abort. With the current, relatively short periods of hospitalization for tuberculosis and the relatively quick recovery, however, this consideration is no longer as important as it used to be.

(6) *Diabetes Mellitus.*[31]—Diabetes, of varying degrees of severity, has often been an indication for therapeutic abortion. On occasion, poor medical control of the disease has indicated the abortion; other times one of the complications of the disease, such as arteriosclerosis, affecting the retina, heart, or brain, has been felt to be severe enough to interrupt the pregnancy. The maternal mortality rate, however, is currently considered to be essentially the same among diabetic patients as with the overall pregnant population. Fetal risk is distinctly increased in the diabetic patient, but this would seem to have little to do with the "health" or "life" of the mother. Loth and Hesseltine have stated that "it should be a rare instance in which the diabetic pregnant patient could not be carried to the time of fetal viability, if not to term, by adequate medical management."[32] As with the other medical indications, the customary legal demand that the "life" of the mother be in danger as a result of the disease necessitating the abortion is not always fulfilled.

---

[31] A disease in which the metabolism (body utilization) of sugars is greatly impaired due to the faulty secretion of insulin by the pancreas.

[32] Loth & Hesseltine, *Therapeutic Abortion at the Chicago Lying-In Hospital*, 72 AMERICAN J. OBSTETRICS & GYNECOLOGY 304, 309 (1956).

(7) Malignancy.—Some physicians feel that pregnancy will adversely affect the patient's medical course when a prior malignancy has been treated. The medical course of the patient with carcinoma[33] of the breast, for example, may be changed by the use of the so-called female hormones, either estrogen or progesterone, which are present in high concentration in the bloodstream of a pregnant patient. The effect of hormones on the patient with carcinoma of the breast, however, is unpredictable since these products sometimes improve the clinical situation and at other times seem to contribute to the progression of the disease. There is little convincing evidence that they either prolong or shorten the patient's life. Majury says that "no convincing evidence has been produced which shows that subsequent pregnancy affects adversely the prognosis in extra-uterine malignancy."[34] A history of carcinoma of the bowel (or, on occasion, carcinoma in other locations) has also been an accepted indication for therapeutic abortion; however, there is no convincing evidence that pregnancy in any way adversely affects the outcome of these neoplastic diseases.

(8) Other Medical Diseases.—Rheumatoid arthritis, hyperthyroidism, lacerated cervix, multiple fibroids,[35] mumps in the first trimester, and other miscellaneous diseases too numerous to mention have also indicated therapeutic abortion. It is difficult to prove that many of these diseases actually threaten the life of the pregnant patient, and social factors often seem to be a prominent consideration in the decision to abort.

B. *Fetal Indications*

No state statute permits abortion because of an expected abnormality or the death of the fetus. Perhaps this is not a surprising fact

---

[33] A malignant tumor or new growth (*i.e.*, a cancer) arising from cells that make up epithelium. Epithelium is the outer covering of the skin and the lining of the body cavities, such as the mouth, the rectum, the interior of the chest, etc.

[34] Majury, *Therapeutic Abortion in the Winnipeg General Hospital*, 82 AMERICAN J. OBSTETRICS & GYNECOLOGY 10, 13 (1961). Other authors have agreed. See, *e.g.*, Holleb, *Breast Cancer and Pregnancy*, 15 CA, A CANCER J. FOR CLINICIANS 182, 183 (1965).

[35] Pertaining to, or composed of, fibrous tissue. Fibroid is frequently used to refer to a tumor of the womb composed of muscle and fibrous tissue.

when one considers that most of the abortion laws were written many years before anything was known about the etiology of fetal defects. Some hospitals, however, are willing to abort a pregnant woman when there is a strong possibility that the baby will be abnormal. For example, the consultant who recommends an abortion may simply state that the danger of fetal malformation due to maternal rubella in the first trimester of pregnancy makes an abortion advisable. On other occasions, however, a psychiatric opinion may be sought, and this specialist may suggest that the patient's mental condition, influenced by the fear of fetal malformation from the rubella, may become suicidal if the pregnancy is not interrupted. Her life is thus endangered. There is little practical difference in these two approaches since the result is the same: interruption of the pregnancy. There are five situations where abortion may be recommended for fetal indications: (1) where there has been an ingestion of certain harmful drugs during pregnancy; (2) where certain viral infections have been contracted by the mother, especially rubella; (3) where the mother's abdomen has been exposed to radiation during pregnancy; (4) where there is a substantial risk of fetal malformation due to genetic factors; and (5) where there is a sensitization to the Rh factor.

(1) Drugs.—The tragedy that occurred following the ingestion of thalidomide by pregnant women both in Europe and in the United States is well known to everyone. The newspaper publicity that surrounded the pregnant woman from Arizona who found it necessary to go to Sweden to obtain an abortion of a fetus presumed and later proved to have been affected by thalidomide brought the problem vividly to the attention of the American public. Thalidomide, however, is not the first drug to cause severe fetal abnormalities. The folic-acid antagonists, employed in the treatment of leukemia, had previously been found to produce severe anomalies because of their metabolic action. Certain other drugs are suspected of teratogenicity, although none is as well established in this regard as thalidomide or the folic-acid antagonists. As the field of developmental pharmacology progresses, however, there seems little doubt that other drugs will be implicated and will further aggravate the legal problem so vividly dramatized by thalidomide.

(2) *Rubella.*[36]—The problem of rubella in pregnancy has also been dramatically reported by the press in recent years. There was an epidemic of rubella in the eastern part of the United States in 1964, and this spread to the West Coast and to Hawaii in 1965. Although many pregnant women who contracted rubella were aborted during this epidemic, it has been estimated that about *30,000 children conceived during the epidemic were born defective.*[37] When one considers how severe the fetal abnormalities following maternal rubella can be, it would certainly seem more desirable from an economic, as well as a humanitarian, viewpoint to have terminated pregnancy when the odds were so relatively high that the child would be abnormal. The actual risk of malformation is unknown, but a summary of the literature indicated a 23.4 per cent risk during the first four weeks of pregnancy, a 21.3 per cent risk in the second month, and, in the third month, a 10.4 per cent risk. After the twelfth week, there seemed to be no increased risk of congenital malformation.[38] The administration of gamma globulin has not been a satisfactory preventative of the disease in the pregnant woman, partially because the commercial lots available vary so markedly in their effectiveness.[39]

Certain other maternal infections are also known to increase the risk of congenital abnormality in the fetus. These diseases, however, are so mild that infection in the mother usually goes unnoticed. At present, in such cases the tragic consequence of a malformed baby seems unavoidable.

(3) *Radiation.*—It is generally agreed that when radiation is given in therapeutic doses to the mother in the first few months of pregnancy, malformation or death of the fetus may result.[40] According to Parlee, "it appears that ionizing radiation in therapeutic

36 Commonly known as German measles.

37 Personal communication from John Sever to the author, October 1965.

38 Warnaky & Kalter, *Congenital Malformations*, 265 NEW ENGLAND J. MEDICINE 993, 999 (1961).

39 Sever, Schiff & Huebner, *Frequency of Rubella Antibody Among Pregnant Women and Other Human and Animal Populations*, 23 OBSTETRICS & GYNECOLOGY 153, 158 (1964).

40 Parlee, *Radiation Hazards in Obstetrics and Gynecology*, 75 AMERICAN J. OBSTETRICS & GYNECOLOGY 327 (1958).

doses in the early months of pregnancy are grounds for the termination of the pregnancy."[41]   Doses of radiation in therapeutic amounts are usually prescribed only for the treatment of malignant neoplastic disease, such as carcinoma[42] of the cervix. Fetal death and extrusion of the products of conception are the usual, but not inevitable, result of such quantities of irradiation. A lesser dose of radiation, such as may be involved in an extensive diagnostic investigation, usually does not produce fetal death, and in most instances does not cause fetal malformation. When extensive diagnostic X-ray is used during the earliest weeks of an undiagnosed pregnancy, some physicians recommend therapeutic abortion. The possibility of having a malformed child under these circumstances does exist, but the actual risk has not been demonstrated. To many distraught parents, any risk is too great. In such cases abortion seems justified on both psychiatric and humanitarian grounds, in spite of the fact that there is little evidence to indicate how many of these children would be deformed.

(4)   *Genetic.*—Therapeutic abortion on genetic grounds is, at the present time, rarely done. As more is learned about inherited diseases, however, there is likely to be an increasing demand from both the physician and the patient for interruption of pregnancy when there is a substantial risk of serious congenital malformation as a result of a likely combination of parental genes.

(5)   *Erythroblastosis Fetalis.*[43]—With the introduction of various methods of transfusing the fetus in utero, the current demand for therapeutic abortion on the grounds that the fetus is likely to die in utero as a result of incompatibility of the Rh factor may soon decrease. The hazard to the fetus in utero, affected by Rh antibodies produced by the maternal organism, is primarily anemia or lack of red blood cells. If this lack can be corrected by transfusing the fetus in utero at periodic intervals, there is a good chance that

---

[41] *Id.* at 332.

[42] For definition of carcinoma see note 33 *supra.*

[43] A hemolytic anemia of the fetus or new born infant, caused by the transplacental transmission of maternally formed antibodies, usually secondary to an incompatability between the blood group of the mother and that of her offspring (usually an incompatability of the Rh factor).

he will be born alive and that modern methods of exchange transfusions will keep him in good health.

C. Psychiatric Indications

Nearly all recent reports on therapeutic abortion practice in the United States indicate an increasing frequency of abortion for psychogenic reasons. Since most state laws require that the "life" of the mother be endangered by pregnancy before abortion may be legally performed, the patient must have exhibited a genuine suicidal tendency to qualify for termination of her pregnancy. In spite of the increase in this type of abortion, there are some psychiatrists who feel that psychiatric indications are not valid. A paper by Dr. Myre Sim, which appeared in the British Medical Journal in 1963, and the correspondence in the same journal which this article provoked, illustrate well the disagreement over psychogenic indications for abortion.[44] Dr. Sim, in the original article, says that "there are no psychiatric grounds for termination of pregnancy."[45] Hoenig, commenting on Dr. Sim's paper, says that "termination of the pregnancy could well be indicated . . . in [certain] cases on psychiatric grounds within the meaning of the law."[46] In answer to this letter of Dr. Hoenig's, Dr. Sim stated that it was really the patient's socioeconomic condition which influenced the psychiatrist to recommend abortion. "If society wants abortion to be easier, it should have the courage to campaign for it honestly and not exploit the psychiatrist, who, I contend, has no factual basis for being associated with the problem."[47]

Rosenberg and Silver sent a questionnaire to a group of psychiatrists to determine their attitudes and practices regarding psychiatric indications for therapeutic abortion.[48] The authors were shocked at the diversity of opinion expressed in the replies. For example, only about 25 per cent of the psychiatrists thought that pregnancy in-

---

[44] Sim, Abortion and the Psychiatrist, 2 BRITISH MEDICAL J. 145 (1963).

[45] Id. at 148.

[46] Hoenig, Correspondence, 2 BRITISH MEDICAL J. 1125 (1963).

[47] Sim, Correspondence, 2 BRITISH MEDICAL J. 1062 (1963).

[48] Rosenberg & Silver, Suicide, Psychiatrists and Therapeutic Abortion, 102 CALIF. MEDICINE 407, 410 (1965).

creased the morbidity of mental illness, but almost two-thirds indicated that they had seen or treated genuine suicidal attempts or psychotic reactions in pregnant patients. A substantial number of the psychiatrists felt that socioeconomic factors, rape, incest, and extreme youth were factors which should indicate abortion. The authors reflect that this liberal attitude on the part of psychiatrists indicates their alignment with progressive social change and suggests that when a psychiatrist recommends therapeutic abortion he is likely to be considering the socioeconomic factors rather than the psychiatric indications.

D. Socioeconomic Indications

Throughout history, socioeconomic indications for interruption of pregnancy have predominated over all other reasons. Some women have been aborted simply because they were afraid of childbirth. Others would not bear children before or after a certain age. Some women aborted to safeguard their beauty, while others aborted because of "improper" paternity. Nomadism made pregnancy inconvenient and led some women to abort themselves. Poverty has played a tremendously important role in the motivation for abortion. With the advent of Christianity, all abortions were considered undesirable, if not criminal, and this was especially true of those done for socioeconomic reasons. Legal abortion for social reasons in civilized societies, therefore, virtually disappeared; there is little evidence, however, to suggest that illegal abortion for the same reasons decreased significantly.

There seems to be little doubt that socioeconomic factors have influenced many doctors to recommend abortion for legitimate medical reasons. In days past when tuberculosis responded slowly, or not at all, to treatment, Taussig felt that factors such as the willingness of the patient to cooperate with rigid therapy, the number of children she had, the amount of help she could get with her children, if any, and other related factors were important in the decision of whether or not to abort her.[49] Cardiac disease, while it

---

[49] TAUSSIG, op. cit. supra note 9, at 293.

may not actually increase the risk of death in the pregnant patient, may make it difficult or impossible for the mother to adequately care for her child. This problem has usually been a most important consideration when the patient has cardiovascular disease, and the same problem exists with many other "medical" indications. Obviously, the fetal indications for abortion are primarily socioeconomic, since few, if any, actually threaten the life of the pregnant patient; however, the social as well as economic ramifications of a severely deformed infant are incalculable. It would seem, too, that socioeconomic factors play a predominant role in the decision to abort psychiatric patients. This widespread consideration of the socioeconomic milieu seems remarkable, since it need not be pointed out that no state law permits abortion on such grounds.

III. CURRENT LEGAL ABORTION PRACTICES IN THE UNITED STATES

A. Changes in the Indications

Nearly all hospital surveys report a decrease in the last twenty to thirty years in the percentage of therapeutic abortions done for medical reasons.[50] Taussig, in his volume published in 1936, lists a myriad of medical indications for abortion.[51] Since the publication of this book, there has been a gradual transition in medical thinking; some diseases formerly considered to be indications for abortion no longer need be. Taussig called tuberculosis, "the most significant indication for therapeutic abortion in point of frequency,"[52] but this disease rarely gives reason to abort today. Of the abortions in a recent Buffalo study, tuberculosis accounted for 33 to 50 per cent of the abortions in the 1940's, about 10 per cent in the 1950's, and none during the years 1958 to 1965.[53] In 1936 Taussig stated

---

[50] *E.g.*, Boulas, *Therapeutic Abortion*, 19 OBSTETRICS & GYNECOLOGY 222, 224 (1962); Colpitts, *Trends in Therapeutic Abortion*, 68 AMERICAN J. OBSTETRICS & GYNECOLOGY 988, 996 (1954); Routledge, *The Present Status of Therapeutic Abortion*, 17 OBSTETRICS & GYNECOLOGY 168, 171 (1961); Russell, *Changing Indications for Therapeutic Abortion*, 151 A.M.A.J. 108, 111 (1953).

[51] TAUSSIG, *op. cit. supra* note 9, at 282.

[52] *Id.* at 292.

[53] Niswander, Klein & Randall, *supra* note 13.

that "recently a tendency toward greater conservation has . . . been manifested with regard to the indications for therapeutic abortion in women with heart disease,"[54] although he felt that it was not infrequently a legitimate indication. The 1965 Buffalo study showed that cardiovascular indications were present in about 15 per cent of the pregnancy interruptions in the 1940's; the incidence decreased to approximately 5 per cent in the 1950's and became practically non-existent in the 1960's.[55]

In 1936 Taussig pointed out that psychiatric indications accounted for only a small percentage of therapeutic abortions, but that such abortions were occurring more often. He quotes Maier as saying that from 1929 to 1931 in Zurich, Switzerland, psychiatrically indicated therapeutic abortions were definitely on the increase.[56] Since Taussig's book was written most of the reports on hospital experience document a gradually increasing percentage of abortions done for what has been recorded as psychiatric indications. In the Buffalo study the psychogenic indications increased linearly from about 10 per cent in 1943 to about 80 per cent in 1963.[57] Although other reports have not shown quite so dramatic an increase, this trend is representative.

An equally dramatic change has occurred in the fetal indications, which were practically unknown before the 1940's. In the Buffalo series the first therapeutic abortion for rubella was done in 1949, and although the incidence has varied from year to year, depending apparently on the prevalence of the disease, rubella has accounted for a significant proportion of abortions since the first case. In 1964, an epidemic year, rubella accounted for 35 per cent of the abortions in the Buffalo study.[58]

Some, but not all, psychiatrists feel that rarely, or indeed never, is psychiatric disease an absolute indication for therapeutic abor-

---

[54] TAUSSIG, op. cit. supra note 9, at 297.

[55] Niswander, Klein & Randall, supra note 13.

[56] TAUSSIG, op. cit. supra note 9, at 313.

[57] Niswander, Klein & Randall, supra note 13.

[58] Ibid.

tion.[59] Yet the number of such abortions gradually increases. A real suicidal risk must be present in the psychiatric patients to legally permit abortion, yet there is good evidence that the suicide rate among pregnant women is considerably lower than among the general population of non-pregnant women.[60] Abortion for rubella is frankly illegal in most states. Many hospitals choose to ignore the law for humanitarian reasons. The physicians doing these abortions feel that the patient has a right to make her own decision concerning a pregnancy which may result in the birth of an abnormal child. It is evident that social factors have become the prime consideration in the decisions to terminate pregnancy for psychiatric indications or for fetal reasons.

It is also noteworthy that, according to most investigators, the private patient is much more likely to have a legal interruption of pregnancy than is the ward patient. Hall reports that at the Sloane Hospital for Women the incidence of therapeutic abortion is four times greater on the private service than on the ward.[61] By sending a questionnaire to sixty-five randomly selected major hospitals, Dr. Hall discovered that this same discrepancy is widespread.[62] The Buffalo study indicates similar trends in support of Hall's findings. In the 1940's, when the majority of abortions were done for medical reasons, the incidences on the ward and private services were about the same. In the 1950's, when medical reasons accounted for fewer abortions, the incidence on the private service rose to twice that of the ward service. In the 1960's, when the number of abortions for psychiatric or fetal reasons rose dramatically, the incidence on the private service soared to better than twenty times greater than that of the clinic service.[63]

The Buffalo series uncovered other interesting trends in relation

---

[59] See Cheney, *Indications for Therapeutic Abortion from the Standpoint of the Neurologist and the Psychiatrist*, 103 A.M.A.J. 1914, 1918 (1934); Sim, *supra* note 44, at 148.

[60] McLane, *Other Aspects of the Abortion Problem*, in ABORTIONS IN THE UNITED STATES 117, 140 (Calderone ed. 1958); Rosenberg & Silver, *supra* note 48, at 409.

[61] Hall, *Therapeutic Abortion, Sterilization, and Contraception*, 91 AMERICAN J. OBSTETRICS & GYNECOLOGY 518 (1965).

[62] *Id.* at 525.

[63] Niswander, Klein & Randall, *supra* note 13.

to maternal age, parity, and marital status of the aborted women. In the decade of the 1940's no girl under twenty years of age was aborted. In the 1950's about 7 per cent of the patients were under twenty years of age, and in the 1960's almost 15 per cent of the patients were in this younger age group. Paralleling the lowering of age has been a change in parity.[64] The proportion of nullipara[65] has increased from about 20 per cent during the 1940's to 36 per cent in the 1960's, nearly a doubling of incidence. The percentage of married patients dropped from 93.3 per cent in the 1940's, to 85.1 per cent in the 1950's, to 58.9 per cent in the 1960's. In recent years, about two out of five of the patients aborted have been either single, separated, or divorced.[66]

The Buffalo patients were also classified on the basis of religion. Only 3 per cent of the total Buffalo population is Jewish, but women of this faith accounted for almost 20 per cent of the therapeutic abortions reported; and about 75 per cent of these abortions were recorded to have been indicated on psychiatric grounds. In contrast, only about half of the abortions of the Catholic patients were done for psychiatric disease. Although the differences were not striking, there were a higher number of Catholics among the non-married group than should have been expected.[67]

Hospitals vary greatly in their abortion policies. At the Los Angeles County Hospital, which treats only clinic patients, Russell reports that from 1946 to 1951 there was an incidence of 1 therapeutic abortion per 2,864 deliveries.[68] At the opposite extreme, one finds reputable hospitals permitting abortion for 1 out of every 35 to 40 deliveries. The variation in the hospitals surveyed by Hall extended from no abortions in 24,417 deliveries to 1 in 36 deliveries.[69] It seems inconceivable that medical opinion could vary so widely. Socioeconomic factors must be playing a major role in the decision to abort in certain institutions. There is no doubt, how-

---

[64] *Ibid.*

[65] A woman who has never given birth to a child.

[66] Niswander, Klein & Randall, *supra* note 13.

[67] *Ibid.*

[68] Russell, *supra* note 50, at 109.

[69] Hall, *supra* note 61, at 525.

ever, that fear of the law frequently interferes with good medical judgment.

In 1965 obstetricians were asked by letter to reveal their thoughts about a proposed change in New York State's abortion law. The chairmen of obstetric departments of the medical schools in the state of New York wished to know how many obstetricians favored a change in the New York Abortion Law in line with the American Law Institute's Model Penal Code of 1959. This latter code has stated that

> a licensed physician is justified in terminating a pregnancy if: (a) he believes there is substantial risk that continuance of the pregnancy would gravely impair the physical or mental health of the mother or that the child would be born with grave physical or mental defect, or the pregnancy resulted from rape — or from incest; and (b) two physicians, one of whom may be the person performing the abortion, have certified in writing their belief in the justifying circumstances and have filed such certificates prior to the abortion in the licensed hospital where it was to be performed, or in such other place as may be designated by law.[70]

Eighty-six per cent of the replying doctors favored changing the law in line with the suggested code.[71] The 1965 session of the legislature failed to change the law, but the proponents of change are girding for a new attempt to liberalize the statute in regard to abortion in the next session of the legislature.

In California a similar endeavor to liberalize the law also failed. A statement encouraging the proposed humane abortion act in California was signed by 1,031 board-certified specialists in obstetrics, pediatrics, psychiatry, and preventative medicine. A similar statement was signed by 150 leading attorneys, 4 deans of law schools, 37 professors of law, members of the Family Law Committee of the State Bar, and the President of the State Bar as an individual. A third statement was signed by about 300 professors of sociology, deans of schools of social work, social workers, clinical psychologists, and others, and still another statement was signed by a large

---

[70] MODEL PENAL CODE § 207-11 (Tent. Draft No. 9, 1959).

[71] Hall, *New York Abortion Law Survey*, 93 AMERICAN J. OBSTETRICS & GYNECOLOGY 1182 (1965).

number of clergymen who favored the adoption of the more liberal abortion law.[72]

One cannot escape the conclusion that a large number of well-informed people feel that the current abortion statutes do not fulfill all the social needs permitted by current moral attitudes. The apparently unalterable position of the Roman Catholic Church does not change these needs. Cardinal Cushing has said that Catholics do not need the law to support their moral principles.[73] If a substantial proportion of the non-Catholic population desire a more liberal abortion law, the legislatures should be so informed.

If more evidence is needed that current laws are being loosely interpreted or completely disregarded, Packer and Gampell's 1959 study of abortion practices in certain California hospitals supplies it.[74] A questionnaire was sent to twenty-nine hospitals with obstetrical services in the San Francisco and Los Angeles areas. It contained eleven hypothetical case histories which the hospital was to process as typical applications for therapeutic abortion. The authors divided the case histories into those that would definitely fulfill legal criteria for therapeutic abortion, those that would questionably fulfill legal criteria, and those considered completely illegal. Ninety-three per cent of the hospitals felt that the case histories posing obviously legal indications for therapeutic abortion would have resulted in an affirmative decision to abort. Eighty-three per cent of the hospitals would have granted abortions for the patients with questionable legal case histories, while 59 per cent would probably have consented to abort those in the frankly illegal group.[75] It seems evident that the conscience of the physician is often in conflict with current legal requirements.

B. Medical Procedures Used to Produce Legal Abortion

A variety of techniques is currently used to produce legal abortion, and many variables influence the choice of a particular tech-

---

[72] Letter from Ruth Roemer to the author, August 1965.

[73] Lader, *Abortion, The Civilized Crime*, True, Sept. 1965, p. 92 (quoting Cardinal Cushing).

[74] Packer & Gampell, *Therapeutic Abortion: A Problem in Law and Medicine*, 11 STAN. L. REV. 417 (1959).

[75] *Id.* at 446.

nique. Length of gestation, combining sterilization with abortion, and the presence of pelvic pathology independent of the pregnancy all influence the physician's choice. A list of the techniques used in the past two decades would include intracervical insertion of a foreign body, such as a hard, rubber catheter or a bougie; simple dilatation and curettage (D & C); hysterectomy; hysterotomy (either vaginal or abdominal); the use of concentrated oxytocin solution; and the injection of hypertonic solutions into the uterus. Analysis of the pregnancy interruptions in the Buffalo study showed that the simple D & C accounted for the majority of the abortions performed.[76] Hysterectomy was used frequently in the 1940's but is no longer commonly used since it is usually considered too radical. It is employed only when the uterus itself is abnormal. The use of bougies or intrauterine catheters has become obsolete since the 1940's. In 1964 concentrated oxytocin was first used, and presently, intra-amniotic hypertonic solutions are also being tried. These later techniques, however, still account for only a small portion of the abortions done. Concomitant sterilization was performed in nearly two out of five patients in the 1940's and the 1950's, but this incidence dropped to one in five during 1960-1964.[77] This decrease in incidence of sterilization can be directly traced to the increase in abortions for rubella, a circumstance which in no way affects future childbearing, and to the increase in the number of unmarried young nulliparous patients, as shown by the Buffalo study.

C. *Hazards of Therapeutic Abortion*

The D & C is a safe operation; of the 320 D & C cases reported in the Buffalo series, only 2 patients became significantly ill.[78] One developed an abscess in the tissue adjacent to the uterus, an infection which responded very rapidly to antibiotic therapy. The second patient developed pelvic peritonitis and a fistula between the bowel and the vagina. She became very ill and required major abdominal

---

[76] Niswander, Klein & Randall, *Therapeutic Abortion: Indications and Techniques* (unpublished paper).

[77] *Ibid.*

[78] *Ibid.*

surgery before she recovered. On the other hand, primary abdominal surgery to effect the abortion (hysterectomy, hysterotomy, D & C, and tubal ligation) is less innocuous. Of 176 such patients, 1 died of heart failure forty-eight hours after surgery because of a severe congenital heart defect, a death which would have occurred even without the abortion.[79] There were 8 operative complications, no more than would be expected with abdominal laparotomies for other indications. These complications included evisceration, thrombophlebitis, pyelitis, wound infection, and two postoperative bowel obstructions. All patients responded to appropriate therapy and recovered.[80]

Bergquist and Kaiser studied the effect of intravenous synthetic oxytocin for induction of labor, a technique which requires a much lower dose of oxytocin than that utilized to produce abortion.[81] They found physiologic changes similar to those observed when naturally occurring oxytocin is given; namely, a drop in blood pressure, an increase in the pulse rate, and certain EKG changes. They concluded, however, that the synthetic oxytocin in the doses they used was apparently safe.[82] The larger doses needed to produce abortion would exaggerate these changes in all likelihood and should be more hazardous. Guttmacher has stated that "because of the potential cardiovascular risk from highly concentrated intravenous oxytocin solutions" he preferred the use of intra-amniotic hypertonic solutions.[83]

The intra-amniotic injection of formalin to produce abortion was first used many years ago, although the use of this drug is known to be hazardous. After World War II, hypertonic saline solution was substituted for formalin; the technique was used widely in Japan and later in other countries.[84] In 1958 hypertonic glucose was substituted and the first successful termination of a mid-trimester

---

[79] *Ibid.*

[80] *Ibid.*

[81] Bergquist & Kaiser, *Cardiovascular Effects of Intravenous Syntocinon,* 13 OBSTETRICS & GYNECOLOGY 360, 361 (1959).

[82] *Id.* at 363.

[83] Guttmacher, *Techniques of Therapeutic Abortion,* 7 CLINICAL OBSTETRICS & GYNECOLOGY 100, 105 (1964).

[84] Wagatsuma, *Intra-Amniotic Injection of Saline for Therapeutic Abortion,* 93 AMERICAN J. OBSTETRICS & GYNECOLOGY 743 (1965).

pregnancy using this solution was accomplished. No ill effects from either modality were reported in the English language literature until recently when a report of a maternal death associated with hypertonic glucose appeared.[85] At least twenty-five maternal deaths related to the use of intra-amniotic hypertonic saline solution have also been recorded.[86]

In summary, therapeutic abortion accomplished by D & C or abdominal laparotomy is safe, although an irreducible minimum of ill effects, including death, will occur. The use of concentrated oxytocin or intra-amniotic injection of hypertonic solutions is too recent to allow objective evaluation at this time.

IV. CONCLUSION

Criminal abortion remains a major public health problem which cannot be ignored. It is doubtful that human nature or human social arrangement will ever permit the avoidance of all unsafe or unwanted pregnancies, and the need for abortion is likely to continue. The legalization of abortion would help to answer this need.

An analysis of the reasons why physicians in the United States recommend legal abortion shows a changing philosophy over the past two decades. As medical disease has demanded less pregnancy interruption, psychiatric disease and risk of fetal malformation have required abortion more frequently. Social factors are apparently an important consideration with these indications. Groups of influential citizens — physicians, lawyers, psychologists, and social workers — are currently encouraging liberalization of the states' abortion laws in order that factors other than the "life" of the pregnant patient may be taken into account.

Legal abortion in a well-equipped hospital is not hazardous, but criminal abortion currently accounts for thousands of deaths annually in the United States. If a realistic relaxation of state laws on legal abortion will decrease this toll of needless deaths, society owes this protection to desperate women.

---

[85] Eastman, *Operative Obstetrics*, 20 OBSTETRICS & GYNECOLOGY SURVEY 776, 777 (1965).

[86] Wagatsuma, *supra* note 84, at 744.

3

Humane Abortion Laws and the Health Needs of Society

Kenneth J. Ryan, M.D.

Although the laws in most states allow interruption of pregnancy in order to protect a mother's life, and although all accredited hospitals have review committees covering the procedure, the medical profession is besieged by legal and moral questions regarding indications for abortions which society demands, but for which no universally acceptable guidelines have been established. These demands for abortion have been based on the possibility of a defective child, illegitimacy, rape, incest, a challenge to the mother's mental or physical health short of immediate, life-threatening conditions, and complex social and economic factors that, in some way, result in a home where the prospective child is unwanted.

In desperation, women seek physicians who will perform an abortion with or without some compliance with legal sanction; barring this, women seek unlicensed practitioners who, in the course of the act, further jeopardize the mother's health and life. The ethical considerations are complex, and although most of society will condone an abortion to save a mother's life, a lesser threat to the mother's life or the child's well-being is often judged inadequate to justify abortion. The central issue is always whether the problems of a given pregnancy can best be solved by the sacrifice of the unborn child.

In Japan, abortion has been allowed upon request as a rather effective countermeasure to population pressures.[1] In Scandinavian countries, abortion laws have been liberalized to include many of the social indications alluded to above.[2] In certain iron curtain countries where religion is no longer a powerful political voice, abortion is freely available.[3] However, it is unlikely that the American Judeo-Christian society will subscribe completely to any of the above solutions.

Whenever surveys of physicians have been conducted, a majority respond in favor of a liberalized abortion law.[4] Physicians, however, may be impressed with the recent, problem cases that provide the greatest moral challenge and may thereby misinterpret the sentiment of the bulk of society. The wide publicity afforded the thalidomide tragedy in Europe, the recent rubella epidemic in America, and the age-old dissatisfaction with dealing with juvenile rape and incest make this a propitious time to open the issues in a public forum. The intent of this article is to critically examine the bases upon which an acceptable code can be established.

I. POSSIBLE BASES FOR AN ACCEPTABLE CODE REGULATING ABORTION

A. Health Needs of Society

While medicine can be narrowly defined as that science involved in the treatment of disease, a more modern interpretation would be that the absence of disease does not constitute health and that medicine should be concerned in a positive way with the health needs of society, rather than responding only to its ills. In this context, the preservation of individual dignity, adequate nutrition, housing and education, and proper attitudes toward life's problems become

---

[1] See George, *Current Abortion Laws: Proposals and Movements for Reform*, in this volume, 1, 3, n. 12.

[2] See Skalts & Nørgaard, *Abortion Legislation in Denmark*, in this volume, 144, 145.

[3] See Hoffmeyer, *Medical Aspects of the Danish Legislation on Abortion*, in this volume, 179, 196-97.

[4] A report from the New York Academy of Medicine indicates that 87.6 per cent of New York obstetricians answering a questionnaire favored a change in the law. N.Y. Times, Jan. 31, 1965, p. 73, col. 5.

essential professional considerations for the physician. The rendering of health services, the planning of family size, and even the outcome of a given pregnancy depend so much upon socioeconomic factors that medicine can no longer consider these functions to be outside its domain. The practice of abortion falls into a category where traditional medicine blends into the total health needs of the community, depending upon a wide range of medical and so-called social problems. Society and physicians, as members of society, have no definitive answers to the question of how appropriate an abortion is for dealing with the many life situations for which it is requested. The problem is cloaked in religious and moral issues, legal tradition, and a strong emotional bias that almost defies a rational approach. This is just as true for those who favor liberalized abortion laws as for those who oppose them. Recently frustrated attempts to revise the laws in California[5] and New York[6] indicate that a majority of voters did not respond in a positive fashion to the reforms offered; and this occurred in the face of the well-known fact that abortions were illegally performed in accredited hospitals without official reproach and in spite of the wide publicity given to fetal deformities due to rubella.[7] Medical students have often asked how it is possible that reputable physicians will perform illegal abortions. The reply the author gives is that society will condone such practices for its own convenience providing that it does not have to collectively assume the moral responsibility for openly justifying them.[8]

As a practicing physician, educator, and pragmatist, the author would suggest that society is ready to revise present laws to conform to those already in existence in several states[9] and the District of

---

[5] For a discussion of the proposed statute, see Packer & Gampell, *Therapeutic Abortions: A Problem in Law and Medicine*, 11 STAN. L. REV. 417, 449-55 (1959). For a history of the fate of this bill, see George, *supra* note 1, at 32-33.

[6] An attempt to liberalize the justification necessary for abortion, PROPOSED N.Y. PENAL LAW § 130.05 (1964), met with subsequent defeat, N.Y. REV. PEN. LAW § 125.05 (1965).

[7] Life, June 4, 1965, p. 24.

[8] Gambling, prostitution, and the handling of traffic deaths are other areas where society has followed a similar course.

[9] ALA. CODE tit. 14, § 9 (1959); MD. ANN. CODE art. 27, § 3 (1957); ORE. REV. STAT. § 677.190 (1963).

Columbia,[10] which permit abortion where necessary to preserve the life and health of the mother. The social and fetal indications for abortion have undoubtedly been deterrents to reform. Ironically, the physician could honestly and effectively deal with all these abortion requests in order to preserve the life and health of the mother if the intent and interpretation of "life and health" are in the broadest sense. The responsibility then becomes an individual one among the family, the physician, and the immediate community. Society in general is not called upon to shoulder the moral burden that in this country, at least, it has been traditionally unwilling to assume.

B. *Status of the Unborn Child*

To the medical profession operating within its present framework, the conceptus, prior to twenty weeks of age, does not have the same legal status as one after that time. Should there be an untimely birth before twenty weeks, the act is considered an abortion, not a delivery, and is not listed on the mother's parity record. A birth or death certificate is not required and the body is handled as a pathological specimen without requiring legal interment.[11] In spite of this altered legal status, state laws allow interruption of even an early pregnancy only when it poses a threat to the mother.[12] In addition, injuries to the fetus, even at this early stage, which result in damage have been the bases for redress in courts of law.[13] The conceptus at all intrauterine ages does, in fact, have some status in society; it is this status which is the pivotal point of all discussions on abortion.

Physicians recognize that the mother's attitude toward her child may change once she feels life near the end of the first trimester of

---

[10] D.C. CODE ANN. § 22-201 (1961).

[11] See, *e.g.*, OHIO REV. CODE § 3705.21.

[12] See George, *supra* note 1, at 6-7.

[13] See, *e.g.*, Daley v. Meier, 33 Ill. App. 2d 218, 178 N.E.2d 691 (1961) (automobile collision); Mallison v. Pomeroy, 205 Ore. 690, 291 P.2d 225 (1955) (automobile collision); Sinkler v. Kneale, 401 Pa. 267, 164 A.2d 93 (1960) (automobile collision); Seattle-First Nat'l Bank v. Rankin, 59 Wash. 2d 288, 367 P.2d 835 (1962) (negligence of physician treating mother during pregnancy).

pregnancy. A recent example was a patient with severe renal[14] disease for whom abortion was recommended by all consultants as a safeguard to her life. Before it could be performed, she felt life and thereupon refused the procedure. This and many other examples suggest that there is a strong cultural force that equates identity with the first-recognized movements of life; prior to this time, abortion can be performed with less remorse. On the other hand, some religious teachings and the strong convictions of many dictate that life begins with conception (joining of sperm and egg) and is inviolate thereafter.[15] It is unlikely that the Western culture, which is so steeped in the traditions of the rights of the individual, will alter the status of the fetus at any gestational age, either legally or emotionally, in a manner which would allow abortion upon demand. The socially required indications for abortion will probably always be important and have a relative scale of values depending on the factors involved.

C. *Fetal Defects*

In most proposals for a more liberal abortion law, provision is made to allow abortion when there is a strong possibility that there will be a grave physical or mental defect in the child.[16] This can be considered either a modern or an ancient concept, depending on one's point of view, since provisions for doing away with defective examples of humanity have been in existence throughout recorded history. In some cultures, the decision for action was made after the child was born, a solution that would be unacceptable to most people today.

It would be difficult to argue against the proposition that all infants should be physically and mentally well-born. There are, today, modern medical techniques for predicting, in some instances, on a statistical basis, when a defective child can be anticipated. The potential for mongolism and various types of severe, hereditary, men-

---

14 This is a disease affecting the kidneys. For a discussion of this disease, see Niswander, *Medical Abortion Practices in the United States*, in this volume, 37, 42.

15 See Drinan, *The Inviolability of the Right To Be Born*, in this volume, 107, 111.

16 See, *e.g.*, PROPOSED N.Y. PENAL LAW § 130.05 (1964).

tal, and physical defects can be uncovered by genetic typing, which will undoubtedly prove to be a useful part of premarital medical advice. In spite of this, couples with such potential for defective offspring may only ask for help after the wife becomes pregnant. On the other hand, families with no known hereditary factors can be afflicted with a deformed child due to environmental factors such as drugs, radiation, or viral infections.

What should be the attitude toward "so-called" fetal indications for abortion? The indications that a child will be deformed are usually statistical. During the early months when most abortions are considered, one can predict deformity only by prior overall experience and not specifically in a given case. For example, the risk of a defective child in a mother who develops rubella in the first trimester of pregnancy is about 20 per cent; but the risk is 60 per cent if she develops the disease in the first few weeks of pregnancy and less than 10 per cent at twelve weeks of gestation.[17]

In a careful prospective study that followed the 227 infants of mothers who contracted rubella during pregnancy, the incidence of mental retardation was no different from that in the general population; 92 per cent of the children were attending regular schools eight to eleven years after birth.[18] Many of the defects of these children were correctable. While these statistics may indicate an overly optimistic attitude, they represent the best information available until the figures from the rubella epidemic in 1964-1965 have been similarly analyzed. How differently parents might respond to the threat of a deformed child if they were presented such data. Should one say there is a 40 per cent chance of a normal child or a 60 per cent chance of an afflicted one?

In this country's rubella epidemic of 1964-1965, many women were aborted with and without good evidence of risk, since other viral infections often masquerade as clinical rubella. Recent laboratory tests have made the diagnosis more secure, but the tests are not

---

[17] Rendle-Short, *Maternal Rubella, The Practical Management of a Case*, 2 LANCET 373 (1964).

[18] Sheridan, *Final Report of a Prospective Study of Children Whose Mothers Had Rubella in Early Pregnancy*, 2 BRITISH MEDICAL J. 536 (1964).

always available when a decision must be made. In the report on the epidemic from a United States Public Health Services Collaborative Study, 10 per cent of the patients reported exposure, 40 per cent of the exposed patients developed rubella, and 10 per cent of those delivered affected children.[19] It is not unlikely that the request for abortion in some quarters was so strong that studies on the value of prophylactic treatment with gamma globulin and prospective statistical evaluation will be impossible. Most physicians and patients wanted to take no chances.

The fear and risk of a deformed child are real, but require an informed medical profession for evaluation. With an acknowledged risk of 60 per cent for a deformed child to be born to a mother with rubella in the first few weeks of gestation, the odds may be more than most parents and society can bear. If an abortion is performed, it in fact is done for the family and society, not for the unborn child. Although some parents and physicians have indicated a desire to abort out of compassion for the child who would bear these defects, this is a difficult moral line to follow. People ask, "How would you like to be born deformed?" The child might reply, "If it is a choice of that or no life at all, I might choose life." One prominent gynecologist made a plea for "someone to speak for the fetus."[20] If someone is speaking for the fetus, he must realize that it might say, "Let me live." Finally, lest one become too concerned with the cult of perfection, remember —

> They say, best men are moulded out of faults,
> And for the most, become much more the better for being a little bad.[21]

The more conservative, less popular, attitude toward fetal defects has been stressed to point out that fetal indications can be a hazardous basis for moral or medical arguments on abortion. It is difficult to justify helping a child by aborting it, if the extent of the defects, or the actual existence of a defect, is not certain but is, instead, based on statistical grounds. One popular rejoinder is that

---

19 Medical World News, Dec. 10, 1965, p. 92.

20 Dr. Allan C. Barnes.

21 SHAKESPEARE, MEASURE FOR MEASURE.

the stakes involved, not the odds, should control. For this reason, the author favors an abortion law that provides for the individual family's needs in a given situation, based on the premise of protecting the mother's health. All fetal indications could be answered on these grounds. No distinction should be made between the mother's mental and physical health in this context since, in modern medical thinking, there is no real difference in terms of both being incapacitating and a potential threat to life.

D. *Needs of the Mother*

(1) The Life of the Mother.—Current practice, in most states, allows abortion to preserve the mother's life.[22] However, with the advances in medical technology, there are now almost no absolute contraindications to pregnancy; the threat to a mother's life with most medical diseases complicating pregnancy is relative, based on many factors besides the primary complicating ailment. For example, a woman with rheumatic heart disease who is financially capable and has help at home, no other children, the capacity to follow medical instructions carefully, and strong motivation might very well breeze through her pregnancy. Her sister with the same degree of heart disease who already has three children, lives on the fourth floor of a walk-up apartment, is incapable of following medical instructions, and is poorly motivated may well succumb either before or after delivery of another child. The point of time is academic.

It would serve no useful purpose to list all of the possible medical threats to a woman's life since the factors involved are complex and each case must be considered individually. Progressive renal failure in pregnancy was once thought to be an absolute indication for abortion, but even this has been treated by dialysis on the artificial kidney with resultant survival of the infant and the mother. However, this involves a dubious, long-range medical success for the mother.[23]

---

[22] See George, *supra* note 1, at 6-7.
[23] See Niswander, *supra* note 14, at 42.

In every large medical center there are instances when all consultants feel that abortion is indicated as a safeguard for a given mother's life, but no specific disease or set of conditions can be singled out as conclusive in all cases. Even the question of the immediacy or remoteness of the threat cannot be resolved with certainty; one is dealing with a probability as in the case of fetal defects. How much risk should one take? Fortunately, the law has not set an arbitrary figure.

Threatened suicide, as a psychiatric basis for recommending abortion, has been the subject of much discussion. Such observations as the very low suicide rate in pregnant women and the probable use of suicide as a threat to obtain abortions, otherwise legally denied, have been used to question the validity of psychiatric indications for interruption of pregnancy. Probability figures cannot determine whether a given patient will commit suicide; however, abuse by a few cannot be used, out of desperation, to discredit the motivation of all physicians dealing in this area. If psychiatric indications are used as a basis for abortion, physicians are concerned with the continued evaluation and treatment of the patient both before and after the procedure.

The threat to maternal life is the current base from which present abortion laws must be liberalized to cope with factors which do not obliterate life physically, but may do so functionally.

(2) Health of the Mother.—Health in the broad sense, as outlined in an earlier paragraph, is a positive concept.[24] Distinctions between physical and mental health are meaningless in terms of modern medical thinking. Health cannot be divorced from socio-economic factors which influence people's lives since health is a product of these conditions. In applying criteria for abortion based on maternal health, the question should be the extent to which the pregnancy threatens the general well-being of the patient. The threat must justify the sacrifice of the child. As with the threat of death, the risk will be relative and should not be subject to specific legislation for all patients.

---

[24] See text accompanying notes 4-5 *supra.*

Although women with heart disease, diabetes, chronic hypertension, a severe neurosis, or an impossible home life may not die with their next pregnancy, it could so disrupt their lives that they are neither effective members of society nor effective mothers. Certainly here, gradations of risk and relative values pertain. As with the threat to a mother's life, there should be no distinction between so-called medical and psychic influences since the latter is part of the former and they both can be devastating to health.

E. Humanitarian or Social Needs

Most humane indications for abortion can be included in this category. Should a twelve-year-old child who is raped or is made a partner to incest be forced or allowed to bear the child? It is inconceivable that society would answer in the affirmative, yet there is no provision for this under the present laws, which allow abortion only where there is a threat to life.[25]

Illegitimacy is a more complex point of departure since "moralists" would have the partners "punished" for socially unacceptable activities. Perhaps this could be individualized on the basis of a thorough medical evaluation of the case. The fear that the availability of abortion will lead to promiscuity is sheer nonsense; the same fear could be, and has been, leveled at contraception without any evidence that, over the course of history, either has significantly modified human behavior in this regard. Recently, there was a teen-age, unmarried patient in the hospital who had had three children. The fact that she was not aborted and did not use contraception may be a "moral" triumph, but it is neither a medical nor a social one.

II. IMPROBABLE BASES FOR ABORTION REFORM

A. Control of World Population

As stated previously, it is unlikely that abortion would be acceptable in this country as a means for controlling population pressures.[26] Unfortunately, until recently, even contraception was

---

25 See George, *supra* note 1, at 6-7.

26 See text accompanying note 1 *supra*.

denied to that segment of the population which needed it most, by ignoring or forbidding it in public health institutions. In spite of the more widespread dissemination of contraceptive information, certain women, at risk, will become pregnant; a humane, effective law for coping with their problem is needed. The means for effective family planning are available and must be made accessible to all within their individual religious and moral convictions. Certainly this will go a long way toward reducing the traffic in abortion, which is an even more involved moral and medical issue.

B. Reduction of Criminal Abortion

As other causes of maternal death decline under the impact of adequate modern medical care, the proportion due to criminal abortion by non-medical practitioners will undoubtedly increase. From both a relative and absolute point of view, the number of maternal deaths due to abortion are as distressing as they are unnecessary. A recent news release indicated that criminal abortions are the leading cause of maternal deaths in New York City.[27] In any large medical center, a sizable number of septic, incomplete abortions are admitted regularly as the result of the activities of unlicensed practitioners who are the last route of appeal for desperate women. However, abortions conducted under modern medical conditions are reasonably safe.

The plea for a liberal abortion law has often been based on the supposition that it would decrease this traffic in criminal abortions. Barring a law that allows abortion upon demand, it is unlikely that this activity can be abolished.[28] Although deplorable, the illegal abortions by unlicensed practitioners and their resultant mortalities provide unlikely bases for society to liberalize laws. The community has not legalized gambling to avoid the criminal element, has not legalized prostitution to avoid venereal disease and blackmail, and has not required a change in standards for the manufacture and operation of motor vehicles to overcome traffic deaths.

---

[27] AMA News, Nov. 29, 1965 p. 1.

[28] In Sweden, the advent of liberal abortion laws was accompanied by a decline in criminal abortion only to be followed by a resurgence due to the time and bother of justifying an abortion before a reviewing committee.

Such a state of affairs would suggest that liberalization of abortion laws will be based predominantly upon other grounds. With such a change in laws, the benefits from decreased criminal interruption of pregnancy would be a welcome relief in any case.

III. CONCLUSION

The medical community has had a much more intimate exposure to the problems of and needs for therapeutic abortion than other segments of society. The patient has generally turned to the physician for help and compassion rather than to the more rigid courts or churches. When medical help was withheld, the patient turned to the non-licensed practitioner in spite of the risks involved. Society has left the burden, by default, at the physician's doorstep.

Abortion should be allowed when pregnancy constitutes a grave threat to the life or health of the mother in the opinion of her physician and two consultant physicians. Whether the fear and despair of rape, incest, illegitimacy, or a possibly deformed child constitute a grave threat to the health or life of a given patient should be decided in such a manner and are properly medical decisions. Physicians would not shun this role; indeed, doctors currently have to deal with these questions without the help of the rest of society or of enlightened legislation. If properly interpreted, a law such as the one outlined above could provide a reasonable basis for physicians to deal with the problem of therapeutic abortion in modern society.

4

Psychiatric Implications of Abortion:
A Case Study in Social Hypocrisy

*Harold Rosen, M.D.**

Any discussion of the abortion problem — and of its psychiatric implications — must of necessity stress the legal and medical hypocrisy involved that is usually so blandly ignored. From 20 to 30 per cent of all pregnancies end in abortion.[1] If a woman, despite exceedingly severe physical or emotional disease, is nevertheless determined to carry her pregnancy to term, she in all probability will be able to do so if all the resources of modern medicine, including modern psychiatry, are employed to treat her. But if she does not wish to carry the pregnancy to term, even the punitive pressure of the official medical code and the various state statutes cannot necessarily force her to do so.

I. THE COMPLEXITIES OF THE ABORTION PROBLEM

Between ten and twenty criminal abortions are performed every fifteen minutes in this country.[2] Estimates of twenty-five hundred

*Portions of Dr. Rosen's article have been reprinted from *The Encyclopedia of Mental Health*, ed. Albert Deutsch and Helen Fishman (New York: Franklin Watts, Inc., 1963), © 1963 by Franklin Watts, Inc. These appear with the permission of the publishers.

[1] Fisher, *Criminal Abortion*, 42 J. CRIM. L., C. & P.S. 242 (1951); Hardin, *Abortion and Human Dignity*, Public Lecture at University of California (Berkeley), April 29, 1964 (Distributed by Citizens for Humane Abortion Laws, San Francisco, Calif.).

[2] Rosen, *Abortion*, Today's Health, April 1965, p. 24.

per day are not unusual,[3] and it may be a great deal more.[4] The majority are performed on married women between thirty and forty years of age, with two or more children, who have conceived by their husbands.[5] Eighty to ninety per cent of all abortions in the United States are performed by competent physicians,[6] on referral from other physicians.[7]

The abortion problem, as Cameron has stated, seems to be "a meeting point of great and, at times, sharply conflicting human needs and interests. . . ."[8] This is understandable. It is historically determined. It must necessarily constitute one of the most contentious of the medical, legal, social, and economic problems which, again to quote Cameron, "lie so vexed upon the conscience of our society."[9] In Baltimore, for instance, white children between the ages of twelve and sixteen, even though repeatedly pregnant, are more apt to have abortions than their colored sisters, who therefore bear a greater number of illegitimate children.[10] Nevertheless, the

---

[3] Id. at 62.

[4] ABORTION IN THE UNITED STATES 178, 180 (Calderone ed. 1958); BATES & ZAWADZKI, CRIMINAL ABORTION 3 (1964); cf. GEBHARD, POMEROY, MARTIN & CHRISTENSON, PREGNANCY, BIRTH AND ABORTION 136-37 (1958).

[5] ABORTION IN THE UNITED STATES 61 (Calderone ed. 1958); Kleegman, Planned Parenthood: Its Influence on Public Health and Family Welfare, in THERAPEUTIC ABORTION: MEDICAL, PSYCHIATRIC, LEGAL, ANTHROPOLOGICAL AND RELIGIOUS CONSIDERATIONS 254, 255 (Rosen ed. 1954).

[6] GEBHARD, POMEROY, MARTIN & CHRISTENSON, op. cit. supra note 4, at 198, 212; ABORTION IN THE UNITED STATES 62-63 (Calderone ed. 1958); cf. Guttmacher, The Legal and Moral Status of Therapeutic Abortion, 4 PROGRESS IN GYNECOLOGY 279 (1963).

[7] ABORTION IN THE UNITED STATES 62-63 (Calderone ed. 1958) (Remarks of G. Lotrell Timanus); Kleegman, Planned Parenthood: Its Influence on Public Health and Family Welfare, in THERAPEUTIC ABORTION: MEDICAL, PSYCHIATRIC, LEGAL, ANTHROPOLOGICAL AND RELIGIOUS CONSIDERATIONS 254, 256 (Rosen ed. 1954).

[8] Cameron, Psychiatric Foreword, in THERAPEUTIC ABORTION: MEDICAL, PSYCHIATRIC, LEGAL, ANTHROPOLOGICAL AND RELIGIOUS CONSIDERATIONS, at xvii (Rosen ed. 1954).

[9] Id. at xviii.

[10] The author is indebted to Dr. Frank Furstenberg (personal communication) for information showing that published statistics do not portray actual incidence of pregnancy since, as is generally conceded, white girls are more likely to have economic resources that the colored do not possess (for abortion, delivery elsewhere, and the like). Despite this, Dr. Furstenberg adds, there are over eight hundred registered deliveries by girls sixteen or under per year in Baltimore of a first child, and an additional two hundred per year by girls sixteen or under of a second or third child. (Vital statistics of

illegitimately pregnant school child, whether white or colored, is almost invariably forced to become a school drop-out. She frequently spends the rest of her life at menial work. The psychiatric problems here obviously are pronounced.[11]

The laws of most of the states could be interpreted to mean that there are *no* legal indications for therapeutic interruption of pregnancy. Forty-four states either ban abortion or permit it for the sole purpose of saving the mother's life.[12] The only psychiatric threat to *life* is suicide; and suicidal patients can be committed involuntarily to psychiatric hospitals where they can remain until delivery. In eight states[13] there is a curious addendum, which apparently has never been questioned: therapeutic abortions are legal if performed to save not only the life of the mother but that of the child with which she is pregnant.[14] This would seem to mean that physicians can legally sacrifice the conceptus to save its life; and this kind of double talk, in at least one instance that has come to the author's attention, has been used psychiatrically to justify recommendation for therapeutic interruption of an emotionally crippling pregnancy that nevertheless was carried to term.

Much of our abortion law, while *perhaps* relevant in 1800, possesses no pertinence whatsoever today[15] except through a process of interpretation over the years with which, unfortunately, far too many psychiatrists, obstetricians, lawyers, and hospital admin-

---

the Baltimore City Health Department, data circulated 1964.) These recidivists, white as well as colored, are going down the line to poverty.

[11] See Rosen, *Abortion: The Increasing Involvement of Psychiatry*, 2 FRONTIERS OF CLINICAL PSYCHIATRY 1, 8 (Dec. 1965).

[12] Committee on Human Reproduction, American Medical Ass'n, A.P. Dispatch, N.Y. Times, Dec. 1, 1965, p. 1, col. 2. See GEBHARD, POMEROY, MARTIN & CHRISTENSON, *op. cit. supra* note 4, at 192; Guttmacher, *supra* note 6, at 285; Guttmacher, *The Legal Status of Therapeutic Abortion*, in THERAPEUTIC ABORTION: MEDICAL, PSYCHIATRIC, LEGAL, ANTHROPOLOGICAL AND RELIGIOUS CONSIDERATIONS 181 (Rosen ed. 1954); Harper, *Abortion Laws in the United States*, in ABORTION IN THE UNITED STATES 187 (Calderone ed. 1958). For a detailed discussion of statutes in American Jurisdictions see George, *Current Abortion Laws: Proposals and Movements for Reform*, in this volume, 1.

[13] Conn., Minn., Mo., Nev., N.Y., Va., Wash., and W. Va. See Eastman, *Liberalization of Attitudes Toward Abortion*, Current Medical Digest, June 1959, pp. 54, 59.

[14] *Id.* at 59; see George, *supra* note 12 at 9.

[15] Eastman, *supra* note 13, at 60.

istrators are unfamiliar or which they ignore. It may perhaps be that they are mindful of Mr. Justice Frankfurter's comments about the M'Naghten insanity rules,[16] for his remarks apply with equal force to abortion: "to have laws which cannot rationally be justified except by a process of interpretation which distorts and often practically nullifies them . . . is not a desirable system. . . ."[17] It can, therefore, be readily understood why abortion laws "are in a large measure abandoned in practice, and therefore . . . shams."[18]

In any case, to the physician, "life" does not imply merely immediate survival — and only immediate survival — but must be considered a long-range process dependent upon health, both physical and mental.[19] That *life* depends on *health*, and that the legal distinction, at least, between the two is extremely doubtful, was specifically stated by the British Court of Law which in 1938 acquitted an obstetrician charged with having performed an abortion on a fourteen-year-old child whom three soldiers had raped and impregnated.[20] Despite the impact of the decision in the case of *Rex v. Bourne*,[21] rape in the United States does not per se constitute a legal ground for interrupting a pregnancy; but some physicians in some hospitals do therapeutically interrupt an occasional pregnancy — extra-legally rather than illegally — for this reason.

During the past ten to fifteen years in prestige hospitals in various parts of the United States, statutory indications for therapeutic abortions have been interpreted to include not only the saving of the mother's life, but also the protection and preservation of her health.[22] This latter indication is potentially an exceedingly elastic one. Pregnancies have also been therapeutically interrupted, *legally*, to prevent serious injury, emotional as well as physical, to the mother, or in an attempt to halt the advance of serious organic or

---

[16] *The Royal Comm'n on Capital Punishment: 1949-1953 Report of the Comm'n, Cmd. No. 8932*, 7 ENGLISH PARLIAMENTARY PAPERS 102 (1953).

[17] *Ibid.*

[18] *Ibid.*

[19] Rosen, *supra* note 11, at 1.

[20] Rex v. Bourne, [1939] 1 K.B. 687. See also WILLIAMS, THE SANCTITY OF LIFE AND THE CRIMINAL LAW 319 (1957); Eastman, *supra* note 13, at 57-58.

[21] [1939] 1 K.B. 687.

[22] Rosen, *supra* note 2, at 24.

emotional disease, or to prevent it.   Socioeconomic factors here have
been given serious psychiatric consideration.[23]

A therapeutic abortion, to define it as it is now performed, is
an abortion performed in order to preserve the physical and emotional health of the pregnant woman, or to save her life, physically
and emotionally.   It must be performed by a physician and under
prescribed conditions that vary, in this country, from state to state
and, within specific states, from hospital to hospital.[24]   The uterus
is evacuated — and this requires stressing — in order to correct, and
only to correct, a pathologic condition that has come into existence
because of the specific pregnancy involved; the developing chorionic
tissue is either potentially or actually damaging and dangerous to
the pregnant patient.   It must be evacuated or excised.   As Guttmacher so succinctly states, the attitude of the physician, theoretically at least, is essentially the basic amoralistic medical attitude so
characteristic of the surgeon in his operative removal of all types of
pathologic tissue for which, at the present stage of medical knowledge, surgical excision is advised.[25]

This, unfortunately, is purely theoretical.   Where pregnancy is
concerned, few physicians can approach the problem neutrally, with
this basic amoralistic medical attitude.   As Mandy[26] states, physicians as a whole "think of abortion in one way, speak and write of
it in another, and in actual practice conform neither to personally
expressed beliefs, nor to established legal or social codes."[27]   In contrast to all other medical procedures, medically acceptable indications for therapeutic abortion vary from physician to physician, from
hospital to hospital, and — even within the same hospital and on
the part of the same hospital board — from day to day.   This is
regrettable, but emotional involvement in the problem on the part

---

[23] Ibid.

[24] Guttmacher, *The Shrinking Non-Psychiatric Indications for Therapeutic Abortion*, in THERAPEUTIC ABORTION: MEDICAL, PSYCHIATRIC, LEGAL, ANTHROPOLOGI-
CAL AND RELIGIOUS CONSIDERATIONS 12, 15 (Rosen ed. 1954).

[25] Guttmacher, *supra* note 6, at 290, 293; see also Hardin, *supra* note 1.

[26] Mandy, *Reflections of a Gynecologist*, in THERAPEUTIC ABORTION: MEDICAL,
PSYCHIATRIC, LEGAL, ANTHROPOLOGICAL AND RELIGIOUS CONSIDERATIONS 248
(Rosen ed. 1954).

[27] Ibid.

of all concerned is so intense that at present no other, more adequate statement can be made. Not infrequently, for instance, the abortion board of one hospital, but not another, may refuse to accept a recommendation for interruption; on nine separate occasions during the past seven years, patients who have been seen in consultation in one hospital have afterwards been therapeutically aborted at adjacent hospitals with, at times, almost the same visiting staff. Illustrative case material, if this were a clinical article, could be cited practically *ad nauseam*.

Basically, this is not the fault of the hospital board, nor is it something for which the individual physician — be he general practitioner, obstetrician, or psychiatrist — can be blamed. The fault lies in the present, almost complete lack of any standard frame of reference; no clear-cut obstetrical, medical, or psychiatric indications for therapeutic interruption of pregnancy have as yet been defined. Ethical and religious considerations play an exceedingly significant role: the devout Catholic, who feels that life begins at the very moment of conception, for instance, will have one approach to the problem, while the Latter Day Saint will have another, especially since he, with his fellow Mormons, believes that life starts only at the moment of birth.[28] For the purpose of this discussion, however, religious considerations will be disregarded.[29]

According to most estimates, between two and three out of every ten pregnancies in the United States end in abortion.[30] These may

---

[28] Devereux, *A Typological Study of Abortion in 350 Primitive, Ancient, and Pre-Industrial Societies,* in THERAPEUTIC ABORTION: MEDICAL, PSYCHIATRIC, LEGAL, ANTHROPOLOGICAL AND RELIGIOUS CONSIDERATIONS 97, 100 (Rosen ed. 1954); see also DEVEREUX, A STUDY OF ABORTION IN PRIMITIVE SOCIETIES *passim* (1955).

[29] This is despite the fact that in Roman Catholic Chile a recent survey showed that 27 per cent of all women admitted to having had induced abortions, and that in predominantly Catholic France the annual number of abortions equals the annual number of live births. See Avendano & Fraundes-Latham, *A Contraceptive Programme in a Latin American Urban Community,* UNITED NATIONS WORLD POPULATION CONFERENCE (Sept. 1965) (in publication); Tabah & Samuel, *Encuesta de Fecundidad y de Atitudes Relativas a la Formaciòn de la Familia,* 2 MEDICO-SOCIALES 19 (1961); see also Hardin, *supra* note 1.

[30] See text accompanying note 1 *supra.* After rapport here was gained with 107 unselected married women patients with two or three children, they were asked, "Have you ever had a legal or illegal abortion?" Fourteen evaded the question. Twenty had not had an abortion, but of these, three had arranged to have it but had had a miscarriage before it could be performed. Sixty-seven had had abortions and then, within

be spontaneous, therapeutic, or criminal. If reported as spontaneous, although illegal abortions are, perhaps, not infrequently so reported, it cannot be considered as either consciously or deliberately induced. A pregnancy may nevertheless be deliberately interrupted — by physical, chemical, or operative means — and the resultant abortion, whether or not it be reported as spontaneous, must then be termed either criminal or therapeutic, depending largely upon whether it has been performed legally or in an extra-legal environment. In either case, someone, somewhere, somehow, for some reason has thought it was indicated. It would otherwise not have been performed.

Socially acceptable indications, however, vary from culture to culture. Attitudes toward pregnancy — and toward its interruption — are incorporated in group mores, in religious tenets, and in legal statutes. Throughout the world, and not in Western culture alone, the approach for the most part has been a conservative one. There are nevertheless glaring exceptions.

As previously mentioned, in the United States nine-tenths or more of all artificially induced abortions, whether therapeutic or criminal, are procured or prescribed for married women, impregnated by their husbands, with three or more children, and over thirty years of age.[31] If legal, they are performed ostensibly for medical or psychiatric reasons; if illegal, the reasons alleged may, perhaps, also be medical or psychiatric. Whether legal or illegal, nevertheless, the reasons, but not the rationalizations advanced, may be, and usually are, socioeconomic. These have been written into the statutes of the various Scandinavian countries;[32] but in the United States, while they frequently influence the attitude of the examining physician and hospital board, they constitute extra-legal rather than legal considerations. Despite their extra-legal nature, it is these

two or three years, had had planned pregnancies, or so they stated. And finally, six stated that they had had abortions and had no desire for any further pregnancy; one of these six had had two abortions.

[31] See text accompanying notes 5-7 *supra*.

[32] ABORTION IN THE UNITED STATES 14, 21, 25 (Calderone ed. 1958) (Comments of Drs. Brekke, Clemmesen, and Af Geijerstam). See generally Skalts & Nørgaard, *Abortion Legislation in Denmark*, in this volume, 144. (Danish *Act concerning Provisions Relating to Pregnancy* is reprinted at 171).

that are most frequently involved. They far outweigh all medical and psychiatric factors combined. However, to the physician, only rigidly defined medical conditions (although far from rigidly stated) determine whether or not sufficient justification can be found for recommending that a specific pregnancy be therapeutically terminated.

Any decision on the part of a competent, conscientious, and ethical physician to interrupt a given pregnancy can be reached only after grave and prolonged deliberation. Legally, in a number of countries and a number of states, it can be advised only if the physical life of the mother would actually be endangered by the continuation of the pregnancy to term.[33] In other countries[34] and in some states as well, this view no longer prevails.[35] And what is *therapeutic* in some states is *criminal* in others. This requires further discussion in the context of present medical, including psychiatric, indications for therapeutic abortion as they now exist in actual hospital practice.

II. THERAPEUTIC ABORTION

A. Medical Indications

So far as specific medical indications are concerned, these have been shrinking consistently during the past several decades. At present they seem well on the way to becoming virtually, if not actually, non-existent. For instance, with the development of thoracic surgery, the utilization of hormone therapy, and the widespread use of antibiotic medication, even those organic conditions such as essential hypertension, tuberculosis, and heart disease, which previously were thought almost invariably to indicate therapeutic abortion, no longer so invariably necessitate the procedure. A majority of women with uncomplicated hypertension can now carry their

---

[33] Schur, *Abortion and the Social System*, 3 SOCIAL PROBLEMS 94, 95 (1955). See generally TIMASHEFF, INTRODUCTION TO THE SOCIOLOGY OF LAW (1936).

[34] *E.g.*, Austria, Cuba, Denmark, Finland, Norway, Switzerland, Japan, and Sweden.

[35] Eastman, *supra* note 13, at 59; Kummer, *Prevention of Psychiatric Complications of Pregnancy and the Puerperium*, 6 AMERICAN PRACTITIONER AND DIGEST OF TREATMENT 1315, 1319 (1955). *But cf.* Russell, *Changing Indications for Therapeutic Abortion*, 151 A.M.A.J. 108 (1953).

child to term if they so desire, and with little or no hazard as far as their own physical well-being is concerned. Interruption of pregnancy because of pulmonary tuberculosis has been declining steadily during the past two decades. Today, in the larger medical centers, obstetricians will rarely see cases of *hyperemesis gravidarum* so severe and so resistant to current methods of therapy as to require interruption. And cardiac surgery is now being performed with increasing frequency on patients with severe heart disease who desire, and are thereby enabled, to carry their child to term. Pregnancy, in other words, need now seldom aggravate organic disease. As Eastman states, it is only that small minority of patients with both rheumatic heart disease and a history of previous cardiac failure who must be excepted from this generalization.[36]

To phrase this differently, if physicians do not wish to force a specific woman to carry a specific pregnancy to term, and if that woman is actually suffering from some severe physical disease then, but only then, the pathological process, provided it falls within certain categories, is in certain hospitals and by certain physicians and hospital boards considered sufficient indication for interruption. In others, it is not — and this needs stressing. This sometimes, surprisingly, has little or nothing to do with the religious construct within which a specific hospital operates, or with the religious convictions of its visiting and resident staffs.

Despite the fact that in this country the law still concerns itself only with the life and health of the mother — and never with that of the unborn child — pregnancies not infrequently are interrupted on medical grounds for so-called eugenic reasons, not because faulty germ plasm is thought present, but because it is felt that temporary, deleterious, environmental influences may ultimately result in the birth of seriously defective offspring. The thalidomide problem is a case in point. Therapeutic radiation to the pelvic organs during undiagnosed early pregnancy, to diminish the size of a fibroid uterus in a patient not suspected of being already pregnant, is considered by a number of obstetricians as sufficient indication for therapeutic

---

[36] Eastman, *Obstetrical Foreword*, in THERAPEUTIC ABORTION: MEDICAL, PSYCHIATRIC, LEGAL, ANTHROPOLOGICAL AND RELIGIOUS CONSIDERATIONS, at xix (Rosen ed. 1954); WILLIAMS, OBSTETRICS 1116 (12th ed. Eastman & Hellman 1951).

abortion. And if the expectant mother contracts German measles before the twelfth week of her pregnancy, this, too, in some hospitals (but not in all) is considered sufficient indication, since it has now been established that between 30 and 50 per cent of all offspring will suffer from severe congenital abnormalities if such pregnancies are carried to term. Yet, even if this be true, one-third of all children born to women whose pelvic organs have been so irradiated, and perhaps one-half of all offspring born to women with rubella, according to statistics so far compiled, show none of the *serious* defects described in the literature. Some women previously irradiated or with rubella, in fact, have determinedly and against even militant medical advice carried their offspring to term. Nevertheless although in a great many hospitals and by a great many obstetricians such potential fetal pathology is now considered sufficient indication for the interruption of a pre-viable pregnancy, this is an extra-legal indication: the law in no state has seen fit to concern itself with the life and health of the developing human organism.[37] Yet no state statute expressly forbids this. Such interruptions, therefore, are not actually *against* the law; they are merely *outside* it, at least so far as the statutes of the individual states are concerned. But only an infinitesimally small number of abortions are performed for this reason.

In any case, in this country during the past two decades, the incidence of therapeutic abortion, at least for purely medical reasons, has declined steadily. Fewer and fewer hospitals unbegrudgingly accept the recommendation to abort, and for a lower and lower percentage of patients.[38] While current medical progress is probably the basic factor here, a number of usually undeclared non-medical factors are also involved. These include occasional threats of legal difficulties[39] — an understandable, but for the most part not con-

---

[37] Schur, *supra* note 33.

[38] Russell, *supra* note 35, at 109; Tietze, *Therapeutic Abortion in New York City 1943-1947*, 60 AMERICAN J. OBSTETRICS & GYNECOLOGY 146 (1950); Wilson, *The Abortion Problem in the General Hospital*, in THERAPEUTIC ABORTION: MEDICAL, PSYCHIATRIC, LEGAL, ANTHROPOLOGICAL AND RELIGIOUS CONSIDERATIONS 189 (Rosen ed. 1954).

[39] Guttmacher, *supra* note 12, at 175; Schur, *The Abortion Racket*, 180 THE NATION 199 (1954).

sciously perceived, fear of untoward professional, administrative, or legal repercussions[40] — and the current, but almost completely disregarded, restrictive legislative statutes.[41]

B. Psychiatric Indications

Whereas the incidence of therapeutic abortions on the basis of medical indications has been on the decline, recommendations for interruption on psychiatric grounds are now on the increase.[42] This is despite the fact that problems posed by the psychiatric evaluation of emotionally sick pregnant patients are so complex that at times clarification seems almost impossible. The psychiatrist, like his medical *confrère*, when examining patients who demand an abortion, not infrequently finds himself at an impasse.

Some of the abortion-demanding pregnant women who are referred for psychiatric evaluation turn out to be emotionally ill patients who happen, coincidentally, sometimes even as a symptom of their emotional illness, to be pregnant.[43] They may attempt to force the obstetrician and psychiatrist to interrupt their pregnancies by threatening either illegal abortion or suicide. If the psychiatrist feels that, as a result of the pregnancy, the depressive tendencies which are present will be intensified to the point of potential or actual suicide, he will of course suggest treatment in a psychiatric hospital. Because of the extreme urgency of their demands and the identification with them by their husbands, which prevents the latter from realizing how emotionally ill their wives actually are, it frequently becomes impossible to treat them as other depressed or potentially suicidal patients would be treated. This recommendation

---

40 Schur, *supra* note 33, at 95.

41 Regan, *The Law of Abortion*, 6 ANNALS OF WESTERN MEDICINE & SURGERY 26 (1952), in LEGAL MEDICINE 834 (Gradwohl ed. 1954); Schur, *supra* note 33.

42 See Kummer, *Psychiatric Contraindications to Pregnancy with Reference to Therapeutic Abortion and Sterilization*, 79 CALIFORNIA MEDICINE 31 (1953); Rosen, *supra* note 11, at 1.

43 Rosen, *supra* note 2, at 63; Rosen, *The Emotionally Sick Pregnant Patient*, 1 J. OF CLINICAL AND EXPERIMENTAL HYPNOSIS 54 (1953); Rosen, *The Emotionally Sick Pregnant Patient: Psychiatric Indications and Contraindications to the Interruption of Pregnancy*, in THERAPEUTIC ABORTION: MEDICAL, PSYCHIATRIC, LEGAL, ANTHROPOLOGICAL AND RELIGIOUS CONSIDERATIONS 219 (Rosen ed. 1954).

is often rejected by patient, by husband, and by parents. Commitment is usually impossible. Most refuse to see the psychiatrist even a second time. As an emergency life-saving measure, the psychiatrist may, therefore, recommend interruption. It should be noted, however, that although one successful suicide does occur every half hour in this country, the suicide rate among pregnant women is less than what would statistically be expected for the population as a whole. The Chief Medical Examiner of the State of Maryland, for instance, could "recall only one pregnancy among the last 700 suicides, although some pregnancies may have been missed, since we do not do an autopsy where the manner and the cause of death are established."[44] In any case, it usually is extremely rare. It nevertheless does occur; and it must, therefore, not be overlooked. Pregnant women do kill themselves. Eight per cent of all women who committed suicide in Sweden during the twenty-year period from 1925 through 1944, for instance, were found on autopsy to be pregnant and in each case, on investigation, their pregnancy was felt to be the precipitating factor in the suicide.[45] Thus, if a recommendation for interruption be rejected by a hospital board, the risk of suicide as a result, at least occasionally, must be incurred. Statements in the available literature denying this reflect either the bias of their authors or a lack of meaningful follow-up on the patient involved.

The psychiatrist may recommend interruption for other reasons as well.[46] Under certain conditions, he feels abortion to be indicated for patients whose previous pregnancies had repeatedly precipitated post-partum psychotic reactions, and this is so regardless of whether or not depressive and potentially suicidal symptoms be present. If assaultive and possible homicidal drives are becoming intensified, it

---

[44] Letter from Dr. Russell S. Fisher to the author, June 10, 1964.

[45] Ekblad, *Induced Abortion on Psychiatric Grounds — A Follow-Up Study of 479 Women*, ACTA PSYCHIATRICA ET NEUROLOGICA SCANDINIVICA, Supp. 99, at 94-95 (1955).

[46] See Brew & Seidenberg, *Psychotic Reactions Associated with Pregnancy and Childbirth*, 111 J. NERVOUS AND MENTAL DISEASES 408 (1950); Ebaugh & Heuser, *Psychiatric Aspects of Therapeutic Abortion*, 2 POSTGRADUATE MEDICINE 325 (1947); Lidz, *Reflections of a Psychiatrist*, in THERAPEUTIC ABORTION: MEDICAL, PSYCHIATRIC, LEGAL, ANTHROPOLOGICAL AND RELIGIOUS CONSIDERATIONS 276, 279, 281-82 (Rosen ed. 1954).

seems a *sine qua non.* Some psychiatrists will recommend abortion for specific patients with manic-depressive or schizophrenic psychoses who, for whatever reason, are not amenable to therapy. Others believe it to be indicated for previously lobotomized patients because of the very decided risk which, so it is felt, pregnancy imposes upon them. If it seems as though a psychotic reaction will be precipitated as a result of the pregnancy or the stress of early motherhood, a great many psychiatrists would make the recommendation for the sake of the expectant mother's emotional and physical well-being. And a fairly large number of psychiatrists are agreed that interruption of pregnancy for psychiatric reasons is indicated in those patients who, because of their very pronounced emotional immaturity, must themselves be babied, cannot be trusted with the responsibilities of an adult, and cannot, in American culture at least, function the way mothers, as adult women, are expected to function. It can be expected that if their pregnancy is not interrupted their emotional disease will crystallize and assume clinical proportions.

For every 500 births in this country, one pregnant or puerperal woman is committed to a psychiatric hospital. To be more precise, pregnancy, childbirth, and the puerperium are precipitating factors thought to account for 2 per cent of all female admissions to mental hospitals.[47] This may help explain the fact that recommendations for interruption on psychiatric grounds now seem to be increasing.

The psychiatrist, like his colleagues in obstetrics and the other medical specialties, however, can, in general, make this recommendation legally only if he feels that the physical or emotional life or health of his pregnant patient will be endangered by carrying the developing organism to term. Nevertheless, he frequently does give serious consideration to the developing organism itself, as do the obstetrician, the internist, and the gynecologist in cases of rubella or of irradiation to the pelvic organs.

As the obstetrician on occasion considers it medically justifiable to recommend interruption of a pre-viable pregnancy on the basis of actual or potential fetal pathology, some psychiatrists do take into

---

[47] Kummer, *supra* note 35, at 1315; Kummer, *supra* note 42, at 32.

consideration the possible effect of an emotionally unstable environment on the developing human being. Child delinquency and criminal psychopathy require serious consideration by everyone. In an exceedingly thought-provoking article, Jenkins discusses children whose mothers had unsuccessfully tried to abort themselves.[48] He comments about those problems of child and adolescent development which constitute so frequent a source of referral to child guidance clinics, and which ultimately culminate in the appearance of socialized or "gang" delinquents, and of unsocialized, aggressive children, in the juvenile court. It should be noted — and this is practically a truism — that the morbid effect of a specific emotionally unhealthy environment on the young child becomes increasingly irreversible as that child grows older. And since schizoid withdrawal in childhood, which so frequently is related to maternal rejection even before birth, is more frequently found in those patients who later develop schizophrenic breakdowns, this in itself becomes one of the most pronounced of the mental health problems with which the country is now faced.

Schizophrenia in this country fills at least one-quarter of all hospital beds — medical, surgical, and psychiatric — as a result of which, "the question of capacity for maternal response and need for emotional support [must] . . . not be overlooked in considering the important problems relating to the question of therapeutic abortion."[49] Nevertheless, when the psychiatrist makes his recommendations, these and other related questions cannot *legally* be taken into consideration, no matter how important they are, and no matter what growing up in an emotionally unstable environment might mean to the child. The established code of ethics of the medical profession and the statutes in force in the various states at present are such that neither this nor any other socioeconomic factor (no matter how pronounced or how compelling) can be considered as a medical (including psychiatric) justification for abortion.

---

[48] Jenkins, *The Significance of Maternal Rejection of Pregnancy for the Future Development of the Child*, in THERAPEUTIC ABORTION: MEDICAL, PSYCHIATRIC, LEGAL, ANTHROPOLOGICAL AND RELIGIOUS CONSIDERATIONS 269 (Rosen ed. 1954).

[49] *Id.* at 275.

Yet psychiatric consultations are of prime importance. More and more women who otherwise would request and obtain abortions, legally or illegally, with psychiatric help, now want and find it possible to carry their pregnancies to term. With some, the desire for the interruption is iatrogenic. This becomes apparent almost immediately after the psychiatric consultation begins. With exceedingly superficial psychotherapy, directed on the one hand toward the patient and, on the other, toward her physician under the pretext of discussing with him the problems involved, the patient is then usually able to carry her child to term. With other patients, whose problems primarily are situational, the desire not to have the child disappears after relatively superficial psychotherapy.

However, if symptoms are precipitated on an hysterical basis in addition, the therapeutic problem becomes much more complicated, especially if pronounced nausea and vomiting are present. At times symptoms — and even attitudes underlying symptoms — can nevertheless be treated successfully in relatively few sessions; but if symptoms become exaggerated, neither psychiatrist nor obstetrician may at times have any choice. And if the patient also has some chronic disease, like diabetes, which she utilizes in her fight against herself and her environment in order to gain her demands, it may be impossible for the psychiatrist to help her attain any actual desire for the continuation of the pregnancy. She may go so far as to utilize her chronic disease in a quasi-suicidal attempt, discontinuing her insulin for instance, going into diabetic coma and acidosis, and requiring even emergency hospitalization. Nevertheless, when recommended for psychiatric reasons, therapeutic abortion, except in emergency situations, can be considered the treatment of choice only if the abortion itself will not prove more traumatic to the patient than the psychological trauma of pregnancy and childbirth. This always requires careful evaluation on the part of the psychiatrist. But untoward reactions to interruption of pregnancy are rare. It should be noted that if interruption is recommended for psychiatric reasons this does not mean that the particular patient, no matter how sick emotionally she may be, will not be able to desire, to bear, and to successfully rear children in the future.

We have in this section considered and listed various indications for therapeutic interruption of pregnancy. These are the ones stressed on certificates forwarded by physicians to hospital abortion boards. Nevertheless, in most cases these are mere rationalizations. The medical, including the psychiatric, indications must be utilized if the abortion is to have legal justification. However, in most cases, the socioeconomic factors are pronounced; and whether the interruption of the pregnancy is legal or extra-legal, the actual indications are, for the most part, socioeconomic.

As Guttmacher states, "The abortion laws make hypocrites of all of us."[50] Taussig comments in detail about what he characterizes as the "frank and universal disregard for a criminal law" — and by implication castigates the law.[51] Every hospital in the United States, prestigious or not, that allows so-called therapeutic abortions is undoubtedly violating the law, unless the process of interpretation that has already been detailed is openly accepted as such. Three-quarters of all California hospitals studied apparently have no objection to scheduling interruptions of pregnancy in their delivery rooms for reasons that would be in violation of the California law on the subject if it were strictly interpreted.[52] The same statement, as Kummer and Leavy stress,[53] can be made about at least 90 per cent of the therapeutic abortions scheduled at one of New York's leading hospitals and in other leading hospitals throughout the country.[54] Yet only nine jurisdictions in the United States have laws that either permit abortion if the health of the pregnant woman is endangered or are so phrased as to allow this interpretation.[55]

---

[50] Guttmacher, *The Law That Doctors Often Break*, Redbook Magazine, Aug. 1959, pp. 24, 25.

[51] TAUSSIG, ABORTION SPONTANEOUS AND INDUCED: MEDICAL AND SOCIAL ASPECTS 422 (1936).

[52] Packer & Gampell, *Therapeutic Abortion: A Problem in Law and Medicine*, 11 STAN. L. REV. 417, 430 (1959). For a summary of this article see Kummer & Leavy, *Therapeutic Abortion Law Confusion*, 195 A.M.A.J. 96, 97 (1966).

[53] Kummer & Leavy, *supra* note 52, at 97.

[54] Guttmacher, *supra* note 50, at 96.

[55] D.C., Ala., Colo., Md., Mass., N.J., N.M., Ore., and Pen. See Kummer & Leavy, *supra* note 52, at 143.

C.   Socioeconomic Factors and Indications

If one reads the literature, a large number of indications will be found for psychiatric termination of pregnancy.   The problem that the psychiatrist finds it necessary to evaluate during his consultation sessions with the patient is that of whether her emotional health will be endangered more if the pregnancy be interrupted or if it be carried to term.   *There is no physiological time limit on interruption.   Pregnancies are being interrupted by saline amniocentesis on psychiatric recommendation in women over twenty weeks pregnant, and the women leave the hospital in excellent physical health a few days after the abortion.*

What the psychiatrist decries is that he so frequently, when asked to see a pregnant patient in consultation, is expected to function as a "troubleshooter."   Professionally, he can recommend termination of pregnancy only if, in his opinion, *psychiatric* problems are involved.   Most of the time, however, the problems involved are socioeconomic rather than what most hospital boards and courts would consider psychiatric.   Nevertheless, an occasional hospital does recognize them.[56]   It is, of course, exceedingly difficult, and at times impossible, to demarcate socioeconomic and emotional factors so as to state that one has no psychiatric basis while the other has.   The total marital situation, the environment in which the child is to be reared, and the financial status of the family all have profound emotional repercussions.

Yet when physicians feel it indicated, they prefer to have the pregnancies of their patients interrupted legally — necessarily through psychiatric recommendation if the medical indication is absent — rather than to have their patients criminally aborted, as are so many hundreds of thousands.   The psychiatrist, as a result, now assumes the major responsibility for deciding whether or not a given pregnancy is legally terminated.

While he dislikes finding himself forced into the untenable position of being asked to make recommendations, or to give decisions, on non-psychiatric grounds, neither does he feel that he can dodge

---

[56] See Schur, *supra* note 33, at 95.

the issue. The patient needs help. Emotional factors in almost every case are profound.

It should be stressed and re-stressed that while socioeconomic conditions per se never legally warrant therapeutic abortion, socioeconomic status, nevertheless, frequently determines whether or not an abortion will be performed and, if performed, whether that selfsame abortion will be therapeutic or criminal.[57] Some physicians are more prone to recommend interruption, for instance, for a cardiac patient who is unwed, on relief, and already the mother of several children than for one with the same degree of cardiac pathology who is married, childless, and well-to-do.[58] On the other hand, the difference between having an abortion or a child (so the cynical and frequently heard non-medical aphorism has it) is the difference between having one to three hundred dollars and knowing the right person or being without funds and the right contacts. This is despite the fact that at least two patients, who, so far as could be judged, previously had had non-legal abortions by competent medical personnel, stated that the legal ones, for which they were now being evaluated, were more costly than their previous illegal interruptions because of consultation and other fees. On the whole, however, throughout the country, fees charged by criminal abortionists are estimated to range from $10 to $6500. The more usual fee is between $250 and $400, depending upon the geographic locale, the abortionist, and the financial status of the patient.[59] A legal abortion for a semi-private patient, especially if that patient have Blue Cross and Blue Shield coverage, should cost much less. The private patient may pay a great deal more. In any case, this reversal of the usual charge is rather rare.

As Kleegman states, by the very nature of things, ward patients are much less likely to have the necessary consultations requested, including the psychiatric, and to have the necessary recommendations made and accepted by a hospital board, than are their more

---

[57] Rosen, *Abortion*, 1 ENCYCLOPEDIA OF MENTAL HEALTH, 9, 14 (1963); Schur, *supra* note 39, at 200; Sontheimer, *Abortion in America Today*, Woman's Home Companion, Oct. 1955, p. 44.

[58] Guttmacher, *supra* note 24, at 21.

[59] Rosen, *supra* note 57, at 13.

well-to-do sisters.[60] Ethical and conscientious physicians decry this fact but nevertheless find it impossible to contravert, even, perhaps, in their own practice. At hospitals where a psychiatrist is assigned to the obstetrical and gynecological service, as at The Johns Hopkins for instance, this inequity disappears. Socioeconomic factors, whether or not they are recognized, are always of prime importance.

III. CRIMINAL ABORTION

Some 10,000 to 18,000 pregnancies are interrupted each year for medical, including psychiatric, reasons. However, there are, perhaps, more than twenty to thirty times as many criminal abortions each year. In some parts of the country these can be obtained so easily that when patients apply for a psychiatric consultation (for the purpose, so they state, of obtaining a psychiatric recommendation to the effect that their pregnancy be interrupted), the very fact that they make such an appointment seems to be almost presumptive proof that they do not wish the abortion, but rather psychiatric help in order to carry their child to term.[61]

Over a million pregnancies, it is estimated, are interrupted illegally in this country each and every year.[62] Abortions statistically reported as spontaneous may, in fact, sometimes be criminally induced. Yet it is rare that an abortionist is arrested and prosecuted. Out of the one- to two-thirds of a million prosecutions that theoretically would be possible, less than five hundred actually take place.[63] There may be a number of reasons for this: abortions no longer endanger life; the cause is an unpopular one; and the procedure is performed on so many women that prosecution and meaningful investigation become impossible.

---

[60] Kleegman, *Planned Parenthood: Its Influence on Public Health and Family Welfare*, in THERAPEUTIC ABORTION: MEDICAL, PSYCHIATRIC, LEGAL, ANTHROPOLOGICAL AND RELIGIOUS CONSIDERATIONS 256 (Rosen ed. 1954).

[61] Lidz, *supra* note 46, at 227; Rosen, *supra* note 11.

[62] ABORTION IN THE UNITED STATES 178, 180 (Calderone ed. 1958) (Report of the Statistics Committee); Fisher, *Criminal Abortion*, in THERAPEUTIC ABORTION: MEDICAL, PSYCHIATRIC, LEGAL, ANTHROPOLOGICAL AND RELIGIOUS CONSIDERATIONS 3, 6 (Rosen ed. 1954).

[63] Rosen, *Abortion*, Today's Health, April 1965, p. 62; Fisher, *supra* note 62, at 3.

Until antibiotics came into general use, there were 2,000 to 5,000 abortion deaths annually. Now, if the operation be performed by competent physicians as it so frequently is, there need be fewer untold sequelae than from a tonsillectomy. Despite all statements to the contrary, unless infection be present — as it frequently is with botch work but seldom is if the abortionist be competent — or unless the abortus can, under certain circumstances, be subjected to pathologic examination, it seems practically impossible to determine whether a given abortion is spontaneous, criminal, or therapeutic. And since infection today so seldom need be present in a criminal abortion, the gathering of evidence for a prosecution is just as impossible.

As a result, since the problem of law enforcement is so pronounced, an occasional district attorney, perhaps in desperation, may sometimes go to untoward lengths in his attempt to secure a conviction. For example, in cities with laws requiring physicians and hospital superintendents to notify their health departments immediately of all abortion cases in which illegal practice is even suspect, prosecuting attorneys sometimes attempt to obtain abortion information through these statutes.

In one such case, the Appellate Division of the New York Supreme Court held that a municipal rule of this kind conflicted with a statutory prohibition against physicians disclosing information professionally acquired from their patients.[64] This was after the Superintendent of Kings County Hospital refused to comply with a subpoena requiring him to produce all hospital records of all patients admitted and treated for either miscarriage or non-therapeutic abortion. If this subpoena had been complied with, mass information would have been given the district attorney on all abortion cases, whether spontaneous or induced, whether legal or illegal. Requiring reports by physicians to authorities could mean, if carried to its logical extreme, the violation of the individual's privilege against self-incrimination as guaranteed by the due process clause of the fourteenth amendment.

It seems of parenthetic interest that, although in Chicago no

---

[64] In the Matter of the Investigation into Alleged Commission of Criminal Abortions in the County of Kings, 286 App. Div. 270, 143 N.Y.S.2d 501 (1955).

such request of physicians has been made, the State's Attorney in 1955 stated that he felt "convinced a large percentage of the medical profession in Chicago is winking at the violation of state abortion laws."[65]   Whether or not this is so, it cannot be denied that "a large segment of the population condones abortion.   They consider it either all right or, at worst, a necessity."[66]   As a result, law enforcement agencies find it "extremely difficult to obtain convictions or substantial sentences for abortionists."[67]   A large segment of the population has had personal experience with the abortion problem, either directly or through some collateral branch of the family.   Law enforcement in this area is practically impossible.   The operation may previously have been performed on the wives or daughters of jurymen, jurists, lawyers, and physicians.   Because referral of pregnant women to an abortionist is widespread, abortion has been characterized in a magazine with a national circulation as the hypocrisy of modern medicine.[68]   A high percentage of abortions — an accurate estimate of number is impossible — are performed by competent physicians.   And a large number of referrals, sometimes direct and sometimes indirect, in all probability come from honest, conscientious, and otherwise ethical physicians in general practice or in the various specialties (not excluding even psychiatry and obstetrics) who, as Kleegman has so frequently stated, "feel impelled to aid those patients for whom they feel an abortion is indicated, but for whom this can be obtained only through an abortionist."[69]   The problem that should be considered is what can be done to eliminate this hypocrisy.

IV.   SUGGESTIONS FOR SOLUTION, OR PARTIAL SOLUTION,
OF THE ABORTION PROBLEM

Prevention of pregnancy through contraception has not proven effective enough.[70]   Most people prefer not to be too candid about

---

[65] Sontheimer, *supra* note 57, at 97, 100.

[66] *Id.* at 101.

[67] *Ibid.*

[68] Guttmacher, *supra* note 50, at 24.

[69] Kleegman, *supra* note 60, at 256-57.

[70] *Id.* at 254.

abortion practices in American society.[71] Everyone would like society to be organized so as to make the practice unnecessary for either therapeutic or socioeconomic and other reasons. Prevention of unwanted pregnancy should be the *sine qua non*. This is not possible, despite the population explosion, in the present state of American culture and at the present stage of psychosocial medical knowledge. Society is, nevertheless, hopefully groping towards this.

In lieu of this, a number of suggestions have been made with a view towards solution or partial solution of the problem. All steps taken in this country have thus far been completely unsuccessful. These include: (a) forced marriage, (b) adoption, foster home, and orphanage care, (c) liberalization by interpretation of existing statutes, and (d) passage of a model abortion law. A few words about each of these is in order at this point.

A. Forced Marriage

Most abortions are performed on married women. Even the most avid proponents of forced marriage realize that this measure can be applied to only a very small proportion of unmarried pregnant women. In most states, the legal age for marriage without parental consent is twenty-one. In some states, it may be as low as eighteen. But this can be waived by the court when it sanctions even a child marriage, provided the bride-to-be presents a physician's certificate of pregnancy.[72] However, neither child marriage nor forced marriage can be considered an answer to the abortion problem.

B. Adoption, Foster Home, and Orphanage Care

"Few save the biological mother," so Cameron states, "have the necessary degree of devotion and sense of continuing responsibility to provide for the needs of the child throughout its growing years. . . . [I]t would seem that immediate separation of the new-born infant from its mother and its placement either in an orphanage or in a foster home . . . will [not] receive much countenance from

---

[71] Sontheimer, *supra* note 57, at 44.

[72] Maryland did this for a thirteen-year-old child in November 1955. Document contained in the files of the author.

public opinion, once the community is fully informed upon the matter."[73] In any case, the founding even of large orphanages has not helped solve the abortion problem.

No one in the technical literature has stressed the heartlessness, the cruelty, and the sadism that the pregnant woman so frequently senses — perhaps correctly, perhaps mistakenly — when physician, minister, or lawyer suggests to her that she carry the child to term and then hand it over, never to see it again, to someone else to rear. Thirty-seven of the last forty-four unwillingly pregnant patients referred here for consultation had, before their referral, adamantly rejected all pressure in this direction. All felt exactly the same way about it. Four of the women — an eighteen-year-old, unmarried girl who had been raped, the daughter of a taxi driver, the sister of a physician, and the wife of a jurist — objected to "farming the child out for adoption." As they termed it, and in exactly the same words, "I'm not an animal." Each asked, "Do you think I could give my baby away after carrying it for nine months? There's a civil rights movement in this country now. A hundred years ago you could take the babies away from slaves. You can't do that now! And you can't turn me into the kind of an animal that would give my baby away!" Or, to quote the jurist, "That's not the problem! It's not whether my wife delivers the child; it's what this pregnancy is doing to her right now and what having this child will mean. She's a warm, loving person. She would never give it up to a stranger if she's forced to have it!"

Pronounced psychiatric factors were present in all four women. During the past eighteen years the author has seen only three patients for whom "farming out" of a child for adoption would not have been emotionally exceedingly traumatic and psychiatrically contraindicated. For some twenty-nine patients who came into psychiatric treatment within one to four years after they had accepted this kind of recommendation, what they considered to be the abandoning of their infants required careful, cautious, and (in all but seven) extensive therapeutic consideration. A woman does not lightly leave

---

[73] Cameron, *Psychiatric Foreword*, in THERAPEUTIC ABORTION: MEDICAL, PSYCHIATRIC, LEGAL, ANTHROPOLOGICAL AND RELIGIOUS CONSIDERATIONS, at xvii, xviii (Rosen ed. 1954).

a baby in a basket on someone else's doorstep, or in a hospital nursery.

C. Liberalization of the Interpretation of Existing Statutes

Hospital administrators, hospital staffs, and conscientious physicians differ, to the greatest possible extent, in their interpretation of statutory requirements for therapeutic abortion. According to one article in the popular press, a large percentage of women who now have criminal abortions in all probability could have their pregnancies legally interrupted somewhere in this country if they had sufficient time, physiologically, to shop from physician to physician, from hospital to hospital, and from state to state.[74]

In a 1966 article Kummer and Leavy in California state, "it is an accepted fact that pregnancies are terminated by reputable physicians in licensed hospitals for reasons other than to preserve the life of the mother, e.g., on health, humanitarian, and eugenic grounds, and thus in open violation of the law."[75] Their next statement may no longer hold. To quote:

> But if these interruptions are performed with concurring written opinions of other physicians and with approval of the hospital's therapeutic abortion committee, there is no trouble from law enforcement officials. We have found no recorded prosecution under such circumstances.

Yet, as this book goes to press, California hospitals and physicians are threatened with criminal indictment for having aborted women who had had German measles early in their pregnancies. The Stanford Law School survey,[76] these authors continue, previously showed

> that three quarters of the reporting California hospitals would allow induced abortion under circumstances tantamount to violation of that state's prohibitory statute. Furthermore, at a legislative hearing in California, where testimony was heard on a bill which would cautiously broaden the exceptions to include pregnancy from rape or incest, and where pregnancy would endanger a woman's health or perhaps result in the birth of a deformed child, nearly every doctor who testified stated that such a law would only legalize what is now practiced in most non-Catholic hospitals.[77]

---

74 Sontheimer, *supra* note 57, at 95.

75 Kummer & Leavy, *supra* note 52, at 97.

76 *Ibid.* See Packer & Gampell, *supra* note 52, at 446-47.

77 Kummer & Leavy, *supra* note 52, at 97.

However, so they add, "hospital authorities and physicians vary widely in their interpretation of the laws and their willingness to place themselves in jeopardy of prosecution."[78]   And because of this, or in order to be certain of being legally safe from prosecution, a large number of hospitals will not permit a therapeutic interruption of pregnancy unless two physicians — if the recommendation is for psychiatric reasons, this means unless two psychiatrists — make the recommendation which then must be presented to an abortion board usually composed of an internist, an obstetrician, a pediatrician, and a psychiatrist.   This adds to the expense to be borne by the patient and necessarily causes additional delay.

No hypocrisy may be involved in this procedure.   However, no state law allows for anything even remotely approximating this. Occasionally, physicians utilize this procedure, with all its attendant delay, in order to get the patient past the twelfth week of her pregnancy, and then tell her — as sixteen patients interviewed later at Hopkins had been told — that the twelve-week physiologic time limit for the procedure had been exceeded and that, as a result, an abortion could not be performed.

Any pregnancy, it should again be stressed, can be interrupted from the moment it has been diagnosed to the moment of spontaneous delivery.   Physicians who maintain that an abortion cannot safely be performed after the twelfth week are either ten years behind in their knowledge of medical practice or are deliberately falsifying medical information to their patients.   There can be no excuse for either.   They have every possible opportunity to keep abreast of current medical, including obstetrical, progress.   If they do not feel that their patient should be aborted, they should in all honesty state so openly and frankly to their patient.

No hospital, incidentally, requires two surgeons to submit certificates recommending that an appendectomy be done, while reserving the right to accept or reject the recommendation after considering it even for several weeks.   At The Johns Hopkins Hospital, it is felt that this analogy to an appendectomy is valid.   There, certificates from two psychiatrists are not required nor is an abortion board es-

---

[78] *Ibid.*

tablished. No state statute, incidentally, requires this. Any therapeutic abortion should be performed with a minimum of red tape or administrative delay.

But this is again a digression. Boards may or may not accept the recommendation. Or there may be resistance to submitting the recommendation to a board — from the husband (who must legally sign permission for the procedure), from other members of the family, from friends, from physicians, or from almost anyone else close enough to the patient to be emotionally involved in the situation. Even psychiatrists are not exempt.

But reliance on the medical profession to relieve the abortion problem by interpreting existing laws more liberally can produce very unsatisfactory and unpleasant results. For example, the parents of a psychotic pregnant girl, who at the time the problem arose was in the closed section of a psychiatric hospital, requested that she be seen in consultation because, although her treating psychiatrist felt that the pregnancy should be interrupted, he stated that he could not make the recommendation because according to him this was against the law. This psychiatrist stated that, "for the sake of the emotional health and life of this girl, she should be aborted." She therefore was seen in consultation. One wonders why he had not himself made the recommendation. It was later made in accordance with the law of the state in which this took place. The recommendation was accepted by the hospital. However, before it could be carried out, the psychiatrist wrote to the girl's parents, the girl, and the hospital, labeling the interruption a flagrant violation of the law and stating that the hospital, the parents, and the girl would be criminally responsible. The hospital and its lawyer decided otherwise.

Further evidence of the insufficiency of attempting to solve today's abortion impasse through more liberal interpretation of existing laws is provided by follow-ups on ten cases in which therapeutic abortion was recommended but rejected — seven by a hospital and three by the husband.[79] Of these cases, one resulted in suicide, six

---

[79] Rosen, *Abortion: The Increasing Involvement of Psychiatry*, 2 FRONTIERS OF CLINICAL PSYCHIATRY 1, 11 (Dec. 1965).

criminal abortions were performed, one patient applied for divorce immediately after the child was born, and one woman, following the birth of the child, killed all her children and herself. The tenth patient, for whom the recommendation was rejected when her husband refused to give his written permission, was later aborted at an adjacent hospital where she registered as a single girl.

Abortion is generally thought of by physicians as a medical problem, but this concept is purely and simply an artifact of present social mores. Physicians are able to make recommendations for interruption; but when they do make such recommendations it is only within the framework of the laws of the individual states in which they happen to practice. They cannot make them otherwise. But because this is a sociological problem and a legislative one for the most part, even when physicians try to meet the problem on medical terms, actual practices become more and more confused.

The problem is analogous to that which the courts so often raise with psychiatrists about whether a specific individual is or is not "insane." There is no such term as "insanity" in the psychiatric lexicon. The term has a social and legal meaning, not a medical or psychiatric one. Two different psychiatrists, therefore, who have examined the same defendant and have reached the same conclusion, when they attempt to speak to a court in terms of "insanity" may as a result give what appears to be conflicting testimony leading to diametrically opposed conclusions. No psychiatrist, it should be remarked, is professionally competent to discuss non-medical and non-psychiatric concepts such as "insanity," even though the law so frequently insists that he must.

The same impasse applies, as far as the psychiatrist is concerned, to the abortion problem. What is a sufficient medical indication to one psychiatrist may not be a sufficient indication to another. The problem can be neither raised nor resolved on purely medical grounds, in view of present abortion statutes. And because of the widespread public demand for abortion facilities, the fact that the law does not necessarily mirror public opinion, although it is amenable to popular pressure, becomes doubly apparent here.

Although Timasheff and Ehrlich were discussing other aspects of legal disequilibrium, Timasheff's comments about the disharmony between real forces and verbal formulae[80] and Ehrlich's emphatic contrasting of the living with the positive law[81] highlight the problem. A great deal of thought must be expended, and a great deal of discussion must take place, before concrete, meaningful suggestions can be made. The fact that between 1,000 and 2,500 abortions are performed each and every day in this country means that in discussion of the subject almost invariably the question is raised as to the usefulness of laws that are as constantly and consistently disregarded by the populace as are the present abortion laws.[82]

D. Passage of More Liberal Abortion Laws

Liberalizing present abortion statutes to include socioeconomic, along with medical and psychiatric, grounds would at the very least seem indicated. A number of proposals have been made. On November 28, 1965, the Board of Trustees of the American Medical Association (AMA) submitted to its policy-making House of Delegates, for endorsement or disapproval, a report (1) urging that appropriate legislation be enacted, wherever necessary, so that all physicians may legally give contraceptive information to their patients, and (2) calling for amendments to state abortion laws "so as to reflect medical conscience and public opinion."[83] This report was prepared by the AMA Committee on Human Reproduction. If adopted by the various states, it could have gone far towards taking the hypocrisy out of the abortion practices of our society. It is to be regretted that on December 1 it was rejected by the House of Delegates.[84] It is inevitable that, in one form or another, it will come up for reconsideration.

The report favored the enactment of legislation so that pregnancies can be legally interrupted in licensed hospitals on written certification by two licensed physicians, neither of whom would be performing the abortion, provided that continuance of the preg-

[80] TIMASHEFF, INTRODUCTION TO THE SOCIOLOGY OF LAW 356-63 (1936).

[81] EHRLICH, FUNDAMENTAL PRINCIPLES OF THE SOCIOLOGY OF LAW 477-85 (1936).

[82] ABORTION IN THE UNITED STATES 181 (Calderone ed. 1958).

[83] Report of Board of Trustees of American Medical Association.

[84] Committee on Human Reproduction, American Medical Ass'n, A.P. Dispatch, N.Y. Times, Dec. 2, 1965, p. 24, col. 4.

nancy gravely impairs the physical or mental health of the mother; or if there is substantial risk that the child will be born with great physical or mental defects; or if the pregnancy has resulted from statutory or forcible rape or incest. This report, therefore, merely grants official recognition to current lay and professional attitudes and practices towards the abortion problem. The total family situation and the ability of the mother to care for the child should likewise be taken into consideration.

V. RECOMMENDATIONS OF AUTHORITATIVE BODIES THAT HAVE STUDIED THE PROBLEM

A large number of concrete proposals about the abortion problem have been made, and a large number of studies have been published. At least two thousand articles and books have appeared on the subject. In England at present, the abortion bill introduced in Parliament by Lord Silkin (November 1965),[85] along with the

---

[85] The bill as passed on second reading in the House of Commons by 223 to 29, July 22, 1966, is as follows:

A BILL TO: Amend and clarify the law relating to termination of pregnancy by registered medical practitioners.

BE IT ENACTED by the Queen's most Excellent Majesty, by and with the advice and consent of the Lords Spiritual and Temporal, and Commons, in this present Parliament assembled, and by the authority of the same, as follows:-

1. (1) Subject to the provisions of this section, a person shall not be guilty of an offence under the law relating to abortion when the pregnancy is terminated by a registered medical practitioner if that practitioner and another registered medical practitioner are of the opinion, formed in good faith-

(a) that the continuance of the pregnancy would involve serious risk to the life or of grave injury to the health, whether physical or mental, of the pregnant woman whether before, at or after the birth of the child, or

(b) that there is a substantial risk that if the child were born it would suffer from such physical or mental abnormalities as to be seriously handicapped; or

(c) that the pregnant woman's capacity as a mother would be severely overstrained by the care of a child or of another child as the case may be; or

(d) that the pregnant woman is a defective or became pregnant while under the age of sixteen or became pregnant as a result of rape.

(2) Except as provided by subsection (3) of this section, any treatment for the termination of pregnancy must be carried out in a hospital vested in the Minister of Health or the Secretary of State for Scotland under the National Health Service Acts, or in a registered nursing home, or in a place for the time being approved for the purposes of this section by the Minister or the Secretary of State.

January 1966 report on abortion of a committee of the Church

(3) Subsection (2) of this section, and so much of subsection (1) as related to the opinion of another registered medical practitioner, shall not apply to the termination of a pregnancy by a registered medical practitioner in a case where he is of the opinion, formed in good faith, that the termination is immediately necessary in order to save the life of the pregnant woman.

(4) A termination of pregnancy performed on the ground of rape shall require the certificate of a registered medical practitioner consulted by the patient freshly after the alleged assault that there was then medical evidence of a sexual assault on her.

(5) The termination performed upon a girl under the age of sixteen shall require her express consent in addition to any necessary consent of her parent or guardian.

2. (1) The Minister of Health in respect of England and Wales, and the Secretary of State in respect of Scotland, may by statutory instrument make regulations to provide:

(a) for requiring any such opinion as is referred to in section 1 of this Act to be certified by the practitioners or practitioner concerned in such form and at such time as may be prescribed by the regulations, and for requiring the preservation and disposal of certificates made for the purposes of the regulations;

(b) for requiring any registered medical practitioner who terminates a pregnancy other than in a hospital to give notice of the termination and such other information relating to the termination as prescribed;

(c) for prohibiting the disclosure, except to such persons or for such purpose as may be so prescribed, of notices given or information furnished pursuant to the regulations.

(2) The information furnished in pursuance of regulations under subsection (1) of this section shall be collected solely by the Ministry of Health or the Scottish Office.

(3) Any person who wilfully contravenes or wilfully fails to comply with the requirements of regulations under subsection (1) of this section shall be liable on summary conviction to a fine not exceeding one hundred pounds.

(4) Any statutory instrument made by virtue of this section shall be subject to annulment in pursuance of a resolution of either house of Parliament.

3. (1) Nothing in this Act shall affect the provisions of Infant Life Act 1939 (protecting the life of a viable foetus).

(2) For the purposes of the law relating to abortion, anything done with intent to procure the miscarriage of a woman is unlawfully done unless authorized by section 1 of this Act.

4. In this Act, the following expressions have meanings hereby assigned to them-

"defective means, in relation to England and Wales, a person suffering from a severe subnormality as defined by subsection (2) of section 4 of the Mental Health Act 1959 and, in relation to Scotland, a person suffering from mental deficiency of the degree described in subsection (7) of section 96 of the Mental Health (Scotland) Act 1960; "registered nursing home" means a nursing home registered under the Public Health

Assembly there,[86] shows to how great an extent revision of the British law on abortion has been overdue. Yet this law is much more liberal than is its American counterpart.

There are two British studies that should be mentioned here. The first is the 1936 Birkett Report on the medical aspects of abortion that was prepared by a committee of the British Medical Association.[87] The second is the Report of the Inter-Departmental Committee on Abortion that appeared later under the joint auspices of the Ministry of Health and the Home Office.[88] These recommended wider dissemination of contraceptive advice by local authorities, clarification of the scope of therapeutic abortion, adequate medical facilities for care of abortion patients, and measures to relieve the financial strain of childbirth.

In the United States, current pressure for the revision of the abortion laws and for their liberalization goes back to 1955, when the Planned Parenthood Federation of America called a three-day conference of specialists in obstetrics, psychiatry, public health, biology, sociology, biostatistics, forensic medicine, law, and demography, to discuss the problem.[89] The majority of those participating signed a statement recommending: (1) the encouragement, through early, continued, and realistic sex education, of higher standards of sexual conduct and of a greater sense of responsibility towards

---

Act 1936, the Public Health (London) Act 1936, or the Nursing Homes Registration (Scotland) Act 1938, and a private hospital registered under the Mental Health (Scotland) Act 1960, or legislation amending or replacing them;

"the law relating to abortion means sections 58 and 59 of the Offences against the Person Act, 1861, and any rule of law relating to the procurement of an abortion;

"The National Health Service Acts" means the National Health Service Acts, 1946 to 1966 or the National Health Service (Scotland) Acts 1947 to 1966.

5.   (1) This Act may be cited as the Medical Termination of Pregnancy Act 1966.

(2) This Act does not extend to Northern Ireland.

[86] This report is discussed in the Manchester Guardian Weekly, Jan. 6, 1966, p. 9, col. 3.

[87] See generally GEBHARD, POMEROY, MARTIN & CHRISTENSON, PREGNANCY, BIRTH AND ABORTION 234 (1958).

[88] Ibid.

[89] ABORTION IN THE UNITED STATES passim (Calderone ed. 1958).

pregnancy; (2) the establishment of consultation centers for women seeking abortion, modeled after the Scandinavian centers now in existence (such consultative centers would operate under joint medical and sociological auspices, perhaps through the sponsorship of state health and welfare departments); (3) the extension under medical supervision of facilities for providing advice on contraception, which would be freely available to all desiring it; and (4) the study of the various abortion laws by authoritative bodies (*e.g.*, the National Conference of Commissioners on Uniform State Laws, the American Law Institute, and the Council of State Governments), which would frame a model law that could, perhaps jointly, be presented to the states to replace existing statutes.[90]

---

[90] Section 230.3 of the Model Penal Code is an excellent proposal with the exception of § (3), which requires one physician to check on another. If the first physician is venal, unethical, or incompetent, his certificate should not be accepted and he should not be on a hospital staff. The section as drafted appears as follows:

(1) *Unjustified Abortion.* A person who purposely and unjustifiably terminates the pregnancy of another otherwise than by a live birth commits a felony of the third degree or, where the pregnancy has continued beyond the twenty-sixth week, a felony of the second degree.

(2) *Justifiable Abortion.* A licensed physician is justified in terminating a pregnancy if he believes there is substantial risk that continuance of the pregnancy would gravely impair the physical or mental health of the mother or that the child would be born with grave physical or mental defect, or that the pregnancy resulted from rape, incest, or other felonious intercourse. All illicit intercourse with a girl below the age of 16 shall be deemed felonious for purposes of this Subsection. Justifiable abortions shall be performed only in a licensed hospital except in case of emergency when hospital facilities are unavailable. [Additional exceptions from the requirement of hospitalization may be incorporated here to take account of situations in sparsely settled areas where hospitals are not generally accessible.]

(3) *Physicians' Certificates; Presumption from Non-Compliance.* No abortion shall be performed unless two physicians, one of whom may be the person performing the abortion, shall have certified in writing the circumstances which they believe to justify the abortion. Such certificate shall be submitted before the abortion to the hospital where it is to be performed and, in the case of abortion following felonious intercourse, to the prosecuting attorney or the police. Failure to comply with any of the requirements of this Subsection gives rise to a presumption that the abortion was unjustified.

(4) *Self-Abortion.* A woman whose pregnancy has continued beyond the twenty-sixth week commits a felony of the third degree if she purposely terminates her own pregnancy otherwise than by a live birth, or if she uses instruments, drugs or violence upon herself for that purpose. Except as justified under Subsection (2), a person who induces or knowingly aids a woman to use instruments, drugs or violence upon herself for the purpose of terminating her pregnancy otherwise than by a live birth commits a felony of

VI.   CONCLUSION

Current abortion practices and current abortion laws in the United States are incompatible with concepts of human dignity.[91] They may, perhaps, have applied between 1750 and 1900.[92] They would be understandable in ancient Sparta, and apply there, but they would have been as out of place in the more mature society of Athens at the time of Pericles and Socrates as they are in America today.[93]

Yet, because of them, physicians today are forced to make medical decisions on moral and socioeconomic grounds. Because of the progress of medical knowledge and medical techniques, present statutory provisions with respect to abortion have little or nothing to do

---

the third degree whether or not the pregnancy has continued beyond the twenty-sixth week.

(5)   *Pretended Abortion.* A person commits a felony of the third degree if, representing that it is his purpose to perform an abortion, he does an act adapted to cause abortion in a pregnant woman although the woman is in fact not pregnant, or the actor does not believe she is. A person charged with unjustified abortion under Subsection (1) or an attempt to commit that offense may be convicted thereof upon proof of conduct prohibited by this Subsection.

(6)   *Distribution of Abortifacients.* A person who sells, offers to sell, possesses with intent to sell, advertises, or displays for sale anything specially designed to terminate a pregnancy, or held out by the actor as useful for that purpose, commits a misdemeanor, unless:

(a)   the sale, offer or display is to a physician or druggist or to an intermediary in a chain of distribution to physicians or druggists; or

(b)   the sale is made upon prescription or order of a physician; or

(c)   the possession is with intent to sell as authorized in paragraphs (a) and (b); or

(d)   the advertising is addressed to persons named in paragraph (a) and confined to trade or professional channels not likely to reach the general public.

(7)   *Section Inapplicable to Prevention of Pregnancy.* Nothing in this Section shall be deemed applicable to the prescription, administration or distribution of drugs or other substances for avoiding pregnancy, whether by preventing implantation of a fertilized ovum or by any other method that operates before, at or immediately after fertilization. MODEL PENAL CODE § 230.3 (Proposed Official Draft, 1962).

[91] Hardin, *Abortion and Human Dignity*, Public Lecture at University of California (Berkeley), April 29, 1964 (Distributed by Citizens for Humane Abortion Laws, San Francisco, Calif.).

[92] Eastman, *Liberalization of Attitudes Toward Abortion*, Current Medical Digest, June 1959, pp. 54, 59.

[93] *Cf.* Kummer & Leavy, *Therapeutic Abortion Law Confusion*, 195 A.M.A.J. 96, 97 (1966).

with present-day, considered medical judgment. Physicians, including obstetricians and psychiatrists, as a result find themselves in a completely untenable and essentially hypocritical position.

The law does not prohibit the surgeon from recommending that an appendix be removed (although appendiceal tissue is composed of living cells) or that a patient be operated on because of cancer. The law does not prohibit any physician from recommending, if he feels it medically (including psychiatrically) indicated, that a specific patient be aborted. But the law at times does prohibit — or can be interpreted as prohibiting — the obstetrician or gynecologist from carrying out a considered medical recommendation for interruption. And it is in this that the hypocrisy of the situation can be seen in its pure form.

Surgeons perform life-saving operations. A good deal of their time, however, is devoted to elective surgery, which can be for something as minor as the removal of a wart, or as major as the excision of a gall bladder. Medical (including psychiatric) indications for interruption of a pre-viable pregnancy can likewise be those of a threat to the emotional or physical life of the patient (and therefore among those necessitating emergency surgery), or they may be less severe and on a par, for instance, with other conditions for which elective rather than emergency surgery is indicated. Most of our statutes, rigidly interpreted, permit only the former. Sterilizing procedures, if requested by our patients, can be performed in either case. But if interruption of a pre-viable pregnancy is requested, the law at present dictates what medical opinion should be. It does not do this when an appendectomy is concerned, or an oöphorectomy.

But over and above all this, the law takes no cognizance of the fact that we are dealing with responsible human beings who should be accorded all the dignity the law accords them in other areas. Women in our society are no longer chattel. Our abortion laws have long, usually faithfully but some times faithlessly, and always inadequately, served to help keep them so. Mature legal consideration of mother, family, children, and society would lead legislatures not to pass more liberalized abortion laws but to abolish such laws altogether.

Mature women, as mature human beings with all the respect and dignity to be accorded mature human beings, should have the right to decide whether or not they wish to carry a specific pregnancy to term. The responsibility for the decision, right or wrong, is already theirs. The extra-legal abortion rate shows that they have already illegally assumed it. It should be theirs *legally*.

Abortion, like sterilization voluntarily requested, is a medical procedure, advisable and indicated for medical (including surgical and psychiatric) pathology, and for familial, sociologic, socioeconomic, and humanitarian reasons.

But this is for the future. Our present hypocritical attitudes, conscious or unconscious as they are, will not allow of this today. The recommendations of the American Law Institute, if adopted, will help take at least some of the hypocrisy out of our present medical and legal approach to the problem.

And this is devoutly to be desired. For our women are not chattel. And human beings should be treated with dignity even by our abortion statutes.

5

The Inviolability of the Right

To Be Born

Robert F. Drinan, S.J.

Every discussion of abortion must, in the final analysis, begin and end with a definition of what one thinks of a human embryo or fetus. If one has, by the application of several principles, come to the conviction that a fetus, viable or not, can be extinguished for the benefit of its mother or its own welfare, rational debate on changing or "liberalizing" existing laws forbidding abortion is not really possible or necessary. For if a person argues from the premise that a human fetus may have its existence terminated for any valid reason, then the only point about which to argue is the validity of the reasons asserted to be sufficient to justify the voluntary extinction of a human fetus. These reasons can have only three sources: (1) the welfare of the fetus; (2) the health or happiness of the mother; or (3) the overall future of the family.

It is unfortunate that debates and discussions over the advisability of changing the anti-abortion laws which now exist in every state have not infrequently tended to polarize the disputants into those who desire to make America's abortion laws more "humane" on the one side and Roman Catholics on the other. Such a distortion of the real issues involved in this matter comes about, in part, because Catholic moral theology and philosophy have retained, more than the teaching of most other religious denominations, the traditional, and until recently, unchallenged view that an abortion is

107

the taking of the life of an unborn but, nevertheless, a real human being.

When a Catholic jurist defends the moral viewpoint of his church, he almost inevitably deepens the distortion that anti-abortion laws in America would be easily modified or repealed but for the existing or expected opposition of Catholics, acting individually and collectively. The impression may also be given that the Catholic jurist is seeking simply to translate the views of his religion into the civil law and, as is sometimes alleged, to impose them on others.

The facts and the real issues are a good deal different from the supposed or the asserted posture of the abortion question as it is being debated, on the one hand, by "liberals" who seek a more "humane" law and, on the other hand, by Catholic spokesmen. This is illustrated by a discussion of the following topics: (1) the several issues which are *not* disputed by any of the parties in the discussion about abortion laws; (2) the areas of agreement between all parties regarding the nature of the fetus; and (3) the arguments on why Anglo-American law should continue its basic public policy of discouraging abortion by making it illegal, either by criminal or civil sanctions.

I. THE NON-ISSUES

A. *Peril to the Mother's Life*

Every state in the union permits an abortion by authorized persons when such action is required to save the life of the mother.[1] Although the morality of such laws is open to question, participants in the current controversy over the advisability of easing the nation's laws proscribing abortion cannot cite as relevant the contention that laws in America forbid physicians from performing an abortion when, otherwise, the life of the mother would be endangered. Furthermore, it is well known that by the employment of generally available medical techniques by competent obstetricians, the dilemma

---

[1] See George, *Current Abortion Law: Proposals and Movements for Reform*, in this volume 1.

of choosing whether to save the life of the mother *or* the life of the child will seldom if ever arise.[2]

B. Abortion Not a Substitute for Birth Control

It is further agreed among all persons concerned with a just and fair law regulating abortion that, if abortion is to be allowed by society, it is understood to be a remedy which should be available only in unusual cases and not as a substitute for the ordinary methods of birth control. Those who favor a relaxation of the law regarding abortion would, in other words, presumably endorse a program of private and public birth control clinics designed to assist women to take measures which would make an abortion unnecessary.

It should be noted in this connection that the available statistics on the financial and marital status of the women who seek an abortion in the United States are not at all satisfactory. It is simply not reliably known how many or what percentage of those seeking an abortion are unwed, poor, married, or financially secure. Consequently, it is not known to what extent the greater availability of contraceptive information and devices would diminish the need for abortion.

C. Abortion of a Non-Viable Fetus Only

It is also beyond contention that the advocates of a liberalized abortion law would in general permit an abortion only of a non-viable fetus. This is the position of the Model Penal Code of the American Law Institute (ALI) where it is proposed that the life of a fetus not older than twenty-six weeks may be terminated if such action can be justified because of the physical or mental health of the mother.[3] This proposed law, which is the most carefully drawn of all the proposals in this area, would, furthermore, justify the abortion of a non-viable embryo because of pre-natal injuries to the

---

[2] See, *e.g.*, Heffernan & Lynch, *What is the Status of Therapeutic Abortion in Modern Obstetrics?*, 66 AMERICAN J. OBSTETRICS & GYNECOLOGY 335-45 (1953).

[3] MODEL PENAL CODE § 230.3 (Proposed Official Draft, 1962).

fetus even if such injuries are not deemed to be detrimental to the mental or physical health of the mother.[4]

Glanville Williams, who is surely one of the most vigorous advocates of the abolition of all legal penalties for abortion, appears to feel that, since virtually no abortions are sought after a fetus is viable, a repeal of the sanctions for abortions of non-viable fetuses would almost solve the entire problem.[5]

D. *Abortion in Rape Cases*

The frequently cited, emotion-laden example of the need for an abortion by a woman who has been raped is also really not relevant to the discussion regarding the liberalization of America's abortion laws. No law in the United States prohibits a doctor from taking appropriate medical measures following a rape to prevent the possibility of a pregnancy. The canon law of the Catholic Church permits such measures on the ground that the rapist is an unjust aggressor and allows that the victim of such aggression may prevent the conception which might result from such conduct. This act of prevention is not abortion but rather the elimination of the possibility of conception.[6]

II. AREAS OF AGREEMENT REGARDING ABORTION AND THE NATURE OF THE FETUS

Both in public opinion and in the law of America, there is a profoundly based consensus that an embryo or a fetus has at least *some* rights. Sharp differences arise not over the nature and extent of the rights of the fetus but rather over the question of whether these rights may be totally subordinated to the rights of the mother whose body contains the fetus.

---

[4] See note 3 *supra*. For a discussion of some of the implications of the ALI proposals see Quay, *Justifiable Abortion — Medical and Legal Foundations*, 49 GEO. L.J. 173-256, 395-538 (1961).

[5] WILLIAMS, THE SANCTITY OF LIFE AND THE CRIMINAL LAW 146-247, at 157-59 (1957).

[6] Most manuals on Catholic moral theology touch on this subject. See, *e.g.*, MC-HUGH, CALLAN & WAGNER, MORAL THEOLOGY (1930).

A. Right To Inherit

One right of the fetus that is clearly guaranteed by the law is its right to inherit *en ventre sa mere.*[7] The exercise of this right obviously depends on the live birth of the fetus; therefore, it is uncertain how much about the law's attitude toward the inviolability of the right of the fetus to survive is actually proven by the recognition, by Anglo-American law, of the right to inherit *en ventre sa mere.*

B. Right to Compensation for Pre-Natal Injuries

The fact that ever more frequently both statutory and decisional law recognize pre-natal injuries[8] as the basis for compensation also has dubious probative value regarding the underlying convictions of the law with respect to the right of the fetus to survive. The development of the right of an infant to compensation for pre-natal injuries does, however, at least prove that the law assumes that this right becomes inchoate or vested in a fetus even if the fetus had hardly been conceived when the injury occurred; every fetus is, therefore, *sui juris* or capable of possessing rights.

C. Right To Be Born

Even among the most vigorous proponents of the repeal of laws forbidding abortion, there appears to be consensus that a fetus has a right to be born[9] unless its extinction can be justified by at least one of the following reasons: its birth would be detrimental to itself, to its mother, or to the family into which it would be born. The fetus, in other words, cannot arbitrarily or capriciously be deprived of its right to be born.

D. Right To Self-Abort

Another area of agreement in the controversy over the fairness of America's abortion laws seems to exist by virtue of the fact

---

[7] See ATKINSON, WILLS 75 (2d ed. 1953).

[8] See PROSSER, LAW OF TORTS 354-57 (3d ed. 1964).

[9] See Leavy and Kummer, *Criminal Abortion: Human Hardship and Unyielding Laws,* 35 SO. CAL. L. REV. 136-38 (1962).

that the advocates of the repeal of these laws apparently would not subscribe to an arrangement by which the woman desiring an abortion could unilaterally and without the advice and consent of any other person terminate her pregnancy. The American Law Institute's proposal, for example, requires the consent of two physicians.[10] Similarly, some proponents of liberalized abortion laws recommend the arrangement operating in Sweden by which a medical-lay commission makes the decision concerning the advisability of an abortion. This same feature appeared in a recent proposal made to the House of Delegates of the American Medical Association (AMA);[11] under a plan urged upon the governing board of the AMA, a physician would be permitted to terminate a pregnancy only if two licensed physicians, neither of whom would be performing the operation, have certified in writing the circumstances that justified the abortion.[12]

There has been little, if any, speculation by the proponents of liberalized abortion laws on the question of what the law should be when medical science discovers a drug which may be safely and effectively self-administered by a woman desiring to procure an abortion. All discussion on the advisability of more liberal abortion laws has, up to the present, assumed that a woman is not able, or should not be permitted, to be the exclusive decision-maker in the process of securing an abortion; an outside agency has been recommended, presumably because the state owes some duty to the unborn fetus or at least some duty to protect a pregnant woman against the consequences of her own unilateral decision — a judgment which may be made in excessive haste or fear. If any of the advocates of eased abortion laws would categorically recommend the free availability of abortifacient drugs (when they will have become safe for self-administration) the underlying position of these proponents of easier abortion laws will become much clearer. If

---

10 See note 3 *supra*.

11 Committee on Human Reproduction, American Medical Ass'n, A.P. Dispatch, N.Y. Times, Dec. 1, 1965, p. 1, col. 2.

12 See N. Y. Times, Nov. 29, 1965, p. 44, col. 6. See also N. Y. Times, Dec. 2, 1965, p. 24, col. 4, for an account of the vote by the AMA to defer action on a report of its Committee on Human Reproduction.

they see no problem in permitting a pregnant woman to abort herself without the advice or consent of any other human being, then the fetus is, in this view of things, simply a quantum of protoplasm with no rights or interests, which the mother may destroy for any reason deemed valid by herself alone. Absent such a position, however, those who would defend existing legal penalties against abortion must argue against adversaries who presumably think that an unborn fetus has *some* rights which the state should protect and preserve. Furthermore, the absence of individuals or legal groups that would advocate that a pregnant woman has the complete and exclusive right to determine whether to have an abortion indicates that those who are dissatisfied with existing legislation forbidding abortion in certain circumstances have not really thought through the central problem — the nature of the non-viable fetus.

E.   Additional Points of Agreement

Other areas of agreement, or partial agreement, exist between those with opposing positions with regard to legislation regulating the availability of abortion. Unfortunately these areas have not emerged in public discussions of this question. The polarization of the contending parties on the basic moral issue probably has been the major reason why little if any consensus has developed on certain legal-moral aspects of the abortion question. One of those aspects, for example, is the question of whether a married woman should have the right to secure an abortion of a non-viable fetus without the advice and consent of her husband. One could devise persuasive arguments on either side of this issue; it must be admitted, however, that if the law is to continue to promote family solidarity, it is questionable whether the law should permit a wife to dispose of an unborn child of a marriage without the knowledge, advice, or consent of her husband — the father of the child unwanted by its mother.

III.   WHY THE LAW SHOULD HAVE SANCTIONS AGAINST THE ABORTION OF A NON-VIABLE FETUS

When one has conceded the principle that the life and rights of a non-viable fetus may be subordinated to the desires or rights of its mother or parents, one must then justify this hierarchy of rights by recourse to one or more of three reasons: (1) the welfare of the fetus; (2) the health or happiness of the mother; or (3) the overall future of the family into which the unwanted child would be born. It may be helpful therefore to analyze each of these three reasons in the light of the justification for abortion drawn from these sources.

A. Future Welfare of the Fetus

One of the reasons regularly advanced to justify abortion is the damage or disability suffered by a fetus because of the sickness of the mother or because of some pre-natal disease contracted by the fetus itself. The assumption is, of course, that it is better to terminate the life of a future person if it is certain (or highly probable?) that he will be seriously deformed, physically or mentally. The proponents of this position do not seem to limit their advocacy of this measure to only those infants who would be forever pitiable, "sub-human" creatures incapable in any way of developing into a fully human person. The thrust of the argument of those who recommend the elimination of defective embryos reaches all future children whose development may have been harmed by the mother taking a drug like thalidomide, contracting German measles, or suffering any other of the known medical conditions which can adversely affect a fetus.[13]

No one can deny the laudable humanitarian intentions of those who seek, by the elimination of anti-abortion legislation, to prevent the birth of those persons who, because of serious pre-natal injuries, cannot enjoy a normal life. At the same time, however, to concede that the life of the fetus, disabled through no fault of its own or of its mother, may be extinguished because it might not attain complete physical or intellectual development is to concede either (1) that the non-viable fetus is really *not* the repository of any inviolable rights or (2) that the strong and dominant members of society may extinguish or terminate the life of those indi-

---

[13] See ST. JOHN-STEVAS, THE RIGHT TO LIFE (1964).

viduals whose physical or mental development may, in the judgment of society, be so substantially arrested that they cannot attain a life worth living.

Clearly no advocate of easier abortion laws will concede the second of these alternatives. He will resist and reject any imputation that by permitting abortion he is by implication permitting infanticide, euthanasia, "mercy-murder," or anything else in the "parade of the horribles" not unknown in the rhetoric of the defenders of existing laws forbidding abortion. But can one logically and realistically claim that a defective non-viable fetus may be destroyed without also conceding the validity of the principle that, at least in some extreme cases, the taking of a life by society may be justified by the convenience or greater overall happiness of the society which takes the life of an innocent but unwanted and troublesome person?

It is submitted that it is illogical and intellectually dishonest for anyone to advocate as morally permissible the destruction of a defective, non-viable fetus, but to deny that this concession is not a fundamental compromise with what is surely one of the moral-legal absolutes of Anglo-American law — the principle that the life of an innocent human being may not be taken away simply because, in the judgment of society, non-life for this particular individual would be better than life.

It is intellectually dishonest to maintain that a defective, non-viable fetus may be destroyed unless one is also prepared to admit that society has the right to decide that for certain individuals, who have contracted physical and/or mental disabilities, non-existence is better than existence. The advocate of abortion who bases his position on the ground that this is best for the fetus would no doubt shrink from this extension of the principle by which he justifies abortion; he would retreat to the familiar ground that the non-viable fetus is not even *medically* a person and, hence, does not possess the same right to survive enjoyed by a human being who has lived outside the body of its mother. But does this distinction really make a difference? Is there any real moral or ethical difference between pre-natal and post-natal life? And is it not possible that medical discoveries will show more and more that fetal life is different from post-natal life only in degree and not in kind? Furthermore, if medical science makes it possible for a fetus to be viable at a time much earlier than the present moment of viability, will the advocates of the abortion of the defective fetus eliminate the distinction that only the non-viable fetus may be aborted?

Abortion performed for the asserted future welfare and happiness of a defective fetus cannot be justified morally or ethically except by the use of a principle which, however attenuated, leads logically to the validation of the termination by society of the life of an innocent but unwanted person. If one does not shrink from that consequence, the discussion has to be extended to a much broader base. But, it is submitted, it is intellectual dishonesty for anyone to advocate the destruction of a defective non-viable fetus without being prepared to accept the far-reaching consequences of the principle which justifies the termination of pre-natal life.

B.   Health or Happiness of the Mother

(1)   *A Mother's Health and Abortion.*—As previously noted,[14] all states permit a therapeutic abortion in order to save the life of the mother.   Although there is no meaningful decisional law on this matter, it is clear that this policy allows a physician to make the indisputably moral judgment that the life of the mother is to be preferred over the life of her unborn child.   It could be argued that, since the law permits physicians to act upon their own moral judgments when a mother's life is at stake, the law should logically permit physicians to make similar moral judgments when the mother's future health, rather than her survival, is in question. If this line of reasoning is correct, it may be that those who oppose the legalization of abortion must urge that the right of physicians to perform an abortion to save the life of a mother be either abrogated or logically extended to a granting of permission to perform an abortion in order to save the health of the mother.   On the assumption which permeates the case of those seeking the legalization of abortion — that society should concentrate on the quality, rather than the quantity, of life it preserves — there would seem to be no

---

14 See note 1 *supra* and accompanying text.

reason why a doctor should *not* be allowed to preserve the health of the mother by performing an abortion.

The medical hypothesis running through this line of argumentation is, of course, open to question. Assuming reasonably modern medical techniques, in how many instances is it likely that the birth of a child will permanently impair the *physical* health of a mother?

Some cases, of course, do exist where the continuation of a pregnancy may bring about a substantial risk, not to the mother's life, but rather, to her future physical health. If there is an inherent right in basic justice for a mother in this situation to request an abortion — and this case is probably the most appealing and compelling reason for a justifiable abortion — how should the law regulate the exercise of this right? The various proposals for changes in America's law regulating abortions silently suggest that the mother's right not to have her health impaired is paramount in this instance and that the state has no duty to speak for, or to protect, the fetus. However appealing such a solution may appear, its implications and consequences need examination.

Every married couple possesses a moral and a legal right to privacy from any undue interference from the state. This right, emphasized by the United States Supreme Court in *Griswold v. Connecticut*,[15] involving the Connecticut birth control statute, should be as broad and as inclusive as is consistent with the good of society. The right to have, or not to have, children and to determine the number of such children are matters in which the state, by general agreement, should not interfere. The welfare of children born to any marriage, however, is, by equally general agreement, a matter of grave concern for the state. Recent controversies over the advisability of statutes designed to curb the physical abuse or the battering of children by mentally upset or emotionally disturbed parents indicate that society feels a deep responsibility to protect children even at the expense of restricting the right to privacy enjoyed by married couples.

For at least a century and a half, this same concern of society

---

[15] 381 U.S. 479 (1965).

and the law for children too young to speak for themselves has been extended to the unborn child by Anglo-American law. The law has taken the position that a married couple may refrain from having children or may restrict the number of their children[16] but that a child, once conceived, has rights which its parents may not extinguish, even if the parents seek only to prevent a permanent impairment of the physical health of the mother.[17]

Once again, the advocates of the right of a mother to an abortion, when confronted with the interest of the state in the child, born or unborn, will take refuge in the medically questionable and logically indefensible position that the unborn child is so different from a child after birth that the state has no right to interfere with a mother's desire to extinguish the life of her unborn child. It appears, however, that if Anglo-American law is to retreat from its present position of extending some, not total, protection to the fetus, it must logically say that the right to marital privacy precludes state interference with an abortion or that the non-viable fetus is not yet sufficiently a human being to merit the protection of the law.

The advocates of the abolition of anti-abortion laws will no doubt urge, as one of the principal arguments, the right to marital privacy as that right is explained in the *Griswold* decision. It is submitted, however, that even the broadest dicta in *Griswold*, and even the most sweeping language in other judicial decisions on the right to marital privacy, do not justify the exclusion of the interest of the state *after* a child has been conceived but not yet delivered. It may be, of course, that courts in the future will extend the right of marital privacy to exclude state interference with an abortion decided upon by a couple. But such a decision would be entirely different from existing decisional law and would, at least logically, have to reject the underlying assumption of present laws forbidding abortion which is, of course, that a non-viable fetus has an inherent and inviolable right to be born even if it is physically or mentally

---

16 Only Massachusetts bans the use of contraceptives. See MASS. GEN. LAWS ANN. ch. 272, §§ 20, 21 (1956).

17 See note 1 *supra*.

defective and even if its birth results in the impairment of the physical health of its mother.

(2) A Mother's Mental Health or Happiness and Abortion.— The various proposals designed to liberalize America's abortion laws, including that of the American Law Institute (ALI),[18] do not attempt to restrict the right to have an abortion to women who might otherwise have an impairment of their *physical* health. Those who would ease existing abortion laws recognize the fact that physical and mental health are so interdependent that it would be unrealistic to state that an abortion is allowable only for threatened damage to *either* the physical *or* mental health of the mother.

When the meaning and scope of mental health are evaluated, however, many problems arise. The legislative history of the section on abortion of the Model Penal Code of the ALI[19] suggests that the term "mental health" is not meant to be used in the proposed law in a narrow or technical sense but rather in a comprehensive way which would permit two physicians to authorize an abortion if in their judgment an operation of this nature would be best for the long-range happiness of the mother. Hence, the term "mental health" of the mother is not intended to be restricted to cases where there is a diagnosis that severe mental depression or some similar psychiatric phenomenon will follow childbirth.

Therefore, in view of the broad authorization which would result if the mental health of the mother became a norm for judging the advisability of abortions, it may be that the married and unmarried mother should be treated differently.[20]

(3) Mental Health of Unwed Mothers.—There is not much scientifically compiled information available on the number and nature of unwed mothers in America. Even less is known about those unwed mothers who terminate their pregnancy by an abortion.[21] As a result, any writer moves into a sea of ambiguities

---

[18] See note 3 *supra.*

[19] MODEL PENAL CODE § 207.11, comment 3 (Tent. Draft No. 9, 1959).

[20] For a discussion of the mental health of married mothers see text accompanying note 22 *infra.*

[21] See GEBHARD, POMEROY, MARTIN & CHRISTENSON, PREGNANCY, BIRTH AND ABORTION (1958).

when he attempts to analyze the factors involved in reaching a pru-
dential judgment on the question of whether more relaxed abortion laws would promote the mental health of unwed mothers.
Among the many factors which should be weighed in coming to a
decision regarding the basic legal-moral policy which America
should adopt with respect to the availability of abortion for unwed
mothers are the following.

(a) *Promiscuity among Single Persons.*—To what extent
would more relaxed abortion laws promote promiscuity among single persons?

(b) *Adoption of Children of Unwed Mothers.*—Should law
and society give greater consideration to childless couples (one out
of ten) who seek an adoptable child?   If so, should the nation's
public policy tend to encourage unwed mothers *not* to destroy their
unborn child but to arrange that the child be born and placed for
adoption?

(c) *Guilt Feelings of the Unwed Mother.*—Who is to assess
the nature and the consequences of the guilt which, according to
reliable and virtually universal reports, comes to an unwed mother
who resolves her problem by abortion?   If accurate psychiatric testimony showed that the vast majority of unwed mothers who abort
their child experience guilt that may have adverse consequences in
their lives and their future marriages, would society be morally
obliged to counsel unwed mothers about the likelihood of guilt before an easy method of abortion were made available to them?   If,
in other words, the mental health of the mother is to be the norm
by which the advisability of an abortion is to be judged, then the
assessment of an unwed mother's prospective mental health following an abortion must include the most careful and comprehensive
evaluation of the impact which a feeling of guilt may have on her
life.

(d) *"Happiness" of the Unwed Mother.*—Since the term
"mental health" in the Model Penal Code of the American Law
Institute[22] actually translates into "happiness," how and by whom

---

22 See note 19 *supra* and accompanying text.

is this broad norm to be interpreted and applied, not merely to the present predicament of the unwed mother but, more importantly, to her entire future life?

Some may object to the relevance of some or all of these factors and urge that the desire of the unwed mother for an abortion should be controlling. As much as one must be sympathetic to this apparently simple solution to a most difficult problem, it should never be forgotten that in modern society the unwed mother is in a position of shame, humiliation, and anguish which is possibly worse than any other human predicament. One may feel that society's attitude of disdain towards the unwed mother is one of hypocrisy, but the fact remains that the pressures and problems confronted by an unwed mother are such that it is not likely that she will be in a position to make rational decisions substantially uninfluenced by fear or panic. Society, therefore, has a very special and unique duty to furnish the most careful counselling to unwed mothers before it allows them to employ a legally approved method of abortion.

The various proposals to modify or repeal anti-abortion laws in America do not distinguish between married and unmarried mothers with respect to the reasons and the procedures by which an abortion would be sanctioned. In view of the very different problems faced by unwed mothers, it is submitted that any new law regulating abortion should take these factors into consideration.

IV. THE WELFARE OF FAMILIES AND ABORTION

One of the recurring ideas in the literature recommending a liberalization of abortion laws is the concept that the coming of an unwanted child into a family may tend to disrupt the relationship of the husband and wife and destroy the unity and solidarity of the family. A persuasive article by an anonymous mother who secured the abortion of an unwanted child, published in the *Atlantic Monthly*, sets forth in a dramatic manner the argument that parents have a right and duty to plan their families, even to the extent of terminating an unplanned pregnancy.[23]

There exists a growing consensus in America that couples

---

23 Atlantic Monthly, Aug. 1965, pp. 66-68.

should be assisted by private and public agencies in the planning of their families. Differences over the morality of various methods of birth control center on means, rather than on ends.

There is a serious question, however, whether there exists a consensus which would support a public policy permitting a married mother to secure an abortion for an unplanned and unwanted pregnancy. Even to discuss such a question requires that one delve into the question of the origins or sources of public policy in America. Who or what groups, and for what reasons, should supply the guidelines for the shaping of the fundamental legal-moral policies underlying American law?

V. CONCLUSION

It is submitted that no logically defensible or rational change of a substantial nature can take place in America's abortion laws unless the proponents of less strict sanctions against abortion confront and resolve the issue underlying all the other issues: what or whose moral values should the law endorse and enforce?

America's laws against abortion derive in large part from the concept of the sacredness and the inviolability of every human being. This concept of the non-violability of the human person clearly has many of its most profound roots in the Judeo-Christian religious tradition. That tradition, in fact, is probably the principal source of Anglo-American criminal law. Not all of the elements of that religious tradition are, of course, incorporated or embodied in the criminal laws of England and America; but the essence or the most fundamental principles of that tradition *are* an inherent part of Anglo-American criminal law. And any change of a substantial kind in America's abortion laws would be a notable departure from that body of Anglo-American law which regulates conduct deemed to constitute a crime against society.

No one can reasonably insist that *all* of the actions now penalized by law should remain as they are. On the other hand, no one, presumably, desires to scuttle the entire fabric of Anglo-American criminal law. But, it is submitted, no one can take a position (allegedly between these two extremes) which advocates abortion

without inevitably sanctioning a basic compromise of principle —
a compromise which could undermine the very foundations of
Anglo-American criminal jurisprudence.

The integrity, the untouchableness, the inviolability of every
human life by any other human being has been the cardinal principle and the centerpiece of the legal institutions of the English-
speaking world and, to a large extent, of every system of law de-
vised by man. However convenient, convincing, or compelling the
arguments in favor of abortion may be, the fact remains that the
taking of a life, even though it is unborn, cuts out the very heart of
the principle that *no one's* life, however unwanted and useless it
may be, may be terminated in order to promote the health or happiness of another human being. If the advocates of legalized abortion
desire to have an intellectually honest debate about the fundamental
change they seek in the moral and legal standards of American life,
they should not fall back on the error of fact that a fetus is not a
human being. They should, rather, face the fact that they are stating that the rights of one or more human beings to health or happiness may in some circumstances become so important that they
take precedence over the very right to exist of another human being.

The inescapable moral issues in the emerging struggle over the
wisdom and fairness of America's abortion laws deserve to be discussed and dissected and eventually resolved. It will be a tragedy
beyond description for America if the question of legislation on
abortion is resolved on sentiment, utilitarianism, or expediency
rather than on the basic ethical issue involved — the immorality of
the destruction of any innocent human being carried out by other
human beings for their own benefit.

6

Jewish Views on Abortion

Rabbi Dr. Immanuel Jakobovits

With the staggering rise in the rate of abortions — the overwhelming majority of them illegal according to most states' laws — and with the motives for such operations now including the fear of abnormal births as well as birth control considerations, abortion has lately become the most widely debated medico-moral subject. What was previously either a therapeutic measure for the safety of the mother or a plainly criminal act is now being widely advocated as a means to prevent the birth of possibly defective children, to curb the sordid indignities and hazards imposed on women resorting to clandestine operators, and simply to contain the population explosion. Under the mounting pressure of these new factors, combined with the widespread violation of the existing laws even by reputable practitioners, there is increasing agitation for a liberalization of these laws, particularly among physicians.[1] Many physicians, individually

---

[1] The New York Academy of Medicine, in a report by its Committee on Public Health, has pleaded that "permissive medical practices based on *sound medical judgment* should be recognized, not forbidden by law . . ." and it recommended an amendment to the State Penal Law "to legalize therapeutic abortion when there is substantial risk that the continuance of the pregnancy would gravely impair the physical or mental health of the mother, or that the child would be born with grave physical or mental defects." The report argued that the present law "places the physician who performs the therapeutic abortion and the hospital where it is done in the position of *breaking the law*, even when they are adhering to what they believe to be *sound medical practice.*" N.Y. Times, Dec. 14, 1964, p. 48, col. 5. (Emphasis added.) A subsequent report indicated that 87.6 per cent of New York obstetricians answering a questionnaire favored the change in the law, and that the President of the Association for Humane Abortion, who called the existing law "inhumane and unrealistic," had admitted that "reputable physicians often perform therapeutic abortions, in respectable New York hospitals, which are not strictly legal." N.Y. Times, Jan. 31, 1965, p. 73, col. 5.

and as organized groups, are pressing for legislative modifications which would give them far more discretionary power than they presently enjoy. They claim that, within some broad general guidelines, the decision whether or not legally to terminate a pregnancy should be left to their judgment. In part, this claim is already being asserted on a wide scale through the establishment at numerous hospitals of "abortion boards," composed solely of physicians, charged with the responsibility of sanctioning all such operations.

In the Jewish view, this line of argument cannot be upheld. The judgment that is here required, while it may be based on medical evidence, is clearly of a moral nature. The decision on whether, and under what circumstances, it is right to destroy a germinating human life depends on the assessment and weighing of values, on determining the title to life in any given case. Such value judgments are entirely outside the province of medical science. No amount of training or experience in medicine can help in ascertaining the criteria necessary for reaching such capital verdicts, for making such life-and-death decisions. Such judgments pose essentially a moral, not a medical, problem. Hence they call for the judgment of moral, not medical, specialists.

Physicians, by demanding that as the practitioners in this field they should have the right to determine or adjudicate the laws governing their practice, are making an altogether unprecedented claim not advanced by any other profession. Lawyers do not argue that, because law is their speciality, the decision on what is legal should be left to their conscience. And teachers do not claim that, as the profession competent in education, the laws governing their work, such as on prayers at public schools, should be administered or defined at their discretion. Such claims are patently absurd, for they would demand jurisdiction on matters completely beyond their professional competence.

There is no more justice or logic in advancing similar claims for the medical profession. A physician, in performing an abortion or any other procedure involving moral considerations, such as artificial insemination or euthanasia, is merely a technical expert; but he is no more qualified than any other layman to pronounce on the rights or legality of such acts, let alone to determine what these rights should be, relying merely on the whims or dictates of his conscience. The decision on whether a human life, once conceived, is to be or not to be, therefore, properly belongs to moral experts, or to legislatures guided by such experts.

I. JEWISH LAW

A. The Claims of Judaism

Every monotheistic religion embodies within its philosophy and legislation a system of ethics — a definition of moral values. None does so with greater precision and comprehensiveness than Judaism. It emphatically insists that the norms of moral conduct can be governed neither by the accepted notions of public opinion nor by the individual conscience. In the Jewish view, the human conscience is meant to enforce laws, not to make them. Right and wrong, good and evil, are absolute values which transcend the capricious variations of time, place, and environment, just as they defy definition by relation to human intuition or expediency. These values, Judaism teaches, derive their validity from the Divine revelation at Mount Sinai, as expounded and developed by sages faithful to, and authorized by, its writ.

B. The Sources of Jewish Law

For a definition of these values, one must look to the vast and complex corpus of Jewish law, the authentic expression of all Jewish religious and moral thought. The literary depositories of Jewish law extend over nearly four thousand years, from the Bible and the Talmud, serving as the immutable basis of the main principles, to the great medieval codes and the voluminous rabbinical *responsa* writings recording practical verdicts founded on these principles, right up to the present day.

These sources, to be detailed below, spell out a very distinct attitude on all aspects of the abortion problem. They clearly indicate that Judaism, while it does not share the rigid stand of the Roman Catholic Church which unconditionally proscribes any direct destruction of the fetus from the moment of conception, refuses to endorse the far more permissive views of many Protestant denominations. The traditional Jewish position is somewhere between these two extremes, corresponding roughly to the law as currently in force in all but five American states, namely, recognizing only a grave hazard to the mother as a legitimate indication for therapeutic abortion.[2]

(1) Abortion in the Bible.—The legislation of the Bible makes only one reference to our subject, and this is by implication:

> And if men strive together, and hurt a woman with child, so that her fruit depart, and yet no harm follow, he shall be surely fined, according as the woman's husband shall lay upon him; and he shall pay as the judges determine. But if any harm follow, then shalt thou give life for life. . . .[3]

(a) The Jewish Interpretation.—This crucial passage, by one of the most curious twists of literary fortunes, marks the parting of the ways between the Jewish and Christian rulings on abortion. According to the Jewish interpretation, if "no harm follow" the "hurt" to the woman resulting in the loss of her fruit refers to the survival of the woman following her miscarriage; in that case there is no capital guilt involved, and the attacker is merely liable to pay compensation for the loss of her fruit. "But if any harm follow," *i.e.*, if the woman is fatally injured, then the man responsible for her death has to "give life for life"; in that event the capital charge of murder exempts him from any monetary liability for the aborted fruit.[4]

This interpretation is also borne out by the rabbinical exegesis of the verse defining the law of murder: "He that smiteth *a man,*

---

[2] The only states in which health risks, too, are recognized as a legal ground for abortion are Alabama, Colorado, Maryland, New Mexico, and Oregon. See ALA. CODE tit. 14 § 9 (1958); COLO. REV. STAT. ANN. § 40-2-23 (1963); MD. ANN. CODE art. 27, § 3 (1957); N.M. STAT. ANN. § 40A-5-3 (1953); ORE. REV. STAT. § 163.060 (1957).

[3] *Exodus* 21:22-23.

[4] *Mekhilta* and Rashi. For a translation of these sources, see 3 LAUTERBACH, ME-KHILTA 66-67 (1935); ROSENBAUM & SILBERMAN, PENTATEUCH AND RASHI'S COM-MENTARY 112-13 (1930).

so that he dieth, shall surely be put to death . . ."[5] which the Rabbis construed to mean "a man, but not a fetus."[6]

These passages clearly indicate that the killing of an unborn child is not considered as murder punishable by death in Jewish law.

(b) The Christian Interpretation.—The Christian tradition disputing this view goes back to a mistranslation in the *Septuagint*. There, the Hebrew for "no harm follow" was replaced by the Greek for "[her child be born] imperfectly formed."[7] This interpretation, distinguishing between an unformed and a formed fetus and branding the killing of the latter as murder, was accepted by Tertullian, who was ignorant of Hebrew, and by later church fathers. The distinction was subsequently embodied in canon law as well as in Justinian Law.[8] This position was further reinforced by the belief that the "animation" (entry of the soul) of a fetus occurred on the fortieth or eightieth day after conception for males and females respectively, an idea first expressed by Aristotle,[9] and by the doctrine, firmly enunciated by Saint Augustine and other early Christian authorities, that the unborn child was included among those condemned to eternal perdition if he died unbaptized.[10] Some even regarded the death or murder of an unborn child as a greater calamity than that of a baptized person.[11] Eventually the distinction between animate and inanimate fetuses was lost; and since 1588, the Catholic Church has considered as murder the killing of any human fruit from the moment of conception.[12]

---

[5] *Exodus* 21:12. (Emphasis added.)

[6] *Mekhilta* and Rashi. For a translation of these sources, see 3 LAUTERBACH, *op. cit. supra* note 4, at 32-33; ROSENBAUM & SILBERMAN, *op. cit. supra* note 4, at 110-10a.

[7] The mistranslation, also followed in the Samaritan and Karaite versions, is evidently based on reading "zurah" or "surah" (meaning "form") for "ason" (meaning "harm" or "accident"). See KAUFMANN, GEDENKSCHRIFT 186 (1900).

[8] See WESTERMARCK, CHRISTIANITY AND MORALS 243 (1939).

[9] ARISTOTLE, DE ANIM. HIST., vii. 3; see 1 CATHOLIC ENCYCLOPEDIA 46-48 (1907).

[10] See 1 PLOSS & BARTELS, WOMAN 483 (1935); 2 CATHOLIC ENCYCLOPEDIA 266-67 (1907).

[11] See 2 LECKY, HISTORY OF EUROPEAN MORALS 23-24 (3d ed. 1891).

[12] See 1 PLOSS & BARTELS, *op. cit. supra* note 10, at 484; BONNAR, THE CATHOLIC DOCTOR 78 (1948).

This position is maintained to the present day.[13] It assumes that potential life, even in the earliest stages of gestation, enjoys the same value as any existing adult life. Hence, the Catholic Church never tolerates any direct abortion, even when, by allowing the pregnancy to continue, both mother and child will perish;[14] for "better two deaths than one murder."[15]

(2) Abortion in the Talmud.—Jewish law assumes that the full title to life arises only at birth. Accordingly, the Talmud rules:

> If a woman is in hard travail [and her life cannot otherwise be saved], one cuts up the child within her womb and extracts it member by member, because her life comes before that of [the child]. But if the greater part [or the head] was delivered, one may not touch it, for one may not set aside one person's life for the sake of another.[16]

This ruling, sanctioning embryotomy to save the mother in her mortal conflict with her unborn child, is also the sole reference to abortion in the principal codes of Jewish law.[17] They add only the further argument that such a child, being in "pursuit" of the mother's life, may be destroyed as an "aggressor" following the general principle of self-defense.[18]

This formulation of the attitude toward abortion in the classic sources of Jewish law implies (1) that the only indication considered for abortion is a hazard to the mother's life, and (2) that, otherwise, the destruction of an unborn child is a grave offense, although not murder.

(3) Abortion in Rabbinical Writings.—Some of these conclusions, and their ramifications, are more fully discussed in later rab-

---

[13] See, *e.g.*, CATHOLIC HOSPITAL ASSOCIATION OF THE UNITED STATES AND CANADA, ETHICAL AND RELIGIOUS DIRECTIVES FOR CATHOLIC HOSPITALS 4 (1949).

[14] See BONNAR, *op. cit. supra* note 12, at 84.

[15] Tiberghien, *Principles et Conscience Morale*, CAHIERS LAENNAC, Oct. 1946, p. 13.

[16] TALMUD, TOHOROTH II *Oholoth* 7:6.

[17] MAIMONIDES, HIL. ROTZE'ACH, 1:9; SHULCHAN ARUKH, *Choshen Mishpat* 425:2.

[18] This is based on a discussion of the Mishnah, TALMUD, *Sanhedrin* 72b. See generally JAKOBOVITS, JEWISH MEDICAL ETHICS 184-91 (1962).

binical writings, notably the prolific *responsa* literature. Before some of these writings are detailed, it should be pointed out that criminal abortion, as distinct from therapeutic abortion, is scarcely mentioned in Jewish sources at all. This omission seems all the more glaring in view of the extraordinary attention given to the subject in Christian literature and other legislation in ancient, medieval, and modern times. Criminal abortion was, with few exceptions, simply nonexistent in Jewish society. Consequently, the legal and moral problems involved were rarely submitted to rabbinical judgment, and their consideration thus did not enter into the *responsa*, at least not until comparatively recent times.[19]

Elaborating on the law as defined in the Talmud and the codes, the *responsa* add several significant rulings. While the status of a child conceived by rape is not discussed, several opinions are expressed on the legality of aborting a product of incest or adultery, both capital offenses in Biblical law. One eighteenth-century authority considered the case of an adulteress different insofar as her capital guilt would also forfeit the life of the fruit she carried.[20] But others maintained that there could be no distinction between a bastard and a legitimate fetus in this respect, and that any sanction to destroy such a product would open the floodgates to immorality and debauchery.[21] A later *responsum* also prohibited such an operation.[22]

Since the Talmud permits the sacrifice of the child to save the mother only prior to the emergence of its head or the greater part of its body from the birth canal,[23] a widely discussed question concerns the right to dismember the fetus even during the final stage of parturition if it is feared that otherwise both mother and child may die. As the danger to the mother usually is likely to occur before that stage is reached, this is mainly a hypothetical question, but it may be of some practical significance in the case of a breech-birth if the child's head cannot be extracted following the delivery of

---

[19] See JAKOBOVITS, *op. cit. supra* note 18, at 181.

[20] EMDEN, RESPONSA SHE'ILATH YA'AVETZ, pt. 1, no. 43. *Cf.* note 53 *infra*.

[21] BACHARACH, RESPONSA CHAVATH YA'IR no. 31.

[22] HALEVI, RESPONSA LECHEM HAPANIM, KUNTERES ACHARON no. 19.

[23] See text accompanying notes 16-18 *supra*.

the rest of the body. Notwithstanding the rule that the child in principle assumes full and equal human rights once the major part is born, and that consequently one may not thereafter save one life (the mother's) at the cost of another (the child's), this particular case may be an exception because (1) the child is liable to die in any event, whether the operation is carried out or not, while the mother can be rescued at the expense of the child, and (2) in the Jewish view the viability of a child is not fully established until it has passed the thirtieth day of its life, so that of the two lives here at stake the one is certain and established, while the other is still in some doubt. This slight inequality in value is too insignificant to warrant the deliberate sacrifice of the child for the sake of the mother if, without such sacrifice, the child would survive; but it is a sufficient factor to tip the scales in favor of the mother if the alternative is the eventual loss of both lives. Hence, with one exception,[24] rabbinical verdicts are inclined to countenance the intervention, provided the physician is confident of the success of the operation.[25]

(4) Deformed Children in Rabbinical Writings.—More recently the tragic problem of abortions indicated by suspected fetal defects has occupied considerable space in rabbinical writings. The recognition of this problem only dates from 1941, when an Australian medical journal first drew attention to the incidence of abnormalities resulting from rubella[26] in the mother during her early pregnancy. Since then, the legal, moral, and religious issues involved have been widely but still inconclusively debated in medical as well as non-medical circles. They aroused much public controversy when it was established that the birth of thousands of

---

24 SOPHER, RESPONSA MACHANEH CHAYIM *Choshen Mishpat*, pt. 2, no. 50. Some authorities left the question unresolved, see EGER, OHOLOTH 7:6; MEIR OF EISENSTADT, RESPONSA PANIM ME'IROTH, pt. 2, no. 8.

25 SCHICK, RESPONSA MAHARAM SHIK, *Yoreh De'ah* no. 155; HOFFMANN, RESPONSA MELAMED LEHO'IL, *Yoreh De'ah* no. 69.

26 German measles. See Gregg, *Congenital Cataract Following German Measles in Mother*, 3 TRANSACTIONS OF THE OPHTHALMOLOGICAL SOC'Y OF AUSTRALIA 35-46 (1941); see also Swan, Tostevin, Mayo & Black, *Congenital Defects in Infants Following Infectious Diseases During Pregnancy*, 2 MEDICAL J. OF AUSTRALIA 201-10 (1943).

deformed babies could be traced to drugs, notably thalidomide, taken by pregnant mothers and when many such mothers sought to have their pregnancies terminated for fear that they would deliver malformed children.

All the authorities of Jewish law are agreed that physical or mental abnormalities do not in themselves compromise the title to life, whether before or after birth. Cripples and idiots, however incapacitated, enjoy the same human rights (though not necessarily legal competence) as normal persons.[27] Human life being infinite in value, its sanctity is bound to be entirely unaffected by the absence of any or all mental faculties or by any bodily defects: any fraction of infinity still remains infinite.

(5) *Monster-Births in Rabbinical Writings.*—The absolute inviolability of any human being, however deformed, was affirmed in the first *responsum* on the status of monster-births. Early in the nineteenth century, a famous rabbinical scholar advised a questioner that it was forbidden to destroy a grotesquely misshapen child; he ruled that to kill, or even starve to death, any being born of a human mother was unlawful as homicide.[28] Indeed, in a somewhat less legal context, a twelfth-century moralistic work referred to a ruling against terminating the life of a child born with teeth and a tail like an animal, counseling instead the removal of these features.[29]

C. Arguments against the Destruction of Defectives

Based on these principles and precedents, present-day rabbis are unanimous in condemning abortion, feticide, or infanticide to eliminate a crippled being, before or after birth, as an unconscionable attack on the sanctity of life. Further considerations leading to this conclusion include the arguments that, conversely, the saving of an unborn child's life justifies the violation of the Sabbath (permitted

---

[27] See MISHNAH BERURAH, BI'UR HALAKHAH, ON ORACH CHAYIM 329:4. An idiot can even sue for injuries inflicted on him. TALMUD, *Baba Kamma* 8:4. Again, the killing of even a dying person is culpable as murder. MAIMONIDES, HIL. ROTZE-ACH 2:7.

[28] ELEZAR FLECKELES, RESPONSA TESHUVAH ME'AHAVAH, pt. 1, no. 53. See ZIMMELS, MAGICIANS, THEOLOGIANS AND DOCTORS 72 (1952).

[29] SEPHER CHASIDIM no. 186 (Zitomir ed. 1879).

only when human life is at stake);[30] that such a child is not in "pursuit" of the mother, thus excluding an important condition for the right to perform a therapeutic abortion;[31] that the interruption of a pregnancy is not without hazards to the mother, particularly the danger of rendering her sterile and the increase in maternal mortality resulting from abortions, as attested by physicians;[32] and that the killing of an embryo, while technically not murder due to a "scriptural decree," yet constitutes "an appurtenance of murder" because "in matters affecting human life we also consider that which is going to be [a human being] without any further action, following the laws of nature."[33]

These considerations would be valid even if it were known for certain that the expected child would be born deformed. The almost invariable doubts about such a contingency only strengthen the objections to abortion in these circumstances, especially in view of the Talmudic maxim that in matters of life and death the usual majority rule does not operate; any chance, however slim, that a life may be saved must always be given the benefit of the doubt.[34]

A similar attitude was adopted in a recent rabbinical article on the celebrated trial in Liege (Belgium) in which a mother and others were acquitted of guilt for the confessed killing of a thalidomide baby.[35] The author denounces abortion for such a purpose as well as the Liege verdict. "The sole legitimate grounds for killing a fetus are the urgent needs of the mother and her healing, whereas in these circumstances the mother's efforts to have the child aborted are based on self-love and plain egotism, wrapped in a cloak of

---

[30] See BACHARACH, *op. cit. supra* note 21. But there is some rabbinical dispute on this opinion. See JAKOBOVITS, *op. cit. supra* note 18, at 279 n.38.

[31] See text accompanying notes 16-18 *supra*.

[32] UNTERMAN, 6 NO'AM (Jerusalem) 1 (1963). Unterman, Chief Rabbi of Israel, refers to medical evidence given him by Professor Asherman, Director of the Maternity Department of the Municipal Hadassah Hospital in Tel Aviv. See also note 43 *infra*.

[33] *Ibid.*

[34] TALMUD, YOMA 84; SHULCHAN ARUKH, *Orach Chayim*, 329:2. See also note 45 *infra*.

[35] ZWEIG, 7 NO'AM (Jerusalem) 36 (1964).

compassion for this unfortunate creature, and this cannot be called a necessity for the mother at all."[36]

D. Psychological Considerations

On the other hand, Jewish law would consider a grave psychological hazard to the mother as no less weighty a reason for an abortion than a physical threat. On these grounds a seventeenth-century *responsum* permitted an abortion in a case where it was feared the mother would otherwise suffer an attack of hysteria imperiling her life.[37] If it is genuinely feared that a continued pregnancy and eventual birth under these conditions might have such debilitating effects on the mother as to present a danger to her own life or the life of another by suicidal or violent tendencies, however remote this danger may be, a therapeutic abortion may be indicated with the same justification as for other medical reasons. But this fear would have to be very real, attested to by the most competent psychiatric opinion, and based on previous experiences of mental imbalance.[38]

II. MORAL AND SOCIAL CONSIDERATIONS

The legalistic structure of these conclusions must be viewed in the context of Judaism's moral philosophy and against the background of contemporary social conditions.

A. The "Cruelty" of the Abortion Laws

At the outset, it is essential, in order to arrive at an objective judgment, to disabuse one's mind of the often one-sided, if not grossly partisan, arguments in the popular (and sometimes medical) presentations of the issues involved. A hue and cry is raised about the "cruelty" of the present abortion laws.[39] Harrowing scenes are

---

36 *Ibid.*

37 MIZRACHI, RESPONSA P'RI HA'ARETZ, *Yoreh De'ah* no. 21.

38 UNTERMAN, HATORAH VEHAMEDINAH 25, 29 (4th ser. 1952); FRIEDMAN, RESPONSA NETZER MATA'AI pt. 1, no. 8; FEINSTEIN, RESPONSA IGROTH MOSHEH *Orach Chayim* pt. 4, no. 88. These authorities permit the violation of the Sabbath for the sake of psychiatric patients.

39 See editorial in N.Y. Times, April 7, 1965, p. 42, col. 2, commenting on CBS TV program of April 5, 1965; see also editorial in N.Y. Times, Feb. 13, 1965, p. 20, col. 2.

depicted, in the most lurid colors, of girls and married women selling their honor and their fortunes, exposing themselves to mayhem and death at the hands of some greedy and ill-qualified abortionist in a dark, unhygienic back-alley, and facing the prospect of being hunted and haunted like criminals for the rest of their lives — all because safe, honorable, and reasonably priced methods to achieve the same ends are barred from hospitals and licensed physicians' offices by our "barbaric" statutes. Equally distressing are the accounts and pictures of pitifully deformed children born because our "antiquated" abortion laws did not permit us to forestall their and their parents' misfortune. And then there are, of course, always heart-strings or sympathy to be pulled by the sight of "unwanted" children taxing the patience and resources of parents already "burdened" with too large a brood.

There is, inevitably, some element of cruelty in most laws. For a person who has spent his last cent before the tax-bill arrives, the income tax laws are unquestionably "cruel"; and to a man passionately in love with a married woman the adultery laws must appear "barbaric." Even more universally "harsh" are the military draft regulations which expose young men to acute danger and their families to great anguish and hardship.

B. *Moral Standards in Society*

All these resultant "cruelties" are surely no valid reason for changing those laws. No civilized society could survive without laws which occasionally spell some suffering for individuals. Nor can any public moral standards be maintained without strictly enforced regulations calling for extreme restraints and sacrifices in some cases. If the criterion for the legitimacy of laws were to be the complete absence of "cruel" effects, we should abolish or drastically liberalize not only our abortion laws, but our statutes on marriage, narcotics, homosexuality, suicide, euthanasia, and numerous other laws which inevitably result in personal anguish from time to time.

So far our reasoning, which could be supported by any number of references to Jewish tradition, has merely sought to demolish the "cruelty" factor as a valid argument per se by which to judge the

justice or injustice of any law. It still has to be demonstrated that
the restrictions on abortion are morally sound enough and sufficiently important to the public welfare to outweigh the consequen-
tial hardships in individual cases.

C.   The Hidden Side of the Problem

What the fuming editorials and harrowing documentaries on
the abortion problem do not show are pictures of radiant mothers
fondling perfectly healthy children who would never have been
alive if their parents had been permitted to resort to abortion in
moments of despair.   There are no statistics on the contributions to
society of outstanding men and women who would never have been
born had the abortion laws been more liberal.   Nor is it known how
many "unwanted" children eventually turn out to be the sunshine
of their families.

A Jewish moralistic work of the twelfth century relates the
following deeply significant story:

> A person constantly said that, having already a son and a daugh-
> ter, he was anxious lest his wife become pregnant again.   For he
> was not rich and asked how would he find sufficient sustenance.
> Said a sage to him: "When a child is born, the Holy One, blessed
> be He, provides the milk beforehand in the mother's breast; there-
> fore, do not worry."   But he did not accept the wise man's words,
> and he continued to fret.   Then a son was born to him.   After
> a while, the child became ill, and the father turned to the sage:
> "Pray for my son that he shall live."   Exclaimed the sage: "To you
> applies the biblical verse: 'Suffer not thy mouth to bring thy flesh
> into guilt.' "[40]

Some children may be born unwanted, but there are no unwanted
children aged five or ten years.

D.   Abortion Statistics

There are, then — even from the purely utilitarian viewpoint
of "cruelty" versus "happiness" or "usefulness" — two sides to this
problem, and not just one as pretended by those agitating for reform.   There are the admittedly tragic cases of maternal indignities

---

[40] SEPHER CHASIDIM, op. cit. supra note 29, no. 520.

and deaths as well as of congenital deformities resulting from our restrictive abortion laws. But, on the other hand, there are the countless happy children and useful citizens whose births equally result from these laws. What is the ratio between these two categories?

If one considers that even with the existing, rigid laws there are well over one million abortions performed annually in the United States (most of them by reputable physicians), it stands to reason that a relaxation of these laws would raise the abortion rate by many millions. In Hungary, for instance, where abortions were legalized in 1956, state physicians have terminated about two million pregnancies since then (in a population of ten million), amounting to three abortions for every live birth.[41] Even allowing for the more widespread recourse to birth control and for some stricter controls in the proposed abortion laws in this country, there can be little doubt that the American abortion rate would soar to at least two or three times the present number (probably a gross underestimate) if the proposed changes were adopted.

Out of the three million pregnancies that would probably be terminated every year, no more than thirty thousand[42] would have resulted in deformed births, while the remaining 99 per cent would have been healthy children, had their mothers been allowed or forced to carry them to term. Subtract from this latter figure the number of mothers whose hazards would be minimized if they did not feel compelled to resort to clandestine operations, and one would still have only a relatively minute proportion of abortions that would be fully justified for the reasons advanced by the advocates of liberalization. Well over 95 per cent, if not 98 per cent, of all abortions would eliminate normal children of healthy mothers. In fact, as for the mothers, the increased recourse to abortion (even

---

41 See N.Y. Times, Oct. 28, 1965, p. 14, col. 3.

42 This is the number of defective births resulting from German measles anticipated for 1965 in the United States. To this number may have to be added anticipated abnormalities for other reasons, but from it would have to be subtracted the considerably larger number of cases in which affected mothers would not resort to abortion, either because of their opposition to abortion or because the condition is undetected during pregnancy. The total of abortions fully justified by actual (not suspected) fetal defects due to factors that could be recognized during pregnancy could thus scarcely exceed thirty thousand.

if performed by qualified physicians), far from reducing hazards, would increase them, since such operations leave at least 5 per cent of the women sterile,[43] not to mention the rise in the resultant mortality rate. One can certainly ask if the extremely limited reduction in the number of malformed children and maternal mortality risks really justify the annual wholesale destruction of three million germinating, healthy lives, most of them potentially happy and useful citizens, especially in a country as underpopulated as America (compared to Europe, for instance, which commands far fewer natural resources).

E. *The Individual's Claim to Life*

These numerical facts alone make nonsense of the argument for more and easier abortions. But moral norms cannot be determined by numbers. In the Jewish view, "he who saves one life is as if he saved an entire world";[44] one human life is as precious as a million lives, for each is infinite in value. Hence, even if the ratio were reversed, and there was only a 1 per cent chance that the child to be aborted would be normal — in fact the chances invariably exceed 50 per cent in any given case[45]— the consideration for that one child in favor of life would outweigh any counterindication for the other 99 per cent.

But, in truth, such a counterindication, too, is founded on fallacious premises. Assuming one were 100 per cent certain (perhaps by radiological evidence) that a child would be born deformed, could this affect its claim to life? Any line to be drawn between normal and abnormal beings determining their right to live would

---

[43] See N.Y. Times report, note 41 *supra*.

[44] TALMUD, *Sanhedrin* 4:5. For this reason, Jewish law forbids the surrender of a single life even if any number of other lives may thereby be saved. MAIMONIDES, HIL. YESODEI HATORAH 5:5.

[45] Estimates of the rate of abnormalities from German measles have varied widely, but none approaches 50 per cent. The rate among live-born babies was recently found to be under 10 per cent, and "one can conclude [from various studies] that the incidences of congenital malformations reported by early workers are fantastically high and incorrect. The recommendation of therapeutic abortion based on those rates is not medically justified." Greenberg, Pellitteri & Barton, *Frequency of Defects in Infants Whose Mothers Had Rubella During Pregnancy*, 165 A.M.A.J. 675, 678 (1957). *Cf.* note 26 *supra*.

have to be altogether arbitrary. Would grave defect in one limb or in two limbs, or an anticipated sub-normal intelligence quotient of seventy-five or fifty make the capital difference between one who is entitled to live and one who is not? And if the absence of two limbs deprives a person of his claim to life, what about one who loses two limbs in an accident? By what moral reasoning can such a defect be a lesser cause for denying the right to live than a similar congenital abnormality? Surely life-and-death verdicts cannot be based on such tenuous distinctions.

F. *The Obligations of Society*

The birth of a physically or mentally maldeveloped child may be an immense tragedy in a family, just as a crippling accident or a lingering illness striking a family member later in life may be. But one cannot purchase the relief from such misfortunes at the cost of life itself. So long as the sanctity of life is recognized as inviolable, the cure to suffering cannot be abortion before birth, any more than murder (whether in the form of euthanasia or of suicide) after birth. The only legitimate relief in such cases is for society to assume the burdens which the individual family can no longer bear. Since society is the main beneficiary of restrictive public laws on abortion (or homicide), it must in turn also pay the price sometimes exacted by these laws in the isolated cases demanding such a price.

Just as the state holds itself responsible for the support of families bereaved by the death of soldiers fallen in the defense of their country, it ought to provide for incapacitated people born and kept alive in the defense of public moral standards. The community is morally bound to relieve affected families of any financial or emotional stress they cannot reasonably bear, either by accepting the complete care of defective children in public institutions, or by supplying medical and educational subsidies to ensure that such families do not suffer any unfair economic disadvantages from their misfortune.

G. *Illegitimate Children*

Similar considerations apply to children conceived by rape. The circumstances of such a conception cannot have any bearing on the child's title to life, and in the absence of any well-grounded challenge to this title there cannot be any moral justification for an abortion. Once again, the burden rests with society to relieve an innocent mother (if she so desires) from the consequences of an unprovoked assault upon her virtue if the assailant cannot be found and forced to discharge this responsibility to his child.

In the case of pregnancies resulting from incestuous, adulterous, or otherwise illegitimate relations (which the mother did not resist), there are additional considerations militating against any sanction of abortion. Jewish law not only puts an extreme penalty on incest and adultery, but also imposes fearful disabilities on the products of such unions. It brands these relations as capital crimes,[46] and it debars children born under these conditions from marriage with anyone except their like.[47]

(1) The Deterrent Effect.—Why exact such a price from innocent children for the sins of their parents? The answer is simple: to serve as a powerful deterrent to such hideous crimes. The would-be partners to any such illicit sexual relations are to be taught that their momentary pleasure would be fraught with the most disastrous consequences for any children they might conceive. Through this knowledge they are to recoil from the very thought of incest or adultery with the same horror as they would from contemplating murder as a means to enjoyment or personal benefit. Murder is comparatively rare in civilized society for the very reason that the dreadful consequences have evoked this horror of the crime in the public conscience. Incest and adultery, in the Jewish view, are no lesser crimes,[48] and they require the same horror as an effective deterrent.

(2) Parental Responsibility.—Why create this deterrent by visiting the sins of the parents on their innocent children? First, because there is no other way to expose an offense committed in private and usually beyond the chance of detection. But, above all, this

---

[46] See *Leviticus* 20:10-20.

[47] See *Deuteronomy* 23:3, and Jewish commentaries.

[48] Compare the juxtaposition of murder and adultery in the Ten Commandments. *Exodus* 20:13.

responsibility of parents for the fate of their children is an inexorable necessity in the generation of human life; it is dictated by the law of nature no less than by the moral law. If a careless mother drops her baby and thereby causes a permanent brain injury to the child, or if a syphilitic father irresponsibly transmits his disease to his offspring before birth, or if parents are negligent in the education of their children, all these children may innocently suffer and for the rest of their lives expiate the sins of their parents. This is what must be if parental responsibility is to be taken seriously. The fear that such catastrophic consequences would ensue from a surrender to temptation or from carelessness will help prevent the conception of grossly disadvantaged children or their physical or mental mutilation after birth.

H. *Public Standards v. Individual Aberration*

In line with this reasoning, Jewish law never condones the relaxation of public moral standards for the sake of saving recalcitrant individuals from even mortal offenses. A celebrated Jewish sage and philosopher of the fifteenth century, in connection with a question submitted to his judgment, averred that it was always wrong for a community to acquiesce in the slightest evil, however much it was hoped thereby to prevent far worse excesses by individuals. The problem he faced arose out of a suggestion that brothels for single people be tolerated as long as such publicly controlled institutions would reduce or eliminate the capital crime of marital faithlessness then rampant. His unequivocal answer was: It is surely far better that individuals should commit the worst offenses and expose themselves to the gravest penalties than publicly to promote the slightest compromise with the moral law.[49]

Rigid abortion laws, ruling out the *post facto* "correction" of rash acts, compel people to think twice *before* they recklessly embark on illicit or irresponsible adventures liable to inflict lifelong suffering or infamy on their progeny. To eliminate the scourge of illegitimate children more self-discipline to prevent their conception is re-

---

[49] ARAMA, AKEDATH YITZCHAK ch. 20, at 41 (b) (ed. Frankfurt a/o 1785).

quired, not more freedom to destroy them in the womb. For each illegitimate child born because the abortion laws are strict, there may be ten or more such children *not* conceived because these laws are strict.

The exercise of man's procreative faculties, making him (in the phrase of the Talmud) "a partner with God in creation," is man's greatest privilege and gravest responsibility. The rights and obligations implicit in the generation of human life must be evenly balanced if man is not to degenerate into an addict of lust and a moral parasite infesting the moral organism of society. Liberal abortion laws would upset that balance by facilitating sexual indulgences without insisting on corresponding responsibilities.

I. *Therapeutic Abortions*

This leaves only the concern for the mother's safety as a valid argument in favor of abortions. In the view of Judaism, all human rights, and their priorities, derive solely from their conferment upon man by his Creator. By this criterion, as defined in the Bible, the rights of the mother and her unborn child are distinctly unequal, since the capital guilt of murder takes effect only if the victim was a born and viable person. This recognition does not imply that the destruction of a fetus is not a very grave offense against the sanctity of human life, but only that it is not technically murder. Jewish law makes a similar distinction in regard to the killing of inviable adults. While the killing of a person who already suffered from a fatal injury (from other than natural causes) is not actionable as murder,[50] the killer is morally guilty of a mortal offense.[51]

This inequality, then, is weighty enough only to warrant the sacrifice of the unborn child if the pregnancy otherwise poses a threat to the mother's life. Indeed, the Jewish concern for the mother is so great that a gravid woman sentenced to death[52] must not be subjected to the ordeal of suspense to await the delivery of

---

[50] TALMUD, *Sanhedrin* 78a.

[51] Maimonides acquits such a murderer only before "a human court." HIL. ROT-ZE'ACH 2:7-8. *Cf.* note 4 *supra*.

[52] In practice Jewish law virtually abolished capital punishment thousands of years ago, as it insisted on numerous conditions whose fulfillment was almost impossible (such as the presence of, and prior warning by, two eye-witnesses).

her child.[53] (Jewish sources brand any delay in the execution, once it is finally decreed, as "the perversion of justice" *par excellence*,[54] since the criminal is sentenced to die, not to suffer.)

Such a threat to the mother need not be either immediate or absolutely certain. Even a remote risk of life invokes all the life-saving concessions of Jewish law,[55] provided the fear of such a risk is genuine and confirmed by the most competent medical opinions. Hence, Jewish law would regard it as an indefensible desecration of human life to allow a mother to perish in order to save her unborn child.

IV. CONCLUSION

This review may be fittingly concluded with a reference to the very first Jewish statement on deliberate abortion. Commenting on the *Septuagint* version of the above-quoted *Exodus* passage,[56] the Alexandrian-Jewish philosopher, Philo, at the beginning of the Current Era declared that the attacker must die if the fruit he caused to be lost was already "shaped and all the limbs had their proper qualities, for that which answers to this description is a human being . . . like a statue lying in a studio requiring nothing more than to be conveyed outside."[57] The legal conclusion of this statement, reflecting Hellenistic rather than Jewish influence, may vary from the letter of Jewish law; but its reasoning certainly echoes the spirit of Jewish law. The analogy may be more meaningful than Philo could have intended or foreseen. A classic statue by a supreme master is no less priceless for being made defective, even with an arm or a leg missing. The destruction of such a treasure can be warranted only by the superior worth of preserving a living human being.

---

[53] TALMUD, *Erakhin* 1:4; TALMUD, TOSAPHOTH, *Erakhin* 7a.

[54] ETHICS OF THE FATHERS 5:8.

[55] SHULCHAN ARUKH, *Orach Chayim* 329:2-4.

[56] See text accompanying note 3 *supra*.

[57] DE SPEC. LEGIBUS 3:108-10, 117-18; DE VIRTUT. 138. But in the latter two passages, Philo himself qualified his statement by calling only a person who killed a child already born "indubitably a murderer."

7

Abortion Legislation in Denmark

Vera Skalts and Magna Norgaard

In Denmark termination of pregnancy has been the subject of special legislation since 1937. Before that time legislation concerning this question had been limited to statutes in the Criminal Code which provided that termination of pregnancy was punishable both for the woman and for those who assisted her.[1] As far as the woman was concerned, even this legal attitude was considerably milder and more liberal than that during the last centuries. This is reflected by the trend in the legislation under which sentences ranged from capital punishment in the seventeenth century to imprisonment up to two years (a sentence which under special circumstances could be remitted and, as time passed, was very often remitted) under the Criminal Code of 1930.[2] Indeed, during the first decades of this century it became obvious that illegal abortion was not considered, by large circles of the population, to be a criminal act on the part of the woman. In most of the rather few cases which were brought into court, the women were acquitted;[3] when the cases were decided by juries, this almost always happened, reflecting the general public

---

[1] CRIMINAL CODE (Denmark 1930); CRIMINAL CODE (Denmark 1866).

[2] CRIMINAL CODE § 242 (Denmark 1930).

[3] See FIRST PREGNANCY COMM'N REP. OF 1936 ON THE LAWFULNESS OF TERMINATION OF PREGNANCY. This report consists of a study concerning eighty-two women who were charged with abortion during a five-year period. Nineteen of these women were indicted. Fifteen of the women indicted were tried by jury and all were acquitted but one who was guilty of infanticide. Four of the women did not want a jury trial and they were found guilty and sentenced. See FIRST PREGNANCY COMM'N, REP., *supra* at 12-13. The report also sets forth the main reasons for withdrawal of the charges against those women who were not indicted.

opinion that the woman ought not to be punished. Furthermore, it was generally known that the abortion, as a "hidden crime," in most cases never came to the attention of the police,[4] and it was a matter of great concern that most of the women who committed this "crime" had their pregnancy interrupted in an unsafe manner by "quacks" at the risk of their life and health.[5]

In spite of the general criminality of abortion, it had been recognized for many years as lawful for a doctor to terminate a pregnancy in special cases if such intervention was necessay to avert serious danger to the life or health of the pregnant woman; this was the so-called "medical indication."[6] In this respect, however, a great amount of uncertainty prevailed among physicians, and highly different attitudes toward this medical indication were adopted.[7]

It was this general uncertainty about the legality of abortion under the medical indication which in 1932 motivated the Medico-legal Council to recommend to the Ministry of Justice that there be undertaken a general review of the question of whether termination of pregnancy should be permitted and, if so, to what extent. The Council also recommended that the Ministry consider the question of whether information on the use of contraceptives should be disseminated by the state.[8] In the same year, the Ministry of Justice established the first Pregnancy Commission;[9] the result was the Pregnancy Measures Act of 1937[10] (Pregnancy Act), which was substantially amended in 1956.[11]

---

[4] See FIRST PREGNANCY COMM'N REP., *supra* note 3, at 24-27, 116-38.

[5] *Ibid.*

[6] See KRABBE, CRIMINAL CODE TEXTBOOK (C.E.G.2d 1935) (the author is a professor of law at the University of Copenhagen). The practice was formulated through judicial fiat, based on the rule of necessity.

[7] See FIRST PREGNANCY COMM'N REP., *supra* note 3, at 5.

[8] *Ibid.*

[9] *Ibid.* The Ministry of Justice established a commission on Nov. 7, 1932, for the purpose of studying: (1) whether intermission of pregnancy ought to be permitted, and if so, to what extent; (2) whether the state ought to subsidize or organize a medical information center for the purpose of preventing the occurrence of unwanted pregnancies; and (3) whether there is reason for amending CRIMINAL CODE § 235 (Denmark 1930) which prohibits the advertising of contraceptive objects and services.

[10] Act concerning Provisions Relating to Pregnancy, Act No. 163 of May 18, 1937, amended by Act No. 89 of March 15, 1939 [hereinafter cited as 1937 PREGNANCY ACT].

[11] Act concerning Provisions Relating to Pregnancy, Act No. 177 of June 23, 1956

Since 1937 the abortion legislation has been subject to review at regular intervals; the application of the Pregnancy Act has been followed closely.[12]   Statistical material concerning both the number of legal and estimated illegal abortions has been published, often together with proposals for preventing abortions, legal as well as illegal.[13]

I. THE EVOLUTION OF ABORTION LEGISLATION IN DENMARK

A.   Danish Attitudes toward Abortion

Much discussion has taken place concerning the extent to which legal abortion should be allowed; but it is generally agreed that although legal abortion is a highly deplorable step which should be prevented as far as possible, there are situations in which abortion is the best solution.   In these cases the woman ought to have the operation performed in a hospital under safe conditions and with the aid of expert medical advice and supervision.

The abortion legislation should be considered as part of the social legislation of the country; and as a preferable alternative to abortion, constructive help and support should be provided to women in unwanted pregnancy so as to encourage them to carry through their pregnancy.   Thus, it is important for women in unwanted pregnancy to be brought into contact with organizations capable of giving help and advice during pregnancy and after delivery.   In Denmark, this is one of the services provided by the Mothers Aid Centers.[14]   Experience has shown that women in unwanted preg-

---

[hereinafter cited as 1956 PREGNANCY ACT].   Reprinted here on p. 171.

[12] See THE MOTHERS AID CENTERS OF COPENHAGEN REPS. (1941-1948).   The Mothers Aid Centers, which have increasingly had the responsibility of administering the Pregnancy Act (see text accompanying notes 32-34 *infra*), publish regular reports on the number of legal abortions recommended by the Centers.   In addition, all cases of legal abortion must be reported to the Board of Health, which publishes the figures regularly.

[13] See, *e.g.*, Henningsen, Skalts & Hoffmeyer, *Mothers Aid and Legal Abortion Since the Pregnancy Act of 1939*, 114 UGESKRIFT FOR LÆGER 502 (1952); Hoffmeyer & Nørgaard, *Incidence of Conception and the Course of Pregnancy*, 126 UGESKRIFT FOR LAEGER 355 (1964).

[14] See text accompanying notes 16-21 *infra*.

nancy are often desperately determined on one thing — to obtain abortion — and are only interested in applying to organizations which are not only capable of assisting them in pregnancy, but which will also consider abortion.[15] For this reason it is important that the Mothers Aid Centers, to some extent, be active in the decision on the request for abortion. The Centers have played an important role in the development of abortion legislation and today hold a central position in the administration of the Pregnancy Act; thus, a brief account of their activities is necessary.

B. Mothers Aid Centers

From the beginning of this century a private organization called "Mothers Aid" assisted single mothers, especially in Copenhagen.[16] Eventually, that work attracted a good deal of attention and ultimately was expanded by the Mothers Aid Act of 1939 to include individual help and advice to all pregnant women and mothers with young children.[17]

Today, eleven Mothers Aid Centers, under the Ministry of Social Affairs, are in operation throughout the country. Financed by the Central Government, their charge, under the relevant legislation, is to provide personal, social, legal, and medical assistance and guidance to pregnant women and mothers, as well as to families with infants and young children. The Centers are in contact with a large proportion of all expectant mothers, married and unmarried alike. The applicants are women from all classes of the population and from all parts of the country. Less than half of the women are married; the remainder are sole supporters.[18]

---

[15] See Skalts, *Termination of Pregnancy and Mothers Aid*, Socialt Tidsskrift, April 1943.

[16] The original Mothers Aid organization was financed by private contributions, whereas the Mothers Aid Centers established by the Mothers Aid Act of 1939 are financed by tax money. In addition, the present Mothers Aid Centers provide help and advice to all pregnant women and to women with young children, whereas the original Mothers Aid offered help and assistance to single mothers only. Furthermore, the original Mothers Aid operated only in Copenhagen whereas the present Mothers Aid Centers are operative throughout Denmark.

[17] Act No. 119 of March 15, 1939, amended by, Act No. 150 of March 30, 1942, Act No. 112 of March 23, 1948, Act No. 176 of June 23, 1956, Act No. 41 of March 1, 1961.

[18] See [1958-1962] MOTHERS AID CENTERS REP. (1963).

The staff of the Centers is comprised of social workers, lawyers, and doctors (chiefly psychiatrists and gynecologists), and there is close teamwork between these professional groups. Characteristic of the work is the personal-psychiatric-medical help which is offered concurrently with economic-practical help. Efforts are made to establish constructive, active cooperation with the applicants in accordance with the principle of self-help.

Family guidance is provided. Direct financial support may be granted, often by way of benefits in kind (*e.g.*, for a layette, for clothes for the pregnant woman, for domestic help during pregnancy and after childbirth). The Centers operate convalescence and treatment homes for pregnant women and mothers with infants.

A number of special programs are provided for self-supporting mothers (*i.e.*, unmarried, widowed, or separated women). The Centers are in touch with 90 per cent of all single mothers.[19] Assistance is granted for maintenance during pregnancy and after childbirth in special homes for pregnant women and mothers, for paternity cases and maintenance orders, and for placing the child in a children's home, in private care, or for adoption. However, no more than approximately 3 per cent of the unmarried clients of the Mothers Aid have their children adopted by strangers — the so-called anonymous adoptions.[20] To the vast majority of self-supporting mothers who keep their children, it is essential that long-term assistance be provided in order to make them better suited to establish a good home for their children. Financial assistance for education, training, or retraining is a very important help to many self-supporters. A small number of such mothers may obtain a flat in special houses with communal facilities — the so-called "collective house" — during the first difficult years after they have become self-supporting mothers. This permits them to settle down and prepare to fend for themselves and their children in the future. The award of a flat in such a house is intended to help during the early difficult period. The Centers consider it quite inadvisable to gather solitary mothers in special blocks of houses for any extended

---

19 From the files of the Mothers Aid Centers.

20 See Nørgaard, *The Mothers Aid Centers During 25 Years,* Socialt Tidsskrift, March-April 1964, pp. 33-64.

period of time. The flats are, therefore, let for a limited period, normally two years.

C. Aid to Women with an Unwanted Pregnancy: The Pregnancy Act of 1937

Women in unwanted pregnancy constitute about one-third of the Centers' clients.[21] The first Pregnancy Act,[22] enacted in 1937, provided for three indications for abortion: (1) the *medical* and *sociomedical* indication, allowing termination of a pregnancy when it involved serious danger to the life or health of the woman; (2) the *ethical* indication, allowing termination of pregnancy where the woman had become impregnated through certain criminal acts; and (3) the *hereditary* indication allowing termination of pregnancy when there was serious danger that the child would suffer from severe hereditary illness or disturbance. While there was general agreement concerning the latter two indications, the first indication was the object of much discussion by the Pregnancy Commission, by Parliament, and by the populace.[23] Besides the medical, the ethical, and the hereditary indications, the majority of the first Pregnancy Commission had proposed a "social" or a "welfare" indication,[24] according to which abortion would be permitted in cases where pregnancy or childbirth involved unavoidable danger of lasting and substantial deterioration of the personal, familial, or social status of the woman. This social indication was, however, rejected by Parliament, where it was emphasized that instead of allowing termination of pregnancy on account of social reasons, it was the duty of the community to meet the motivating social difficulties, whether they were of a financial character or based on a rigid attitude in the community towards unmarried mothers.[25] However, a purely medical indication seemed too restrictive. The

---

21 From the files of the Mothers Aid Centers.

22 1937 PREGNANCY ACT.

23 See Skalts, *Pregnancy Act and Mothers Aid Act*, Socialt Tidsskrift, Jan.-Feb. 1957, pp. 1-24.

24 See FIRST PREGNANCY COMM'N REP., *supra* note 3, at 77.

25 See, *e.g.*, STEINCKE, SHALL ABORTION BE EXEMPT FROM PUNISHMENT? (Copenhagen, 1949).

result was that the original, purely medical indication was changed
to a medicosocial indication by the omission of the words "on account of illness" from the act.[26] Thus, "other reasons" could under-
lie the danger to the woman's life or health.[27] Circulars distributed
by the Board of Health and the Ministry of Justice about the time
of the enactment of the law mentioned, as examples of such "other
reasons," chronic malnutrition, exhaustion due to many confine-
ments, suicidal attempts, and depression, but not necessarily pathological depression.[28]

The decision on abortion should be made by two physicians, one
of them, normally, the woman's own doctor.[29] In special cases certain additional requirements have to be met, one of which is having
a special impact on the development of abortion legislation: in cases
where the danger to the woman's life or health is due to reasons
other than illness, it is a condition for termination of pregnancy
that the Mothers Aid Center certify that the woman has been given
information on the help and support that would be available to her
during pregnancy and after childbirth.[30] The rationale for this requirement was clear: in those cases where the indication for abortion
was not purely medical, but rather where social, economic, familial,
or personal reasons were prevailing, an attempt should always be
made to solve these problems and avoid abortion. For this purpose
the Mothers Aid Center was the proper organization. This point of
view was considered so important that the effective date of the
Pregnancy Act was postponed for eighteen months so as to permit
the establishment of Mothers Aid Centers; thus, both the Pregnancy
Act and the Mothers Aid Act came into effect in 1939.[31]

---

26 The original text of the § 1(1) of Bill concerning Provisions Relating to Pregnancy (1937) provided that abortion is permitted "when intermission of pregnancy is
carried out in order to avert a present danger, due to illness, to the life of the woman
or to lasting and considerable deterioration of her health." Section 1(1) of the 1937
PREGNANCY ACT provided that abortion is permitted "when intermission of pregnancy
is necessary to avert a grave danger to the life or health of the woman."

27 1937 PREGNANCY ACT § 2.

28 See Board of Health Circular, March 25, 1939 (unpublished); Ministry of Justice
Ruling, January 23, 1940 (unpublished).

29 1937 PREGNANCY ACT § 3(1).

30 1937 PREGNANCY ACT § 2(1).

31 Act No. 84 of March 1938, § 1, in which the effective date of the 1937 PREG-

Through the combination of the Pregnancy Act and the Mothers Aid Act, the foundation was laid for intensive work by the Mothers Aid Centers with women in unwanted pregnancy. During the first ten years, the number of women who applied to the Centers for legal abortion increased rapidly.[32] Some women came on their own initiative; but between 80 and 90 per cent were referred by their doctors, who generally preferred to bring their patients into contact with the Mothers Aid Centers,[33] which, with their social-gynecological-psychiatric staff, were in a better position to give impartial expert opinions on the abortion question and had far better facilities for providing help and support. Furthermore, the Pregnancy Hygiene Act of 1945 provided that physicians were under an obligation to refer to the Mothers Aid Centers any woman who expressed a desire for termination of pregnancy because of personal, social, or economic difficulties.[34]

As time passed, it became increasingly necessary for the Mothers Aid to build up its staff and establish sociomedical teamwork whereby social workers would determine the kind of economic, social, or personal strain under which the woman was suffering so that doctors could decide whether or not the woman in question could bear the burden of that strain physically and psychically. In making these determinations, both the social workers and the doctors always considered the possibility of helping the woman carry her pregnancy to term either by means of sociomedical treatment or by various forms of social, economic, or personal support. If the Mothers Aid found that there was no indication for abortion, they so informed the woman; if, on the other hand, they found that abortion ought to be recommended, they arranged for the woman's hospitalization and sent the hospital detailed reports from the social worker and doctor. In nearly all of these cases the hospitals followed the recommendations of the Mothers Aid Centers; thus, in practice, the administration of the Pregnancy Act has rested with the Mothers Aid Centers.

NANCY ACT was postponed from April 1, 1938, to Oct. 1, 1939.

[32] See Nørgaard, *supra* note 20.

[33] See, *e.g.*, [Jan. 1933] MOTHERS AID CENTERS REP.

[34] Act No. 472 of Oct. 1, 1945, § 1 (2).

D. Present Abortion Legislation: The Pregnancy Act of 1956

(1) *Conditions under the First Pregnancy Act.*—In the first decade after the enactment of the Pregnancy Act of 1937 there was a considerable increase in the number of legal abortions in the country.[35] This was not surprising for the period immediately following the first liberalization of abortion law. At the same time, the number of illegal abortions also increased.[36] The rise in legal and illegal abortions was probably partly due to the difficult situation during the years of the Second World War period. This increase might also have been caused by the fact that the general measures of help for pregnant women and families with children contained in the Pregnancy Act of 1937 and the development of the practical-economic facilities of the Mothers Aid Centers were far from being carried out to the extent proposed in the discussions at the time of passage of the Pregnancy Act. And still another reason might be that information on the use of contraceptives was not available to the extent proposed by the first Pregnancy Commission.

At this time a controversy concerning the Pregnancy Act developed. Some contended that the increasing number of legal abortions indicated that the law was being interpreted too liberally. According to others, the increase indicated that the law was not being interpreted liberally enough. Furthermore, the drafting lacked clarity; indeed, the wording of the first indication left a good deal to interpretation.[37]

The Mothers Aid Centers were, to a great extent, drawn into the discussions about the abortion problem. Many women, their families, and family doctors expressed the opinion that the Centers were too restrictive in recommending abortion. On the other hand, hospital physicians, gynecologists, and surgeons, who performed the operations, often expressed the opinion that the Mothers Aid Centers

---

[35] See Fenger & Lindhart, *The Number of Abortions in Denmark 1940-1950,* 114 UGESKRIFT FOR LÆGER 617-21 (1952).

[36] See Oram, *The Number of Criminal Abortions,* 115 UGESKRIFT FOR LÆGER 1367 (1953).

[37] In the situation where there may be grave danger to the health of the woman the doctor determines whether the danger actually exists. This determination may be a matter of the doctor's personal opinion, especially in ascertaining whether nervousness or general weakness constitutes a grave danger.

were too liberal.[38] This opinion is not surprising since this latter group only saw the women who were recommended for abortion by the Mothers Aid Centers, but not the many women who were refused such recommendation.

(2) The Second Pregnancy Commission.—The increasing discussion surrounding the abortion question resulted in the appointment of a second Pregnancy Commission in 1950.[39] Again, the great problem of the indications for abortion was considered on an official level, and the different attitudes of the populace were clearly reflected in the proposals of the Commission. Four different proposals were made by the Commission members:[40] (a) *one member* found that the question of abortion could only be decided by the woman herself and recommended "free abortion";[41] (b) *one member* recommended that the medical indication should be limited to cases of illness (*i.e.*, a strict medical indication) with the ethical and hereditary indications being maintained;[42] (c) *four members* recommended a social or welfare indication in accordance with the indication proposed by the majority of the first Pregnancy Commission;[43] and (d) *the majority* (ten members) of the Commission found that the indications set out in the Pregnancy Act of 1937 ought to be maintained without any radical changes.[44]

The majority found that the law had been interpreted fairly

---

38 See Rydberg, *The Legal Abortions*, 114 UGESKRIFT FOR LÆGER 690 (1952).

39 Appointed by the Ministry of Justice, January 9, 1950. The purpose of the Commission as stated by the Ministry of Justice was to examine the need for amending the legislation on pregnancy by analyzing the past ten years' developments and experience. The Commission was also to study and determine what tasks and means should be conferred upon the Mothers Aid Centers, and how the cooperation between the Centers, the public authorities, and the physicians should take place. In addition, the Commission was to study whether the state should subsidize or organize a medical information center which would operate to prevent unwanted pregnancies, and if so, recommend how this should be established. Finally, the Commission was to study the value and the mode of operation of the sexual clinics. See SECOND PREGNANCY COMM'N REP. NO. 96 OF 1954 ON AMENDMENTS OF LEGISLATION CONCERNING PREGNANCY.

40 See SECOND PREGNANCY COMM'N REP., *supra* note 39, at 96.

41 *Ibid.*

42 *Id.* at 122.

43 *Id.* at 92.

44 *Id.* at 67.

well, but that since there had been some doubt concerning the extent and meaning of the medical and medicosocial indication, a clarification of the section relating to this indication was necessary. A very limited and clearly defined extension of the indications was proposed; the extension related primarily to women who suffered from severe physical or psychic defects.[45] The bill proposed by the majority was passed by Parliament almost without change.[46]

The question of the interpretation of the Pregnancy Act of 1937 was also taken up by the second Pregnancy Commission. The Commission thoroughly investigated the practice of the Mothers Aid Centers during the preceding ten years and found that the rise in the number of abortions was due to a complexity of reasons,[47] and that this trend was in no way the result of a misinterpretation of the legal provisions of the 1937 act.[48] The majority of the Commission proposed that, as a general rule, the Mothers Aid Centers should make the decisions in abortion cases with the assistance of medical experts — a proposal which was, in fact, a legalization of the actual practice developed since the first Pregnancy Act.[49] This proposal was adopted in the Pregnancy Act of 1956.[50]

II. LEGAL ABORTION UNDER THE PREGNANCY ACT OF 1956

A. The Legal Indications for Abortion

The new act did not involve any essential changes in the opportunity for termination of pregnancy and caused no increase in the

---

[45] *Ibid.* The Minister of Justice can, after the issuance of a statement from the Central Board (see note 58 *infra*), grant permission to interrupt a pregnancy even if the conditions mentioned in § 1 of the Bill concerning Provisions Relating to Pregnancy (1937) (see note 26 *supra* and accompanying text) are not fulfilled, provided that extraordinary circumstances exist for interrupting the pregnancy (see text following note 55 *infra*).

[46] 1956 PREGNANCY ACT § 1.

[47] This is true except as to one member of the Commission. See note 43 *supra* and accompanying text.

[48] See SECOND PREGNANCY COMM'N REP., *supra* note 39, at 34.

[49] *Id.* at 69.

[50] 1956 PREGNANCY ACT § 3(3).

number of legal abortions. The Pregnancy Act provides for legal termination of pregnancy in four main groups of cases: (1) where termination of pregnancy is necessary to avert any serious danger to the life or health of the woman; (2) where the woman has become impregnated through various criminal acts specified in the act; (3) where the child is likely to be born with any serious form of mental illness, mental deficiency, or any serious physical abnormality or disease; and (4) where because of serious physical or psychic defects or other medical reasons the woman is deemed unfit to take proper care of her child.[51]

(1) Where Termination of Pregnancy Is Necessary To Avert Serious Danger to the Life or Health of the Woman.—The clarification proposed by the Pregnancy Commission resulted in an amplification of the provision in the 1937 act. In evaluating the danger, due consideration must now be given to all relevant circumstances, including the conditions under which the woman must live. Consideration is to be given not only to her physical and mental health, but also to any condition of physical or psychic weakness, present or threatening.

This provision is based on the principle that the condition of health and the opportunities for taking curative measures should be viewed in the light of the living conditions of the patient. It is still required, however, that there be serious danger to the life or health of the woman. No matter how poor the social, economic, and matrimonial conditions may be, they will never in themselves be sufficient ground for abortion. Thus, the act does not provide for any social or welfare indication, but the medical indication is sociomedical in principle.

(2) Where the Woman Has Become Impregnated through Various Criminal Acts.[52]—This is the so-called ethical indication. Sexual intercourse with a child under fifteen years of age is such a criminal act under the Danish Criminal Code;[53] a girl who has become pregnant before the age of fifteen may always obtain a

---

[51] 1956 PREGNANCY ACT § 1(1).

[52] 1956 PREGNANCY ACT § 1(1)(2).

[53] CRIMINAL CODE No. 126, § 222(1) (Denmark 1930), with later amendments.

legal abortion, provided her pregnancy is not too far advanced. Termination of pregnancy due to incest or rape is also permitted; however, in the case of pregnancy by rape, it is a prerequisite that the offense be reported to the police and that they do not dismiss it as false. However, it is not a condition precedent to the abortion operation that a court shall have affirmatively decided the question of the guilt of the rapist. The time limitations for termination of pregnancy would make it impossible to await this decision.

(3) *Where the Child Is Likely To Be Born with Any Serious Form of Mental Illness, Mental Deficiency, or Any Serious Physical Abnormality or Disease.*—This is the so-called heredity indication. The evidence of such hereditary risk is normally obtained through a prognosis supplied by the Institute of Human Genetics at the University of Copenhagen.[54] Included here are risks due to prenatal or fetal injuries, for instance, those resulting from rubella[55] or thalidomide.

(4) *Where the Woman Is Deemed Unfit To Take Proper Care of Her Child.*—This provision, which was introduced in 1956, has special reference to conditions where, by reason of any severe mental or physical defect (mental deficiency, severe defects of character, severe physical disability), the woman is not able to care for her child, and where termination of the pregnancy is not indicated for health or hereditary reasons. In principle, it is a social indication, it being the interests of the child, not of the woman herself, that are safeguarded. In accordance with its terms, the provision has been applied in only a few cases. The current debate about extending the range of indications has touched upon the possibility of applying a broader construction to this provision so as to include, for instance, a larger number of mentally retarded persons.[56]

Before any legal abortion may be performed, it is a requirement that the woman desire the termination of her pregnancy. If by

---

[54] This institute, which receives reports on all cases of serious hereditary disease and on all admissions to psychiatric institutions, and other pertinent information, is in possession of extensive material relating to the genetic conditions of the individual family.

[55] This disease is commonly known as German measles.

[56] The problem was discussed at the University of Copenhagen in May, 1965.

reason of mental illness, mental deficiency, or any other reason she is incapable of understanding the significance of the intervention, the application for abortion may be made by an appointed guardian (*e.g.*, by the person in charge of a mental hospital or an institution for mental defectives).[57]

B. *Procedure for Obtaining Abortion under the 1956 Act*

When a woman wants a termination of her pregnancy, the general procedure is for her to apply to the nearest Mothers Aid Center. The Center then begins an exhaustive fact-finding procedure, the goal of which is to provide the decision-makers with all available information pertinent to the indications discussed above.

(1) *Investigation by the Mothers Aid Centers.*—The Mothers Aid Center provides an overall picture of the woman and her total situation through social and medical examinations, visits to the home, interviews with the woman's husband (possibly the father of the child) or the parents or other relatives of the young girl, and through correspondence with the woman's own doctor or perhaps with the above-mentioned University Institute for Human Genetics. Attention is continually given to the question of whether it will be possible, through social and/or medical measures, to prevent abortion.

In some cases examinations performed outside of a hospital will not provide a sufficient basis for deciding whether the woman will be able to go through with her pregnancy. In such cases, hospitalization in a psychiatric or other hospital ward may be required. Of great importance in this context is a special type of treatment and observation home operated by the Mothers Aid. These homes are small and cozy with no mark of a hospital-like atmosphere. The homes have a matron and assistants who are trained nurses and work in close cooperation with the social and medical personnel of the Mothers Aid. The attitude is positive, constructive, and therapeutic. The social worker, psychiatrist, and gynecologist pay regular visits to the homes; and because of the therapeutic attitude, the homes

---

[57] 1956 PREGNANCY ACT § 2(2).

provide extremely good opportunities for observation of pregnant women, often better than a psychiatric ward. Furthermore, living at one of these homes will often be less of a strain on the woman than hospitalization would be.

(2) Decision by Medicosocial Boards.—When the necessary examinations are finished — this requires, on the average, about two weeks — the justification of legal abortion is made by medicosocial boards which are linked to the eleven Mothers Aid Centers in the country.[58] There is a total of twenty such boards, each covering a particular geographical area.[59] Each board is comprised of three members: a graduate in law or a social worker representing the Mothers Aid, generally the person in charge of the Center that has handled the applicant's case; a psychiatrist, usually the one who has been in charge of the medical examination of the patient by the Mothers Aid; and a surgeon or a gynecologist, normally the person in charge of one of the hospital wards where the operation, if any, is to be performed.[60] Any termination of pregnancy must be unanimously approved by the board.[61] This composition ensures representation of gynecologic, psychiatric, and sociolegal expert knowledge. The collaboration of the members of each board has proven excellent, and the system is valuable in that it promotes a closer understanding between the professional groups concerned. As mentioned earlier,[62] a certain tension was sometimes formerly noticeable between psychiatrists and the Mothers Aid on the one

---

[58] Mothers Aid Centers, Act No. 176 of June 23, 1956, on Amendments of Act No. 119 of March 15, 1939 on Mothers Aid Centers § 6A(1)(2). According to § 3 of the act, one Central Board is established which coordinates the work of the boards connected with the Mothers Aid Centers. The Central Board acts as consultant to the boards and on the whole aims at a uniform practice concerning intermission of pregnancy. The three members of the Central Board — a director of a Mothers Aid Center or a "social practitioner" with knowledge of the work of the Mothers Aid Centers; two medical doctors, one of whom must be a specialist in psychiatry and the other a specialist in gynecology or surgery — are appointed for a period of four years by the Ministry of Social Affairs.

[59] More than one board is established at many of the Center locations. For instance, at the Mothers Aid Center of Copenhagen, five boards are established. See Mothers Aid Centers § 6A(1), Act No. 176 of June 23, 1956.

[60] Mothers Aid Centers § 6A(1), Act No. 176 of June 23, 1956.

[61] Mothers Aid Centers § 6A(2), Act No. 176 of June 23, 1956.

[62] See text accompanying note 38 *supra*.

hand, and surgeons and gynecologists on the other, the latter being informed only of the cases in which abortion was recommended. Now that all cases, including those ending in a refusal, are submitted to the boards, that tension has disappeared.

There is one exception to the general rule that questions concerning termination of pregnancy shall be decided by the boards of the Mothers Aid. Where it has been ascertained by a hospital that, because of illness, the life or health of a woman is in serious danger, referral to a Mothers Aid Center is not required, the hospital superintendent being considered competent to decide on termination of the pregnancy.[63] This permits the general practitioner to send his abortion-seeking patients to a hospital. However, only a small proportion of legal abortions are carried out under this provision. Of the 3,970 legal abortions performed in Denmark in 1963, 3,346 took place on the basis of board decisions, while 624 were decided by physicians.[64] Of the latter 624 cases, however, more than 200 had first applied to the Mothers Aid, which had arranged for their hospitalization for further observation.[65]

(3) The Abortion Operation.—The operation may be performed only by a central or local government hospital, or by a private hospital that receives public grants.[66] In Denmark, this means virtually all hospitals.

Apart from the cases in which there is serious risk to the life or health of the woman, a pregnancy cannot normally be terminated after the expiration of the sixteenth week of gestation.[67] Under the Pregnancy Act of 1937 this time limit was three months,[68] but was extended by the 1956 act because of the various factors involved in the consideration of the promptness with which abortion cases should be decided. For example, there must be sufficient time for examinations and observation, if required. Furthermore, it may be useful for the woman to have time to reflect and reconsider the

---

[63] 1956 PREGNANCY ACT § 3(2).

[64] Notice to the Mothers Aid Center from the Board of Health (unpublished).

[65] From the files of the Mothers Aid Centers.

[66] 1956 PREGNANCY ACT § 3(1).

[67] 1956 PREGNANCY ACT § 1(2).

[68] 1937 PREGNANCY ACT § 1(2).

decision to have the abortion performed, since the initial decision
may have been made when the feelings of panic and depression during the first few months of her pregnancy were present.

On the other hand, intervention should, as far as possible, be
made at an early stage of the pregnancy. In recent years, special
attention has been given to investigations, carried out in Denmark[69]
as well as abroad,[70] which seem to indicate that the risk attending
the operation increases considerably as the pregnancy becomes more
advanced. This consideration has led to speedier decisions.

(4) Residency Requirement.—A few years ago, after the
Mothers Aid had been approached by a number of foreign women
seeking legal abortion in Denmark, it was decided that termination
of pregnancy in Denmark would, in principal, be confined to women
ordinarily residing in Denmark.[71] Now, pregnancy of nonresident
women may be terminated only on purely medical grounds, as approved by the superintendent of the hospital to which they are
sent.[72] Thus, there is every reason to advise nonresident women
against going to Denmark to seek an abortion; virtually all of them
will have to leave Denmark in the same condition in which they
came.

C. Accomplishments of the Mothers Aid Centers

Since only 10 to 15 per cent of legal abortions are performed
without the assistance of the Mothers Aid Centers, a survey of the
work done by these Centers will give an almost complete picture of
abortion practices in Denmark.

(1) The Applicants.—Since about 1950 between 7,000 and
8,000 women per year have applied to the Mothers Aid Centers for
abortion.[73] In 1964, the number of applications for abortion in-

---

[69] Discussed at professional conferences (unpublished).

[70] See, *e.g.*, Tietze & Lehfeldt, *Legal Abortion in Eastern Europe*, 175 A.M.A.J. 1149-
54 (1961).

[71] Ruling by the Ministry of Justice to the Mothers Aid Centers, Sept. 23, 1959
(unpublished).

[72] *Ibid.*

[73] See Nørgaard, *The Mothers Aid Centers During 25 Years*, Socialt Tidsskrift,
March-April 1964, pp. 33-64.

creased to about 8,200[74] while the number of live births rose from about 77,000 to 82,400.[75] In the year 1963-1964, 66 per cent of the applicants were married, 24 per cent of them were unmarried, while 10 per cent were divorced, separated, or widowed. With regard to the relative age distribution of expectant mother applicants, the clientele of the Centers includes many women under twenty years of age and relatively many aged thirty-five and over. This indicates that pregnancy in these age groups frequently gives rise to special problems and difficulties.

The women are from all social strata and from all walks of life, but certain trends seem to be significant. There is a certain predominance of spouses of non-skilled workers, while few women married to farmers are represented. The housing conditions of many of the women are below the average standard. And finally, a comparison with the average number of children in families of the general population shows that the women who seek abortion have a comparatively large number of children and many have aborted previously.[76]

(2) The Incidence of Abortion Recommendations.—For a number of years about half of the applicants have been recommended for termination of their pregnancy; in almost all cases this was followed by an operation.[77] The following table shows the disposition of abortion applications by the Mothers Aid Centers in recent years.

The last few years have shown an increasing incidence of recommendation of abortion. This is probably due to the fact that the women and their doctors are becoming increasingly familiar with the practice of the Mothers Aid Centers, so that only those women who

---

[74] From the files of the Mothers Aid Centers.

[75] See THE DANISH STATISTICAL DEP'T, 1964-1965 STATISTICAL YEAR BOOK: NUMBER OF LIVE BIRTHS, table 24. The exact figures are: 1962 — 77,803; 1963 — 82,413.

[76] See REP. ON MOTHERS AID CENTERS 35, 89 (1963).

[77] According to § 3 (4) of the 1956 PREGNANCY ACT the chief physicians may deny to carry out the operation. In such cases the woman can be hospitalized in another hospital by arrangement with the Mothers Aid Center if necessary. This seldom occurs.

	1958-1959		1960-1961		1963-1964	
	abs. fig.	%	abs. fig.	%	abs. fig.	%
Indication for abortion made by medicosocial board _____	3,323	43	3,482	46	3,739	51
Indication for abortion made by hospital superintendent _____	374	5	237	3	197	3
Indications, total: _____	3,697	48	3,719	49	3,936	54
Abortion refused or the woman changes her mind _____	3,701	49	3,619	48	3,066	42
Spontaneous abortion prior to decision, etc. _	258	3	228	3	258	4
Total applicants for abortion* _____	7,656	100	7,566	100	7,260	100

* Women changing their minds before medical examination by the Mothers Aid or found not to be pregnant are not included.

have some chance of getting a favorable recommendation from the Centers apply to Mothers Aid.

The following table gives a breakdown of the bases used for granting applications for abortion in the year 1963-1964.

	1963-1964	
Indication	abs. fig.	%
Medical (made by medicosocial board) _____	3,210	81
Medical (made by hospital superintendent) _____	197	5
Medical indication, total _____	3,407	86
Ethical _____	45	1
Hereditary _____	181	5
Combined medical and hereditary _____	151	4
"Defect" _____	87	2
Various combinations _____	65	2
Total indications for legal abortion _____	3,936	100

Since 1956 the incidence of legal abortion and the indications therefore have been very much the same.[78] As shown by the above table, the medical indication occurs most frequently. The cases of

[78] See REP. ON MOTHERS AID CENTERS (1963).

ethical indications are rather few, and more than half of these involve girls under fifteen years of age.[79]

The "defect" indication is found in few cases. It has been applied, for example, to severely psychopathic or mentally deficient women or to women suffering from a very severe physical disability.[80] Recently, discussions have indicated that some people feel that the defect indication has been interpreted too strictly by the sociomedical boards of the Centers; in particular, it has been argued that mentally deficient women should almost always be covered by this provision.[81] Investigations concerning this question are presently being undertaken.[82]

The incidence of recommendations for abortion varies considerably with the age of the woman, the expected strain on the woman, the applicant's marital status, and the woman's housing conditions. This is largely due to the predominance of the medical indication in the number of recommendations and the effect of these factors on the woman's health.

(*a*) *The Age of the Woman.*—The incidence of recommendations for abortion increases greatly with advancing age.[83] While only 24 per cent of the applicants in the fifteen- to nineteen-year age group were recommended, the percentage for women aged forty and over was 73.

(*b*) *The Expected Strain on the Woman.*—The increasing strain on the woman, which attends an increasing number of childbirths, is also reflected by a higher incidence. While only 28 per cent of the women who had not formerly given birth to a child were recommended for abortion, the percentage was 58 for women with three to four previous childbirths and as much as 75 for women with seven or more previous childbirths.

(*c*) *The Applicant's Marital Status.*—The incidence of recommendations for abortion varies with the marital status of the woman; a relatively larger number of married and formerly married women

---

[79] *Ibid.*

[80] From the files of the Mothers Aid Centers.

[81] See note 56 *supra.*

[82] The investigations are being conducted by the Mothers Aid Center in Copenhagen.

[83] See note 78 *supra.*

are recommended than of unmarried women.[84] This fact is naturally accounted for by the fact that married, or formerly married,
women are, on the average, considerably older and have been subject to a heavier strain, for example by previous pregnancies. While
53 per cent of the women who were married or had been married
were recommended for abortion, the incidence was only 31 per cent
for unmarried women.[85] This seems to show rather clearly that the
law provides no special social or welfare indication.

(d)   The Woman's Housing Conditions.—While 47 per cent
of the applicants who did not live in overcrowded flats were recommended for abortion, the rate was 60 per cent for women occupying
such flats.[86] This demonstrates that women living under bad housing conditions are, for that reason and by reason of other co-existent
difficulties, undoubtedly subject to relatively more severe stress that
may endanger their health.

In regard to occupation, there is no difference in the incidence
of recommendation for housewives and for women working outside their homes. Fifty-three per cent were recommended in both
groups.[87]

(3)   Effects of a Denial of Legal Abortion.—It is of great interest to know what happens to the women who are denied a legal
abortion by the Mothers Aid. Do they abide by the decision or do
they try another way out? At intervals, the Mothers Aid has made
follow-up inquiries into the situation of such women through the
cooperation of national registrars, by an examination of hospital
files, and the like. These studies provide information on the women
with whom the Mothers Aid is not in contact after a denial.
Obviously, a great amount of secrecy has to be observed in such inquiries, so the outcome of a number of cases has remained unknown.
However, recent investigations have shown that the applicants who
received a refusal, increasingly and in a large measure, go through
with their pregnancy and that many of them keep in contact with

---

84 *Ibid.*
85 *Ibid.*
86 *Ibid.*
87 *Ibid.*

the Mothers Aid during their pregnancy and for the first year or so after their child is born.

The following table shows what became of 3,700 women whose applications for abortion in 1958-1959 were refused, or who changed their minds.

Course of pregnancy	abs. fig.	%
The child born	2,988	81
Aborted	598	16
Legal abortion, etc. (at a later date)	29	1
Unknown	86	2
Total	3,701	100

These follow-up investigations seem to show that, once an unwillingly pregnant woman has contacted the Mothers Aid and has been refused legal abortion, she is, nevertheless, normally prepared to go through with the pregnancy. It is relatively rare for her to resort to any other solution. This low incidence of illegal abortion by women who have first contacted the Mothers Aid and have been denied an abortion seems to show that the Mothers Aid program is an effective deterrent to illegal abortion.

Even though a relatively small proportion of the women applying to the Mothers Aid have their pregnancy terminated illegally, the fact remains that there is still a large number of women who fail to consult a doctor or the Mothers Aid, resorting instead to illegal abortion.[88]

III. CRIMINAL ABORTION UNDER THE PREGNANCY ACT OF 1956

As previously mentioned, illegal abortion has for many years not really been considered a crime on the part of the woman.[89] The point of view has for many years been that constructive help, treatment, and advice, so as to motivate the woman not to abort, is a far better way of prevention than is punishment. The second Pregnancy

---

[88] See Hoffmeyer & Nørgaard, *Incidence of Conception and the Course of Pregnancy*, 126 UGESKRIFT FOR LÆGER 355 (1964).

[89] See text accompanying note 4 *supra*.

Commission discussed the possibility of entirely abolishing punishment of the women.[90]   The Commission, however, had no doubt that the persons who helped the woman should be subjected to a rather severe sentence; but it was felt that it would be legally difficult to establish a system by which the helper would be punished, while the woman herself, who had perhaps urged the helper to undertake the operation, would be completely exempt from punishment.[91]

A.   Punitive Provisions of the Pregnancy Act of 1956

A woman who interrupts her pregnancy, or who has it interrupted, knowing that the conditions for legal abortion do not exist, is subject to imprisonment up to three months.[92]   In special and extenuating circumstances, the sentence may be remitted.[93]   As previously mentioned, only a few cases have come to the attention of the police.   In most of these cases the charge was dismissed; and in the very few cases in which the woman was convicted, the sentence was suspended.[94]

The helper is liable to a considerably greater punishment.   If the helper is a licensed medical practitioner, he is liable for imprisonment up to two years.[95]   In aggravated circumstances, the penalty is imprisonment for a term of up to four years;[96] if abortion is carried out without the permission of the woman, the penalty is imprisonment for a term of up to twelve years.[97]

If the helper is not a licensed practitioner, he is liable to imprisonment for a term of up to four years;[98] in the aggravated cir-

---

[90] See SECOND PREGNANCY COMM'N REP. No. 96 OF 1954 ON AMENDMENTS OF LEGISLATION CONCERNING PREGNANCY 64-66.

[91] Ibid.

[92] 1956 PREGNANCY ACT § 6(1).

[93] Ibid.

[94] See SECOND PREGNANCY COMM'N REP., supra note 90, covering thirty-three cases, all of which resulted in suspended sentences.

[95] 1956 PREGNANCY ACT § 6(3).

[96] Ibid.

[97] Ibid.

[98] 1956 PREGNANCY ACT § 6(4).

cumstances referred to above, the term may run as long as eight and twelve years, respectively.[99]

The law also provides for the punishment of the man who has impregnated the woman and has failed, in spite of her appeal to him, to give her reasonable support, provided that this factor has greatly influenced her decision to terminate her pregnancy.[100] Further, a requisite for the prosecution of illegal abortion is the establishment of paternity.[101] The punishment may be imprisonment for a term not exceeding one year.[102] This last provision has been applied in only a few cases.[103] This provision emphasizes the responsibility of the father, its purpose being largely preventive.

B. Incidence of Illegal Abortion

Even if few illegal abortions come to the attention of police and the courts, it is a fact that their number is great; however, since they are rarely reported, it is difficult to reliably estimate the incidence of illegal abortion. Various studies, however, have been made to that end. A recent Danish study found that the number of illegal abortions amounted to nearly 15,000 a year — three or four times the number of legal abortions.[104] Even though it was found in this study that the last 10 years seemed to have brought a slight decrease (10 to 14 per cent) in the number of illegal abortions, the figure is still far too high and presents a very serious problem to the national economy as well as to the individual, to whom it brings much unhappiness and suffering. Considerable discussion is under way concerning the methods of preventing illegal abortions.

C. Prevention of Illegal Abortions

As already mentioned, proposals for free or more liberal allowance of legal abortion were made by both the first and second

---

99 *Ibid.*

100 1956 PREGNANCY ACT § 6(2).

101 *Ibid.*

102 *Ibid.*

103 This fact is a verbal unofficial communication which cannot be documented by case law.

104 See Hoffmeyer & Nørgaard, *supra* note 88, at 403.

Pregnancy Commissions.[105] This view is still advanced on various sides on the ground that the large number of violations of the abortion law shows that it is no longer in accordance with the general sense of justice.[106]

However, the majority viewpoint for many years has been that abortion must be a "last resort."[107] Rather than amending the Pregnancy Act, the conditions underlying unwanted pregnancy, not the least of which is the lack of help and support, should be remedied. This view is in agreement with the point of view of the Mothers Aid Centers, who know by experience that a number of women in originally unwanted pregnancy can be encouraged to change their minds and carry through their pregnancy; the Centers are convinced that a much greater number ought to be helped and could be helped, if satisfactory means of help and support were available. Possible means for increasing the help and support are (1) an expansion of the Mothers Aid, (2) an expansion of the contraceptive clinics, and (3) an increase in general sexual guidance.

(1) Expansion of the Mothers Aid.—There is no doubt that a country's family policy is an essential element in solving the abortion problem and that the existence of effective services in connection with pregnancy and childbirth and for families with children are of particular importance. Regarding the single mother, it is of prime importance to promote societal acceptance of, and respect for, both herself and her child.

But individual help (*i.e.,* personal help and support, family-counseling, practical-economic help) as given by the Mothers Aid Centers continues to be indispensable to a number of women who for special reasons have problems concerning their pregnancy. However, the Centers still provide a rather limited service; funds and facilities for offering individual help ought to be greatly expanded. With such an expansion, women would realize that they might obtain effective help in their special difficulties from the Mothers Aid.

---

105 For the Commissions' attitude see text accompanying notes 26-27, 45 *supra.*

106 See text accompanying notes 24-30, 39-50 *supra.*

107 See Hoffmeyer, *Medical Aspects of the Danish Legislation on Abortion*, in this volume, 179.

(2)   Expansion of Contraceptive Clinics.—At the same time, measures ought to be taken to help women avoid unwanted pregnancies. A good deal of progress has been made along these lines in Denmark during the last few years. Since 1961 the Mothers Aid Centers have operated contraceptive clinics which are available to all women.[108]   In addition, these clinics conduct experiments with new and effective means of birth control. Clinics have also been established by other organizations, such as the Association of Planned Parenthood. General medical practitioners are increasingly giving contraceptive advice to their patients and, according to a new bill,[109] the advice is likely to be given free of charge when combined with a preventive health examination in connection with pregnancy and childbirth. However, since the aim is that all women, even those without difficulty, will be able to receive proper contraceptive advice, the facilities throughout the country are still too limited.

(3)   Increasing Sexual Guidance.—At the same time, sexual guidance, widely disseminated through the schools, churches, physicians, and Mothers Aid Centers ought to be established. Sex education may indeed be said to be the responsibility of parents, but it is a fact that many homes are either unable to cope with this problem or need help. Sex information should be given in an open, matter-of-fact manner, always stressing the personal responsibility of the individual. However, this whole problem, as important as it may be for the abortion problem, is outside the scope of this article. Therefore, it shall only be mentioned that in 1961 the government appointed a commission[110] to inquire into the need for information, ethical guidance, and counseling services in the field of sex.[111]   Since

---

108 See Rosen, *Intrauterine Contraceptive Devices*, 93 AMERICAN J. OBSTETRICS & GYNECOLOGY 896 (1965).

109 PROPOSED BILL (Jan. 10, 1965), drafted by the Minister of the Interior.

110 The Commission was established by the government in November 1961, because of the importance of sexual questions both in personal development and in the safeguard of sound family life.

111 Order of the Prime Minister's Department, Nov. 1, 1961. The purpose of the committee shall among other things be (1) *to* study and estimate valid legislation, existing activities concerning information and counseling, including information in schools; (2) *to* arrange necessary studies — especially concerning youth-problems —

its appointment, the commission has been carrying out an extensive research program with a view toward obtaining an idea of the knowledge, conduct, and attitudes of the population in that field. A number of special investigations relating to conscripts, aborting women, women who have given birth, and pregnant teen-agers have been undertaken. Finally, two counties have started practical experiments of intensified information and guidance.[112]

IV. CONCLUSION

The relatively successful approach to the abortion problem in Denmark is largely a result of two factors — attitude and system. First, for many years efforts have been made to face the problems associated with undesired pregnancy. Attention has regularly been called to statistical data; the problem of abortion has been subjected to thorough study and consideration on the theory that pretending that the problem does not exist will not bring its resolution any nearer. A thorough consideration and discussion of the problems will provide better opportunities for making recommendations to improve the conditions and also for drafting the best possible legislation in this field.

The second advantage is that work with women in unwanted pregnancy and the disposition of applications for abortion are placed with organizations established for the specific purpose of helping and advising women both during pregnancy and after childbirth, namely, the Mothers Aid Centers. A close cooperation between the Centers and the family doctors is established, with the express purpose of helping the women in the best possible way. However, it is of great importance that an incentive to contact these Centers be generated in unwillingly pregnant women, so that the facilities of the Mothers Aid can be more effectively utilized by the community in the work

---

of the actual knowledge of the population concerning sexual matters, including knowledge of contraceptives and of the sexual behavior (existing norms) in various age groups; and (3) *to* give proposals partly to improvement and coordination of existing activities of information and counseling, partly to possible new initiative, included possible legislation. *Ibid.*

112 The counties are Ribe and Sorø. These projects were financed by state-provided funds and in cooperation with the committee.

of preventing abortions. In this way, the abortion problem is seen in the proper light — as part of the social and family legislation of the country. Open discussion combined with a general and comprehensive program of help and guidance will be important and necessary means of meeting the abortion problem.

APPENDIX

ACT CONCERNING PROVISIONS RELATING TO PREGNANCY*

WE, FREDERIK THE NINTH, by the Grace of God King of Denmark, the Wend and the Goth, Duke of Schleswig, Holstein, Stormarn, the Ditmarsh, Lauenburg and Oldenburg.
Do hereby proclaim: The Folketing has adopted, and We have given Our Royal Assent to the following Statute:

SECTION 1.

Subsection 1. A woman may have her pregnancy interrupted in the following cases:

1) When the interruption of the pregnancy is necessary to avert grave danger to the woman's life or health. In evaluating this danger, due consideration shall be given to all relevant circumstances, including those conditions under which the woman must live, and not only to her physical and psychic health, but also to any condition of physical or psychic weakness, present or threatening.

2) When the woman has been made pregnant under such circumstances as are dealt with in the Civil Criminal Code of April 15, 1930, Section 210, or Section 210 cfr. Section 212, as well as when the pregnancy is the result of a violation of the woman's sexual freedom under such circumstances as are referred to in Sections 216-223 of the Criminal Code, or in the aforementioned Sections as related to Section 224.

3) When there is imminent danger that the child, as the result of a hereditary taint or due to injuries or illness suffered in the

---

* Translation by Dilling.

fetal stage, might suffer from insanity, mental deficiency, other grave mental derangement, epilepsy, or serious and incurable abnormity or physical disease.

4)   When, in very special cases, it is presumed that the woman will be unfit to take proper care of her child due to serious mental or physical defects or other medically indicated conditions.

Subsection 2.   Legal abortion in the cases referred to in Section 1, Subsection 1, Clauses 2-4, may normally not be carried out after the end of the sixteenth week of pregnancy.

Subsection 3.   If the pregnancy is the result of a violation of the woman's sexual freedom under circumstances referred to in the Criminal Code's Section 216; Section 217, Subsection 2; Sections 218 and 221, or these sections as related to Section 224, legal abortion may not be carried out unless the crime has been reported to the police and such report — having been duly investigated by the police — has not been dismissed as false.

Subsection 4.   If legal abortion is to be carried out because of the hereditary taint referred to in Section 1, Subsection 1, Clause 3, and these genes originate from the woman, sterilization of the woman may be carried out in connection with the interruption of the pregnancy without special permission, provided that the woman agrees to it and no special reasons argue against it.   The provisions of Section 2, Subsections 1 and 3, shall apply in such cases.

Section 2.

Legal abortion may not, unless justified by grave danger to the woman's life or health as the result of illness, be carried out until the following conditions have been complied with:

1)   If the woman is under 18 years of age or has been declared incapable of managing her own affairs, the consent of those who hold parental custody of her or of her guardian shall be obtained unless decisive circumstances argue against it.

2)   If the woman, due to unsoundness of mind, mental deficiency or other causes is unable to understand the consequences of the operation, the petition for legal abortion may be made by a special guardian appointed thereto by the Social Welfare Committee

or, if she is under public care in a State Institution or other Approved Institution as provided by Section 67 of the Social Welfare Act, by the director of the Institution.

3) If the woman is married and cohabiting with her husband, the latter shall be given an opportunity to make a statement, unless special circumstances argue against it.

SECTION 3.

Subsection 1. Legal abortion may be carried out only by an authorized medical officer in a State or Municipal Hospital, or in a private hospital receiving public grants or to which patients are sent at public expense.

Subsection 2. If the danger to the woman's life or health in the cases referred to in Section 1, Subsection 1, is due to illness, and this has been established in one of the hospitals mentioned in Subsection 1 above, the Chief Physician of that hospital may make the decision on the necessity for the interruption of pregnancy.

Subsection 3. Should a woman in other cases desire the interruption of her pregnancy, she must apply to a Mothers Aid Center for a legal abortion. The Mothers Aid Center will establish whether the conditions, set forth in Sections 1 and 2, for legal abortion have been fulfilled, and in the course of so doing should ordinarily obtain information from the woman's usual physician. Further, the Mothers Aid Center should consult with a specialist in medicine to the required extent, obtain a statement from the Institute of Genetic Biology or have the woman admitted to a hospital or a suitable home for observation or treatment. Decision as to whether legal abortion may be carried out will then be made in compliance with Section 6A, Subsection 1 of Act No. 119 of March 15, 1939 concerning Mothers Aid Centers, as amended by Act No. 176 of June 23, 1956, by a Joint Council consisting of 2 physicians and the director of the Mothers Aid Center or some other member of the staff of the Center with similar training.

Subsection 4. When decision to permit legal abortion has been made, the woman shall on request be admitted to the hospital (hospital department) under which she belongs. The Chief Physician of the hospital (hospital department) shall be entitled to submit the question of carrying out the operation to the Council referred to in Section 6A, Subsection 3, of Act No. 119 of March 15, 1939, concerning Mothers Aid Centers, as amended by Act No. 176 of June 23, 1956, for guidance. Should the Chief Physician refuse to carry out the operation, the patient may be sent to another hospital, if necessary by order of the Mothers Aid Center in question.

SECTION 4.

The medical officers mentioned in Section 3 as well as the staffs of the hospitals referred to in Section 3 are under obligation, in accordance with the provisions of Section 263 cfr. Section 275 of the Civil Criminal Code, to observe professional secrecy concerning the matters pertaining to private life of which they may gain knowledge or which they may surmise in connection with the question of legal abortion, unless they are by law under obligation to make a statement, or unless they act in the warranted service of the public interest or of their own interests or of those of others.

SECTION 5.

He who, for use in making decisions as to whether the conditions for legal abortion have been fulfilled, testifies to something of which he has no knowledge, or who willfully gives erroneous information, is liable to penalties in accordance with the provisions of Section 162 of the Civil Criminal Code.

SECTION 6.

Subsection 1. A woman who interrupts her own pregnancy, or who has it interrupted by a person who is not a licensed medical practitioner, is liable to punishment by fine even though the conditions prescribed in Section 1 may have been fulfilled. If she herself interrupts her pregnancy, or if she has it interrupted, knowing that the conditions for legal abortion do not exist, the punishment is imprisonment for up to 3 months. Under special and extenuating circumstances sentence may be remitted.

Subsection 2. Should, in the course of proceedings instituted for the prosecution of illegal abortion by a woman who has become pregnant out of wedlock or her helpers, or of attempted illegal abortion by her helpers, such information come to light that it must be held to be established who has made her pregnant, that person shall be liable to a prison sentence of up to 1 year, under extenuating circumstances be liable to imprisonment, if it be proved that he, despite the fact that the woman has appealed to him for personal or economic assistance, has failed to give her such support and aid as would be reasonable in the circumstances, and that this omission has materially influenced her decision to interrupt her pregnancy.

Subsection 3. A licensed medical practitioner who interrupts a pregnancy or gives assistance thereto, knowing that the conditions for legal abortion as set forth in Section 1 hereof do not exist, is liable to a prison sentence of up to 2 years. Under aggravating circumstances, especially when the act has led to the death of the woman or has caused appreciable injury to her body or health, the penalty shall be up to 4 years in jail. If legal abortion in accordance with Section 1 is performed without the statutory requirements of Sections 2 and 3 having been fulfilled, the penalty shall be imprisonment or in extenuating circumstances a fine. If an abortion is performed without the consent of the woman, the penalty is a sentence of up to 12 years in jail.

Subsection 4. He who, without being a licensed medical practitioner, shall interrupt a pregnancy or give assistance thereto, is liable to a penalty of up to 4 years in jail. In aggravating circumstances, especially when the act has been performed for profit, or if it has led to the death of the woman or has caused appreciable injury to her body and health, the penalty shall be up to 8 years in jail. In case of the offense being repeated, or if the offender has acted without the consent of the woman, the penalty is up to 12 years in jail.

Subsection 5. The above penalties do not apply to offenses committed through negligence.

SECTION 7.

He who, by duress as defined by the Civil Criminal Code's

Section 260, or by threats of economic loss or of injury to her family or social standing, or by promise of reward, induces a pregnant woman desirous of completing her pregnancy to interrupt that pregnancy, even though legal abortion may be performed in accordance with the provisions set forth for it, is liable to a term of up to 2 years in jail; however, the penalty shall be up to 4 years in jail if the interruption of the pregnancy is performed by a person who is not a licensed medical practitioner.

SECTION 8.

Liability to penalty for the offenses dealt with in Section 6 and 7 become statute-barred in accordance with the provisions of Sections 93 and 94 of the Civil Criminal Code of April 15, 1930. Indictment pursuant to Section 6, Subsection 1, cannot, however, take place if more than 1 year has passed after the abortion has been induced.

SECTION 9.

Subsection 1. The expense in connection with legal abortion shall be borne by the person in question. If she has no means to do so, the expense will be defrayed by the Treasury or, if she is under the care of one of the Welfare Institutions mentioned in Section 66 of Act No. 181 of May 20, 1933, by the Institution in question.

Subsection 2. In the case mentioned in Section 3, Subsection 4, last sentence, such part of the expense which would have been incurred in connection with hospitalization and operation in the hospital in the woman's own parish of domicile will be defrayed in accordance with Subsection 1 above. The Minister of Home Affairs can stipulate rules to the effect that the expense incidental to the woman's hospitalization in that hospital where the operation is carried out shall be refunded in part or in toto by the hospital in the woman's own parish of domicile.

Subsection 3. The respective Mothers Aid Center may, if special considerations for the woman argue in favor of it, sanction that the operation be carried out in a hospital away from the woman's parish of domicile. In such case the expense incurred thereby will be defrayed in accordance with Subsection 1 above.

SECTION 10.

Subsection 1. To municipalities or private societies which undertake the task of organizing and running Sexual Hygiene Counselling Clinics (or Family Counselling Services) for the general public the State may grant subsidies for half the amount expended.

Subsection 2. If the counselling services undertaken by private societies or organizations are closely linked with particular municipalities, the State may make its subsidies dependent upon the participation of the municipalities in question in the defrayment of the costs with one-half of the amount of the State grants.

Subsection 3. The grants of the State subsidies referred to in Subsections 1 and 2 hereof are met by appropriations on the Annual Budgets.

SECTION 11.

Subsection 1. Articles or substances that serve to prevent pregnancy may only be sold if approved by the Minister of Justice after consultation with the Public Health Board. If necessary, the Minister of Justice may, after consultation with the Minister of Trade, fix the prices, which shall be clearly marked on the wrapping, and can rule the necessary measures for carrying out an effective limitation and control of prices in connection with permission to sell the above-mentioned articles or substances. The articles and substances in question may be sold only by pharmacists or by dealers who have been authorized by the medical officer after consultation with the police.

Subsection 2. Commercial examination of urine samples with a view to detection of pregnancy may only be carried out by medical practitioners and pharmacists and by persons duly thereto authorized by the Board of Health.

Subsection 3. Violations of the provisions of this Section are punishable by fines.

SECTION 12.

Subsection 1. The Minister of Justice shall lay down more explicit rules for carrying this Act into effect.

Subsection 2. Violations of the rules laid down by the Minister of Justice for the carrying into effect of the provisions made in Sections 1-4 of this Act are subject to penalties of fines or imprisonment for up to 3 months.

SECTION 13.

Subsection 1. This Act goes into force on October 1, 1956.

Subsection 2. Simultaneously Act. No. 164 of May 18, 1937 concerning Provisions Relating to Pregnancy etc., as amended by Act No. 89 of March 15, 1939, and Section 235, Subsection 2 of the Civil Criminal Code of April 15, 1930, cfr. Order No. 215 of June 24, 1939, are repealed.

Subsection 3. The Government is authorized by an Order in Council to put this Act into force for the Faroo Islands, if necessary with such amendments as the special conditions of the Islands may require.

Subsection 4. Until such time as Mothers Aid Centers or similar institutions can be set up in Greenland, legal abortions in Greenland in the cases dealt with in Section 3, Subsection 3, shall be possible after consultation between the medical officer who is to perform the operation, and another licenced medical practitioner.

Given at Christiansborg Castle, June 23, 1956
Under our Royal Hand and Seal.
FREDERIK R.

8

Medical Aspects of the Danish Legislation

on Abortion

Henrik Hoffmeyer, M.D.

In 1956 the Danish legislature amended the Pregnancy Act of 1937[1] and established a system, still in effect, whereby the legal indications for an abortion are to be decided by a three-member sociomedical board attached to the Mothers Aid Centers.[2] This amendment was a departure from the 1937 act, which provided that two doctors — one being the patient's private doctor and the other the surgeon who was to eventually perform the operation — had to decide whether an abortion was indicated. The purpose here is to examine some of the medical problems connected with the administration of the amended Danish abortion law.

I. REASONS FOR THE ADOPTION OF THE 1956 AMENDMENT

The Pregnancy Act of 1937[3] required that a woman must have applied to a Mothers Aid Office for help before permission for an abortion would be granted.

---

[1] Act concerning Provisions Relating to Pregnancy, Act No. 163 of May 18, 1937, as amended by Act No. 89 of March 15, 1939 [hereinafter cited as 1937 PREGNANCY ACT].

[2] Act concerning Provisions Relating to Pregnancy, Act No. 177 of June 23, 1956 [hereinafter cited as 1956 PREGNANCY ACT] reprinted in Appendix to Skalts & Nørgaard, *Abortion Legislation in Denmark*, in this volume, 144, 171 [hereinafter cited as Appendix].

[3] 1937 PREGNANCY ACT § 2(1).

In the years following the adoption of the 1937 act, more and more women applied to Mothers Aid, most of them being sent by their private doctors for the purpose of having the Centers decide upon the need or desirability of an abortion. The reasons for the increased numbers of women applying for abortion are many: (1) the general practitioners preferred not to be involved in the decisions on indications; (2) the individual doctors often had limited experience and sometimes were pressured by their patients; (3) the surgeons who were to perform the abortions did not feel inclined to follow an indication from the general practitioner without having another examination by an expert; (4) the psychiatric wards, most often responsible for expert examinations, were overcrowded and therefore inclined to recommend that examinations be done by the Mothers Aid consultant; and (5) the Mothers Aid Centers, because of the nature of their organization, with its facilities for giving social advice and financial support, were better fit for giving advice on abortions than were hospitals.

About 80 per cent of all recommendations for abortions were made through Mothers Aid Centers which, because of this demand, had to enlarge their medical departments.[4] Because of this increase in the use and popularity of the Centers and because of the Centers' facilities for ruling on indications for abortions, the legislature in 1956 changed the procedure for deciding on abortions, giving the power to make that decision to the three-member medicosocial boards of Mothers Aid.[5]

II. PRE-ABORTION PROCEDURE UNDER THE PRESENT DANISH ABORTION LAW

The primary goal of the abortion legislation is to persuade women to carry through with their pregnancies whenever possible. The performance of an abortion is only a secondary goal when all other help-measures fail. This goal is demonstrated by the fact that

---

[4] From the files of the Mothers Aid Institute.

[5] 1956 PREGNANCY ACT § 3(3), Appendix p. 173. For a discussion of how decisions were made before the 1956 amendments, see Skalts & Nørgaard, *supra* note 2, at 150 n. 29.

pregnancy legislation[6] and the Mothers Aid legislation are not simply exceptions to the penal code but are, rather, separate and specific laws providing for the support of pregnant women and mothers.

A. Medical, Psychiatric, and Social Investigations

The Danish statute provides specific procedures which are to be followed when a woman applies for a legal abortion.[7] The woman, whether or not she is sent by her doctor, first sees the social worker, who writes a detailed case history. On one of the following days, she submits to a gynecological examination including laboratory tests. After her examination, she will see one of Mothers Aid's psychiatrists; if necessary, she is asked to return later for a further psychiatric interview. The social worker then conducts an investigation that includes visiting the husband, or the alleged father, and other relatives, and collecting information from other institutions which the woman might have visited.

The medical department of Mothers Aid also conducts an investigation, checking with any hospitals and practitioners that might have treated the patient. If the woman's medical condition so warrants, she may be referred to the Institute for Human Genetics.

B. Conference of Medicosocial Boards

After all the investigations are completed, a team conference is conducted among the doctors, social workers, and lawyers connected with the case. At each of these conferences the board members discuss the possibility of having the patient carry through with her pregnancy. In some cases further examinations are deemed necessary and often admittance to a hospital for observation is indicated. Generally, however, it is preferable to observe the woman during a stay at one of the more "home-like" sub-institutions of the Mothers Aid instead of sending the patient to a hospital. In many cases the patient will change her mind during this stay.

---

[6] 1937 PREGNANCY ACT; see Skalts & Nørgaard, *supra* note 2, at 144-46, 149-51.

[7] 1956 PREGNANCY ACT § 3(3), Appendix p. 173.

C. Report of Findings and Board Decision

When all of these examinations are completed, a "Discussion and Summary" is written by the psychiatrist and the social worker. This report is written in an objective manner and sets forth the recommendation as to whether the pregnancy should be interrupted or carried through. Copies of all reports are sent to the members of the board. It should be mentioned that these reports sometimes run up to twenty pages, represent a heavy strain on office personnel, and require a large number of working hours for the many staffs involved.

Another important element which must be considered is that most of the women who come to the Centers are under a great deal of emotional stress, which is not lessened by the procedure and examinations of Mothers Aid. The board knows that those who have a strong desire for an abortion, or who do not consider their chance for legal abortion to be very great, may resort to having it performed illegally in order to avoid the stress combined with the legal procedure. For these reasons the boards may take abbreviated measures when they are needed.

The boards meet once a week. At times they will ask for further examination or even turn to the central board for advice.[8] When the board has made its decision, a detailed letter is sent to the woman's private doctor giving the reasons for the decision and suggestions for further treatment and help.

III. INDICATIONS FOR ABORTION UNDER THE ACT

A. The Medical Indication

The main criterion under the law is a "grave danger to the woman's life or health."[9] This provision states that the conditions of life which the woman has to endure must be taken into consideration.[10] However, this does not imply that there is any social indication for abortion. It is only a reflection of a generally adopted medi-

---

8 See Skalts & Nørgaard, *supra* note 2, at 158 n.58 and accompanying text.

9 1956 PREGNANCY ACT. § 1(1) (1), Appendix p. 171.

10 See Skalts & Nørgaard, *supra* note 2, at 155.

cal principle that the assessment of the patient's state of health and the indications for therapeutic measures always must be matched to the conditions of her life. The provision, moreover, provides that threatening "states of weakness" have to be considered.[11] Then, at least theoretically, it should not be necessary to prove any present illness or weakness — only that the threat of carrying through with the pregnancy and of having another child will seriously threaten the life or health of the pregnant woman.

Since the medical indication is the one most commonly used, it is important to examine it in detail. The type of cases which come under this provision include convention conflicts, stress syndromes, and stress syndrome of housewives.

(1) Convention Conflicts.—Quite a large proportion of women applying for legal abortions are experiencing what is called a "convention conflict." The pregnancy itself or the expected child provokes a conflict between the woman and the conventions of the social group to which she belongs.

There can be numerous variations of such conflicts. Typical situations can be found in very young teen-age girls, young unwed women, married women who have had extra-marital relations, married women more than thirty-five or forty years of age who are ashamed of showing that they are still sexually active, separated or divorced women, and widows. Some of these situations are apt to produce "reactive depressive states." However, contrary to what was originally believed, these depressions are rarely very deep. Most often the reaction could better be characterized as a "panic-reaction" created by the fear of not being able to cope with the demands and the responsibility of a future motherhood. These reactions are often dramatic and can come close to psychotic states. However, most often these women can be made to look after their daily jobs, thereby diverting their attention, and to speak about matters other than the pregnancy. When an application for legal abortion has been finally rejected, and the pregnancy advances to the fourth or fifth month, the panic normally declines. A realistic adjustment to

---

[11] 1956 PREGNANCY ACT § 1 (1) (1), Appendix p. 171.

the situation takes place when the woman begins to prepare for the baby's arrival by picking out baby clothes and the like. At times, suicidal threats or superficial suicidal acts are made, but most often these are a part of the appeal for a legal abortion. The degree of appeal, dramatic or hysterical traits, as well as other characteristics of the reaction depend upon the specific personality type of the individual woman. In some rare occasions more severe psychotic reactions of a depressive nature can occur. Here the suicidal danger is much more typical; but during the years it has been observed that these women, owing to the psychotic inhibition and their lack of adjustment to reality seldom seek the aid of a doctor or the Mothers Aid Center. When they do seek aid, they are most often brought by a relative or friend who realizes the seriousness of the situation.

Through the years it has been found with increasing frequency that the background of the "panic reaction" could be characterized as a "conflict of ambivalence." The more pronounced panic reactions are found in women who have passed their adolescence, women who under other circumstances certainly would have been enjoying a pregnancy, and women who have well-developed and mature maternal feelings. The panic arises as a consequence of the conflict between the positive (*e.g.*, ethical) feelings toward the conservation of the pregnancy and the realistic assessment of the heavy burden which the continuation of the pregnancy will bring about. The instructive and ethical impulses toward the continuation of the pregnancy are experienced as terrible dangers confronting the women with all the fears of reality. As a defense, she is apt to completely repress the factors favoring the continuation of the pregnancy in order to be able to carry through her strong, one-sided advocacy for legal abortion.

Seen against this background it is quite clear that the strength of the indication for legal abortion could not be determined by the strength of the emotional reaction. Danish doctors and psychiatrists, perhaps, cannot completely acquit themselves for not doing so. But in discussions with surgeons, who traditionally — and this is well understandable — are more resistant to interruption of pregnancy, it was indicated that the strong emotional reactions and the suicidal threats could make an impression sufficient to convince them to perform the operation. However severe the depressive reaction might be, there is always the possibility that contraindicating factors might be of such an importance that an abortion ought not to be performed. Only a thorough psychiatric examination can clear this up. To the extent that the "ambivalence conflict" plays a role, the strength of the emotional reaction will more likely be inversely proportional to the strength of the indication for legal abortion, since it reflects the strength of the motivations for preserving the pregnancy.

In addition to the women presenting the pronounced affective reactions, there is another group of women in similar "convention conflicts" in whom the pregnancy-conserving motives are so strong that there is no doubt about their wish to continue the pregnancy. They apply to the Mothers Aid late in their pregnancy to have practical and legal advice and help. Finally, another (and perhaps much larger) group exists in whom the motive for abortion is absolute and other motives so weak that there is no doubt about the decision that the pregnancy must be interrupted. They do not want to talk to any authority and consider medical and social preliminary investigations as red tape. They, therefore, immediately turn to illegal methods. They also acknowledge that case workers and doctors might activate their repressed counter-conceptions and postpone the decision until the pregnancy has progressed to a point where the emotional balance is normally changed in favor of the baby.

A specific group which is subject to these "convention conflicts" is the teen-age girl. It is generally thought today that sexual relations are commonly started at an earlier age, that premarital sexual relations are more common in larger circles of the population, and that social conventions of the youth groups (especially with regard to relations between the sexes) are more liberal. Still, experience shows that girls who become pregnant early in their teen-age years (before the age of seventeen) generally represent a specific group, characterized by emotional isolation and frustration in their parental relations. The different reasons for this fact shall not be discussed here. In addition, very authoritative, as well as liberal and pseudo-modern, attitudes held by the parents produce an environment making the girl feel lost, isolated, and frightened to such a degree that she compensates by engaging in premature sexual relations. More specific psychological disturbances, either in the girl herself (neurotic, pseudo-neurotic, or psychotic states) or in the family pattern, may also explain why a girl begins having premature sexual relations. The compensatory or neurotic types of premature sexual relations, however, are generally characterized by being started at an age premature to the rest of the physical and psychological development. Too often the partner is one who is not socially or emotionally able to support the girl when she becomes pregnant.

The psychological reactions encountered with this type of girl are very often only superficial. Rather often she looks forward to having a baby, a further compensation for loneliness. Psychologically, she is usually reflecting the serious reaction of desperate parents. If the pregnancy is carried through, very often the girl's mother will, for the first few years, also function as the real mother of the child.

The termination of a pregnancy, under the Danish law, on the basis of "convention conflicts"[12] is rarely allowed. In some cases the difficulty in distinguishing between psychotic depression and "panic reaction" might be an indication for the interruption of the pregnancy even if the mere diagnosis of psychotic depression does not necessarily indicate the interruption. In some other cases, facts relevant to other provisions of the legislation might supplement medical reasons for interrupting the pregnancy. By and large the attitude toward this type of psychological reaction to an unwanted pregnancy has changed during the time the legislation has been effective. A more objective and sober attitude on the part of officials has been adopted as it was realized that suicides and the development of chronic psychopathology were rare in these cases.

(2) *Stress Syndromes.*—The condition which is the primary cause for legal abortions in Denmark has been named the "stress syndrome." This is a more or less chronic condition existing before the unwanted pregnancy, and interruption of the pregnancy can be granted to prevent a further development of the syndrome.

---

[12] Board of Health Circular, March 25, 1939 (unpublished); Ministry of Justice Ruling, January 23, 1940 (unpublished).

In the discussions during the first decades of the legislation's existence, between the surgeons and gynecologists on the one hand and the psychiatrists and social workers on the other hand, it was realized by the latter that they had to try to re-define the conditions found in a considerable number of women applying for legal abortions. As previously mentioned, there was a tendency to label these conditions as psychotic depressions.[13] In some cases, however, the psychological reaction to the pregnancy was only very slight; in other cases, the reaction represented health conditions which, from a common, general medical point of view, seemed most urgently to demand a legal abortion. By using common medical diagnostic techniques it was difficult to tell what sort of illness these women had and to label them with some "main diagnosis." They seemed to have many separately unimportant illnesses.

Most of the women belonging to this group are married, have two, three, or four children, and are living under some form of stress owing to poor housing conditions, economic difficulties, marital problems, illness, or defective or maladjusted children. Very often the core of the problem is represented by the husband who is ill, disabled, a poor breadwinner, or perhaps addicted to alcohol. Obviously, these conditions get progressively worse with each new weight laid on the shoulders of such a woman. Furthermore, in some cases, the mental or physical resistance beforehand may be impaired by hereditary or other factors or as a result of previous illnesses.

Depending upon the resistance in the individual case, symptoms of what has been called "insufficiency" will develop sooner or later. The diffuse word "insufficiency" is used intentionally as this condition does not cover any known clinical notion. This condition occurs as a result of confinement or of some other increase in the stress to which she is subjected. In the milder cases, the "insufficiency" will disappear in a short time, perhaps as a result of some social or medical provision supporting or relieving her. At this point the Mothers Aid attempts to offer some relief. But if the stress increases or continues, the "insufficiency" will also continue

---

[13] See p. 183 *supra.*

and may change from an intermittent to a chronic type, which in severe cases can be disabling.

The "insufficiency" is caused by physical and mental symptoms, and by diseases such as varicose veins, chronic infections in the genital organs and the lungs, and arthritis. Symptoms of a psychosomatic nature are muscular tensions, migraine headaches, and the like. The mental symptoms are typically fatigue, irritability, sleep disturbances, anxiety states, and increased reactivity. If, beforehand, there has been specific neurosis, the symptoms often develop and manifest themselves in an intensified way during such an "insufficiency state." Such women, of course, often show a minor resistance to the constant stress situation. Thus there is no contrast between the sociological and the psychological analyses of the situation since they represent explanations in different, but supplementary, levels.

An investigation of the pathology appearing in women applying for legal abortion shows that the pathology is varied and is in no way only of a psychiatric nature. In an investigation at Mothers Aid counting all possible diagnoses of any importance in 200 randomly selected women applying for legal abortion, 594 diagnoses were counted — 322 psychiatric and 272 somatic (physical) diagnoses.[14] The psychiatric diagnoses were comprised of 55 per cent neurotic and neurasthenic states, 23 per cent behavior disorders or psychopathic states, 10 per cent mental deficiences, and only 8 per cent reactive depressions. The remaining 4 per cent was comprised of different minor groups.[15] The somatic diagnoses were comprised of 28 per cent general diseases, such as emaciation, anemia, obesity, and metabolic disorders; 17 per cent neurological diseases such as headaches, migraines, sequela after earlier concussions, and meningitis; 14 per cent gynecological diseases; 9 per cent varicose veins; and 5 per cent for each of the following: lung diseases, kidney diseases, and ear and eye diseases.[16]

---

[14] Hoffmeyer, *The Medical Work in the Mothers Aid Institution*, 119 UGESKRIFT FOR LÆGER 1396-1403 (1957); Hoffmeyer, *Pregnancy Legislation and Mothers Aid Legislation*, 119 UGESKRIFT FOR LÆGER 1528-33 (1957).

[15] *Ibid.*

[16] *Ibid.*

The characteristic property of this complex of symptoms is that it appears uniformly, repeating itself almost identically from case to case both with regard to symptoms and to course, appearing to be a real disease but with features that cut across common clinical notions or concepts. It is understandable only from a holistic point of view. Somatic and mental symptoms, the previous medical and social history, and the social and family background are combined in one entity. It must be understood that the sum total of singly unimportant symptoms or diseases under certain conditions could represent a serious state of health. The patient and her illness must be evaluated on the basis of her history and her social background. The doctor working in a clinic is accustomed to analyzing his cases and to isolating the causes for the disease. In a social-disease field, the doctor has to integrate and synthesize to understand the influence of pathological factors in order to evaluate the ability of the person in question to solve her conflict under the circumstances in which she has to live.

In several cases it has been possible with the means and facilities of Mothers Aid to offer material assistance in the form of a cash grant, domestic help, a rest cure, or medical or psychological treatment in order to prevent a disastrous development. In other cases the view has been taken that, if the pregnancy were continued, these women would run a serious risk that the "insufficiency" would develop into a chronic, irreversible, and disabling condition — a condition that would mean insufficiency to meet the demands made upon them as mothers and housewives. In such cases legal abortion, possibly combined with sterilization, has sometimes been indicated.

(3) *Stress Syndrome of Housewives.*—The "stress syndrome of housewives" seems to appear in two slightly different types. One type is dominated by social, financial, and housing problems. In these cases physical symptoms in addition to the stress are often predominant. The other type more often appears in middle-class women who are not directly threatened by social destitution due to the pregnancy, but who are motivated to seek an abortion through the fear of a reduction in their standard of living; they are anxious to preserve the level generally accepted for their social class. This area has been a matter of controversy in discussions of the abortion pol-

icy since the abortions help people to obtain empty, materialistic goals. Still, it must be remembered that the ambitions of the middle class are responsible also for the many positive material as well as cultural achievements of the modern welfare society. In a country such as Denmark, families with more than three or four children find it difficult to maintain the generally accepted standard of living for most working and middle-class families. The emotional forces requiring the maintenance of this level of social prestige are of considerable strength and are mobilized when the threat to it becomes realistic. The stress represented by this fear, when in effect for years, seems to be able to produce similar "stress syndromes" as previously described.[17] The physical symptoms in these cases are developed to a minor degree and the psychological and emotional symptoms are dominant.

It might be asked why contraceptive measures, in a country with liberal access to information on, instruction in, and purchase of contraceptives, do not prevent unwanted pregnancies to a larger degree. The answer must be that while contraception certainly prevents the unwanted pregnancies, the "stress syndromes," the fear of pregnancy, and the frigidity in countless numbers of cases, there still remain groups to whom conventional contraceptive methods are not acceptable and who prefer to take the risk of an unwanted pregnancy. Perhaps modern developments in the field of contraception will at least change the picture to some degree.

Several factors have been shown to affect the medical or sociomedical indications for legal abortion. Women applying for legal abortion are brought through an unwanted pregnancy into a social or personal conflict complicated by some sort of mental or physical pathology. The pathology influences the ability of the woman to cope with her conflict. It is most often the total — minor or major — pathology and not the single disease which creates the problems. Therefore, a synthetic and integrating description and evaluation is a prerequisite for a correct estimation of indications and contraindications for legal abortion.

The main criterion for legal abortion is a medical one, *i.e.,*

---

[17] See pp. 186-89 *supra.*

serious danger to life or health. It is, therefore, in no way contrary to the legislation when married women, more often than unmarried ones, have legal abortions performed, even if the latter group encounters greater external difficulties. Sometimes a woman living in good social conditions and with only a few children will obtain an abortion more easily than a poor woman with many children. These simple facts are very often badly misunderstood by critics who forget that the indication is medical and not social.

The assessment of the danger to life or health cannot be based only upon an observation of the present emotional state. The immediate reaction to an unwanted pregnancy is highly dependent upon personality traits influencing sensitivity and reactivity and tells very little about the ability that the woman might have for overcoming her conflict and for coping with the situation in the long run.

Experience has shown that those who most need abortions are women with chronic conditions which very often started years before the present pregnancy appeared. Pregnancy, delivery, and the stress combined with the raising of a further child can severely aggravate the chronic "stress syndrome of the housewives."

When assessing the condition of a woman who is applying for legal abortion, it must be remembered that these women are often repressing their anxiety and what they tell is often a plea in advocacy of their case. Sometimes one has the impression that the more detailed the examinations, the more one-sided and persistent the argument of the woman. Thus, it is necessary that care be taken not to create situations which are too artificial and which thereby bring the patient into a "controversy" or "opponent" position vis-à-vis doctors and advisors.

The aftercare of women who had applied for legal abortion showed especially that these women very often were more ambivalent than the immediate impression indicated. Therefore, it is of the utmost importance that doctors and social workers engaged in the evaluation of women applying for legal abortion have an opportunity to follow up their cases.

B. *The Ethical Indication*

No specific medical problems are attached to this rarely used provision. For a discussion of this area, see Chapter 7 in this book, which deals with Danish abortion laws.[18]

C. The Eugenic or Hereditary Indications

This provision provides that serious fetal damage, whether caused by genetic disturbance or by damage to the fetus during the gestation period, can be the reason for legal abortion.[19] Among the causes of fetal damage are rubella virus, toxoplasmotic infections, syphilitic infection, Rhesus-negativity, radiation, teratogenic chemical compounds, and genetic factors.

(1) *Rubella Virus.*—It is now known that rubella infections[20] in a woman during the first trimester of pregnancy might cause serious physical and mental disturbances to the fetus. There is no reason to go into detail with regard to the many medical complexities involved in this area. It is enough to say that the defects caused by the rubella virus in fetuses might be very disturbing. Although the frequency of such defects has varied in different epidemics, it is estimated to be at least 10 to 20 per cent during the first three months of pregnancy, with no risk after the fourth month.[21] It is necessary to establish the diagnosis of rubella with as much certainty as possible. Therefore, a careful and unbiased diagnosis from a doctor who examined the patient when she was ill is a necessity in each case.

Legal abortion in cases of rubella in the pregnant woman represents only a preventive measure. In such cases it is extremely important to set stringent requirements upon the quality of the indication for legal abortion and also to stress the importance of possible contraindicating risks. During 1957 there were three cases in the Copenhagen Mothers Aid where childless women, because of rubella, had legal abortions performed which, unfortunately, were complicated by such serious secondary genital infections that the women became sterile. This, of course, represents only a coinci-

---

18 See Skalts & Nørgaard, *supra* note 2, at 155, 162-63.

19 1956 PREGNANCY ACT § 1(1) (3), Appendix p. 171.

20 Commonly known as German measles.

21 From the files of the Mothers Aid Institute.

dence, but it highlights the urgent demand for convincing evidence when recommending legal abortion as a preventive measure.

(2) Toxoplasmotic Infections.—In quite a few cases there is the risk of fetal damage to the brain of the fetus as a consequence of toxoplasmotic infection in the mother.[22] This is still a subject of research, but the danger to the fetus seems only to exist when the mother has recently contracted her infection. Difficulty arises because the disease causes only very slight symptoms in an adult person so the woman is likely to overlook the infection, which is very widespread in the population.

(3) Syphilitic Infection.—Syphilitic infection is rarely a reason for legal abortion since preventive treatment can be given during the pregnancy. In Denmark such prophylactic treatment is mandatory for all pregnant women who have ever had a syphilitic infection.

(4) Rhesus-Negativity.—The risk of damage to the fetus or the newborn child as a consequence of Rhesus-negativity in the blood type of the mother is of decreasing importance as a reason for legal abortion. In all cases of Rhesus-negativity in a pregnant woman the titers of antibodies in her blood are measured at regular intervals during her pregnancy. Only in cases where antibodies are increasing to a very high level are legal abortions permitted, and then only after it is shown that previous miscarriages and post-natal deaths have undermined the psychological resistance of the woman in question. Otherwise, these women are admitted to deliver in clinics specially equipped for performing replacement transfusions after the child has been born and where they can stay without charge.

(5) Radiation.—In some cases radiation damage to the fetus has been the reason why a woman has applied for legal abortion. It has been argued in a very few cases that the risk of genetic disturbances in one of the parents caused by radiation exposure of the sex glands at an earlier date should be grounds for legal abortion.

---

[22] The disease caused by infection with the protozoan.

In most of these cases the source of radiation has been an X-ray apparatus. In such cases the amount of radiation is carefully evaluated through a detailed analysis of the procedures during exposure. Some quantitative limits have been established, and exposure surpassing these limits has sometimes been accepted as grounds for legal abortion. In order to avoid occurrences of this kind, all hospitals have established in the past few years regulations aimed at preventing, as far as possible, exposure of the reproductive organs to radiation, especially in women who have recently ovulated.

(6) *Teratogenic Chemical Compounds.*[23]—Last among the teratogenic noxes sometimes indicating legal abortions are the teratogenic chemical compounds. The thalidomide catastrophe did not affect the Scandinavian countries to any considerable degree. In a few cases an attempt was made, through cautious X-ray examinations, to estimate the development of the fetus before considering the possible indication for legal abortion. As long as thalidomide was still obtainable, it was rather easy for a woman attempting to deceive the board to insist that she had used the drug. The general conclusion from the thalidomide catastrophe in Denmark has been to warn doctors, as well as the public, against any use of drugs during the first trimester of pregnancy unless such use is urgently needed.

(7) *Genetic Reasons.*—As to the genetic reasons for legal abortion, what has been said generally concerning the teratogenic noxes also holds true. In follow-up investigations the number of women who regret an earlier legal abortion is highest where the abortion was motivated by hereditary reasons.[24] As mental defectives and psychopaths are especially prominent in this group, these reactions should perhaps not be of too much importance. Still, it

---

[23] Some reports seem to indicate that viruses other than the rubella virus can also have a teratogenic effect on the fetus. There is no reason to go into detail regarding these still not completely established relations other than to say that the most common and widespread types of viruses like the common cold virus, the influenza viruses, and others do not seem to have any notable teratogenic effect. It is, of course, of the utmost importance that experts acquainted with the results of modern research are always heard in doubtful cases and in fields where research is rapidly progressing.

[24] From the files of the Mothers Aid Institute.

must be emphasized that the hereditary prognosis must be as well established as possible before a legal abortion is performed. In the field of psychiatry, human genetics has not developed to the extent necessary to make it possible to establish any certain prognosis in many cases of neurotic or behavioral disorders. Unfortunately, these are the most common conditions appearing in the families of women applying for legal abortion. More objective reasons for legal abortion could be obtained if hereditary factors were considered together with the social factors responsible for the circumstances under which the expected child will have to grow up. Here again an integration of biological and social factors is necessary.

The Institute of Human Genetics at the University of Copenhagen maintains a central registry where all criminal cases, as well as admittances to psychiatric institutions, are listed. The Institute also maintains a registry of most Danish families with the more pronounced hereditary diseases. In cases where hereditary indications might be present, a thorough report on the hereditary background is given by the Institute to the Mothers Aid.

The possible contraindications also have to be emphasized. In one case, a woman was very frightened by the fear of developing schizophrenia since some distant relations had this disease. Quite different hereditary factors among her closer relatives made a hereditary indication for legal abortion possible. However, it was necessary to refrain from using this to prevent her from feeling that her suspicions had been confirmed.

D. *The Defect Indication*

While the indications based upon this provision are described in another article in this symposium,[25] it should be emphasized that this provision theoretically concerns what could be called "social" indications. A legal abortion based upon this provision is not intended to cure or protect the woman herself, but is for the benefit of her child for whom she is supposedly not able to care. This makes an abortion based upon this provision somewhat humiliating to the woman in question. Most often, however, the woman does not

---

[25] See Skalts & Nørgaard, *supra* note 2, at 156, 162-63.

recognize what provision the board used in deciding upon the indication. In a few cases, relatives or social authorities have persuaded
a woman, poorly equipped both physically and mentally, to apply
for abortion under this defect provision. However, each case has
to be assessed on the basis of its own, particular facts.

IV. TIME LIMITS FOR ABORTION UNDER THE
PREGNANCY LEGISLATION

The pregnancy act provides that a legal abortion should be performed before the sixteenth week of pregnancy when the abortion
is based upon the provisions concerning ethical, hereditary, and defect indications.[26] However, there is no limit with regard to the
medical or sociomedical indications. In urgent medical cases involving a vital danger to the pregnant woman, an abortion is possible at any time during the pregnancy. In practice, however, abortions are very rarely performed later than the eighteenth to twentieth week of pregnancy.

Originally the government proposed to set the limit at the twentieth week. The Mothers Aid would then have had more time to
persuade the woman to continue with her pregnancy. Moreover,
it was realistically thought that many women would change their
minds since the pregnancy would be so far advanced that they
might feel the baby moving in their womb. A lobby of gynecologists opposed such a late limit, and the government changed its
mind, fixing the limit at the sixteenth week. Today it might be
argued that the limit ought to be as early as the twelfth week. Recent statistics have shown that the frequency of complications and
the mortality rate are considerably increased when operations have
been performed after the twelfth to the fourteenth week of pregnancy. Of special interest were the figures published by Dr. C.
Tietze comparing mortality rates in Hungary and Scandinavia.[27]
Hungary has unlimited legal abortions, but the operation has to be
performed before the twelfth week of pregnancy. Mortality rates

---

[26] 1956 PREGNANCY ACT § 1(2), Appendix p. 172.

[27] See Tietze & Lehfeldt, *Legal Abortion in Eastern Europe,* 175 A.M.A.J. 1149
(1961).

in connection with legal abortion operations in Hungary are considerably lower than the same rates in the well-equipped Scandinavian hospitals.[28]

It was found in Denmark that when applying for legal abortions 60 per cent of the applicants did so before the tenth week, 17 per cent between the tenth and twelfth week, 15 per cent between the twelfth and sixteenth week, and 6 per cent after the sixteenth week.[29]

V. AFTERCARE PROGRAM

A. *Contraception and Sterilization*

The decision of the board granting an abortion is the starting point for the aftercare program. Much emphasis has been placed upon the prevention of unwanted pregnancies. Thus, after termination of the pregnancy by abortion or birth, the woman is always urgently invited to utilize the contraception service of the gynecological clinic of the Mothers Aid Centers. Due regard is paid to the many psychological and ethical facets involved in contraception.

The gynecological clinic of the Copenhagen Mothers Aid Center has been engaged in comprehensive research programs on oral contraceptive methods and intrauterine devices in collaboration with the New York Population Council. Where contraceptive measures are deemed not suitable for physical, psychological, or social reasons, a voluntary sterilization might, in some urgent cases, be the necessary consequence. In fact, about 30 per cent of all legal abortions are followed immediately by sterilization since the two operations are so often similar.[30] Sometimes, however, the sterilization will be postponed until a later date — for those who go to term with their pregnancy, to the puerperal period. In a few cases the husband will have a vasectomy performed either because he is carrying the hereditary burden or as a substitute for the wife who is too weak to be operated upon.

It is surprising that a considerable number of women have ap-

---

28 *Ibid.*

29 From the files of the Mothers Aid Institute.

30 *Ibid.*

plied for voluntary sterilization. It is commonly supposed that this reflects a widespread and strong motivation for effective and narrow family size limitation and simultaneously a general distrust of conventional contraceptive methods which are deemed inadequate and psychologically disturbing. It is hoped that the modern contraceptive methods now under development will better fit the needs and thus be a substitute for some of the sterilizations. Sterilization in Denmark can be obtained in four different ways: (1) where a surgeon's approval, based on medical indications (health reasons), is given without any formal procedures, provided that the operation is medically indicated as a prophylactic or therapeutic measure;[31] (2) where social and eugenic factors are the main reasons for sterilization and application to the Ministry of Justice is made and accepted;[32] (3) where an application is made to the Ministry of Social Affairs on the basis of feeble-mindedness;[33] and (4) where the woman requests it after her pregnancy has been legally terminated because of her hereditary status.[34]

Eighty per cent of the sterilizations are performed without formal procedures based on medical indications.[35] Most cases have been investigated and assessed by the Mothers Aid Centers and the abortion boards, even if they do not have any legal basis for expressing their opinion. However, this procedure is generally accepted and is approved in a committee proposal to a new comprehensive sterilization law now in preparation.

B. Family Therapy

Another important field of aftercare is family therapy. Acknowledging the fact that the troubles of the individual woman very often depend upon some kind of family problem, it was recog-

---

[31] Report on Sterilization and Castration submitted by a committee established by the Ministry of Justice on December 30, 1958, No. 353 (1964).

[32] Act on Sterilization and Castration, Act No. 176 of May 11, 1935.

[33] Act on Feeble-Minded Persons, Act No. 171 of May 16, 1934, amended by Act on Care for Feeble-Minded and Other Persons Especially Deficient in Intelligence, Act No. 192 of June 5, 1959. While the earlier act was replaced by the 1959 act, the latter specifies that §§ 6-9 of the 1934 act are still valid.

[34] 1956 PREGNANCY ACT § 1(4), Appendix p. 172.

[35] From the files of the Mothers Aid Institute.

nized that real assistance should also involve an offer to help to solve the family situation. In many cases a team comprised of case workers, psychologists, psychiatrists, and lawyers invite the whole family of the woman who applied for abortion — whether or not the application was turned down — to come in for counselling, guidance, or therapeutic sessions. The type of treatment depends upon the kind of family problems. While budget problems are the most typical problems, some families are also faced with neurotic family interaction. Most often the family members are seen individually. Sometimes the work will go on for several years, and disappointments are not uncommon in this complicated field. However, a follow-up study has shown that about 60 per cent of these cases definitely improved.[36] In some cases a new pregnancy had appeared in the follow-up period and had been welcomed by the family, thereby supposedly avoiding applications for legal abortions. Because of a lack of staff and appropriations in this area, this type of aftercare has developed only to a limited degree and most of the aftercare is done according to more conventional methods of social work. The family-centered work, however, seems to attack the abortion problem closer to its roots, and it is hoped that Mothers Aid can develop this program further.

VI. RESEARCH

It is not possible, even briefly, to report upon the whole field of research covering legal abortions. However, an attempt will be made to give a concentrated report of some of the more important research results and of some relatively little-known information.

A. The Clientele of an Illegal Abortionist

Some years ago, an illegal abortionist was arrested in Copenhagen. His mode of operation consisted of having women write to his post office box asking him to come and see them. After his arrest, the police collected well over one hundred such requests and appeared with a social worker from the Mothers Aid who offered these women support and advice. A detailed investigation showed

---

[36] HOFFMEYER, FAMILIEN OG SAMFUNDET (1964).

that in about 20 per cent of the cases the women were able to obtain a legal abortion.[37] These women were badly informed or were too pessimistic to believe that they could be helped. Forty per cent of the women decided willingly to continue their pregnancies when supported by the Mothers Aid. The most surprising result was that 10 per cent of the women were not pregnant. The quack most likely would not have registered this and would have performed his operation.

In another study,[38] the number of illegal abortions in Denmark was estimated to be between 12,000 and 15,000 with the number of births being about 80,000, and the number of legal abortions being close to 4,000 a year.

B.   *Comparison between Children of Those Turned Down on Abortion Requests and Those Who Made No Applications*

In a study by Forssman and Thuwe from Gothenburgen, Sweden, two groups of children were compared at the age of twenty.[39] The one group was comprised of children born of mothers whose application for legal abortion twenty years earlier had been turned down. The other group was comparable to the first but their mothers had not applied for legal abortion. The study was retrospective and indirect, as the children were not seen by the investigators. All kinds of retrospective materials were collected from social, educational, and medical institutions. The incidence of social and psychological maladjustment during childhood and adolescence and of several other negative factors was considerably higher in the first group.

This result shows that the destiny and interests of the child are best provided for in the legislation. As mentioned previously, this is only done in the provision covering "defect" or handicapped

---

[37] HOFFMEYER, TIDSSKRIFT FOR PRAKT. LÆGERNING OG SOC. MEDIC. NO. 9 (1965).

[38] Hoffmeyer & Nørgaard, *Incidence of Conception and the Course of Pregnancy*, 126 UGESKRIFT FOR LÆGER 355-71 (1964).

[39] Forssman & Thuwe, *A Social-Psychiatric Follow-Up Study on 120 Children Born After an Application for Legal Abortion Was Refused*, 14 NORDISK PSYKIATRISK TIDSSKRIFT 265-79 (1960).

pregnant women.[40] And, as was also mentioned, an indication based upon such considerations is more of a "social" indication.

C. Follow-up Investigations

One might expect that follow-up studies would be able to highlight the effects of legal abortions. Especially in Sweden, where the regulations concerning legal abortion are nearly the same as in Denmark, quite a number of such studies have been published. However, the results are difficult to interpret. Groups of women who had legal abortions are barely comparable to the groups whose applications were turned down. Furthermore, the pregnancy of many years ago becomes blurred with later happenings and later pregnancies in the memories of the studied women, making it often very difficult to isolate the effect of the topical pregnancy. Rather often, the woman forgets that she applied for an abortion five or ten years previously.

In a follow-up study at Mothers Aid in Copenhagen, 427 consecutive cases were studied.[41] After five years, 180 women who had had their applications for abortion turned down were asked their opinion as to what effect the denial had on them. Those who were absolutely happy numbered 31; those who were only moderate in their satisfaction due to serious troubles in managing the child numbered 40; and another 40 were only moderately satisfied due to difficulties during the pregnancy. Only 29 were not able to make up their minds because their children had been placed in adoptive homes, nursing homes, or similar organizations. The number of mothers who affirmatively stated that they did not care for their babies and did not feel anything for them was only 13. Most of these women were psychopathic or mentally defective.

The study also included 126 women who had had a legal abortion performed. Five years later, 112 were absolutely happy and 5 regretted the action. A more complicated viewpoint was held by 9. Of 21 admitted illegal abortions, after five years, 16 were absolutely

---

[40] See note 25 *supra* and accompanying text.

[41] See HOFFMEYER, *supra* note 37.

satisfied and 3 regretted the abortion; 1 had a more complicated point of view.

The conclusion was that about 80 per cent are satisfied in all groups, and around 20 per cent are dissatisfied. Those who were turned down, however, seemed to make certain reservations. It must be remembered also that the natural attachment to the child, even though unwanted originally, may overshadow later complications. Höök, in Sweden, made a follow-up study seven and one-half to twelve years after 249 women had had their applications for legal abortions turned down.[42] Illegal abortions had been obtained by 12 per cent, while 69 per cent stayed with their child and 40 per cent were pregnant again within three years. At the follow-up interview, 73 per cent were satisfied, while 27 per cent maintained that the pregnancy ought to have been interrupted. Only 22 per cent found that the refusal had been the right way out. Höök found more satisfied women among the psychologically normal women than among the psychologically deviating women. In 24 per cent of the cases, symptoms of mental insufficiency developed. It was concluded that women with neurotic conflicts generally ran a greater risk of developing "insufficiency states" in connection with unwanted pregnancy than normal women.

Ekblad made a follow-up study in Stockholm that involved 479 women who had an abortion legally performed.[43] At the follow-up date 64 per cent were absolutely satisfied, 10 per cent had found the procedure and operation disagreeable, 14 per cent had had slight self-reproaches, and 11 per cent had had severe self-reproaches. Only 1 per cent developed psychic insufficiency inhibiting their working capacity slightly. Many of the women became pregnant again very soon thereafter.

Much discussion has been brought about by a study by Amark and Arén from Sweden.[44] They examined 162 women who gave

---

[42] Höök, *Refused Abortion: A Follow-Up Study of 249 Women Whose Applications Were Refused by the National Board of Health in Sweden*, ACTA PSYCHIATRICA SCANDINAVICA SUPPLEMENTUM No. 168 (1963).

[43] Ekblad, *Induced Abortions on Psychiatric Grounds*, ACTA PSYCHIATRICA ET NEUROLOGICA SCANDINAVICA SUPPLEMENTUM 99 (1955).

[44] Arén & Amark, *The Prognosis of Granted But Not Performed Legal Abortions*, 54 SVENSKA LÄKARETIDNINGEN 3709 (1957).

birth after having had an application for legal abortion accepted. The abortion had, for different reasons, not been performed — some were too advanced in their pregnancy, some withdrew their applications, and in some cases the surgeon refused to operate. Of this group, 142 kept their babies, with 21 per cent of these developing poor psychic health, and 37 per cent improving their psychic health by the follow-up date as compared to its state when they applied for the legal abortion. This study has been considered a convincing argument against the current abortion policy. It could, however, be doubted that this material is not comprised of women who are especially ambivalent in their wish for an abortion.

VII. CONCLUSION

The Danish abortion legislation is part and parcel of a general social legislation for the support of families, mothers, and their children. It has always been emphasized that abortion, first and foremost, was to be controlled by means of general, positive social and family policies. So far some goals have been reached, but there is still considerable work to be done with regard to the development of the Mothers Aid staff, especially in the area of the more complicated and time-consuming family services, family treatment, and the like.

It has been argued that society is willing to spend quite a large amount of money on staff to sort into "yes'" or "no" groups the women applying for legal abortion. Society feels its conscience cleared when this is done as equitably as possible. However, it seems much more difficult to obtain government funds for monetary support of the families and for staff for therapeutic and counselling activities. Thus, the administrative work seems to take precedence over the more constructive work.

The still high number of illegal abortions, the difficulties in interpretation of results from follow-up studies, and the results from the Forssman and Thuwe study[45] showing a preponderance of maladjusted children born by women whose applications for legal abortion were turned down, all point out the unreasonableness of pre-

---

[45] See note 39 *supra*.

serving regulations which distinguish between positive and negative indications for legal abortions. Is it possible to realistically assess vaguely defined sociomedical "insufficiency states" and to differentiate between cases with a serious and a light prognosis? Could one not operate a clear "social" or "welfare" provision as well? Or would it be possible to have no limitation at all? These questions are not easily answered. Experience has shown that it is possible to differentiate on medical grounds between sociomedical cases with a bad and a good prognosis. But the cost of performing this differentiation is high because of the time necessary to prepare the cases thoroughly.

"Social" and "welfare" provisions are often proposed. They could be based upon clearly defined criteria (e.g., size of income, housing conditions, number of children). Such automatic limitations would never do justice to real-life situations; however, using more general definitions such as "welfare" would make it necessary again to establish some committee or board with the authority to make decisions.

The problem with the use of social criteria is that doctors are not especially qualified to apply them and would certainly refrain from participating. The doctors prefer the sociomedical principles described above, since it is on medical grounds that doctors are able to make estimates. Furthermore, it is felt that unlimited abortions, or abortions on "social" grounds, would expose some women to a danger, namely, that they could be subjected to pressure from the husband, the fiancé, or other relatives. Moreover, the common, temporary mental depression of the first months of pregnancy certainly would induce some women to apply for an abortion which they later would regret.

Important also is the fact that as long as the indication for legal abortion is medically motivated, the collaboration of the whole medical profession can be preserved. If we leave the medical context, many surgeons and gynecologists certainly would refrain from performing the operations.

In Denmark there is, for the time being, no tendency to change the current provisions. However, a very vivid discussion is occurring and large circles of the population are arguing that the granting of legal abortion ought to be more liberal. Research projects have been started and will soon be published. The government has established a broad committee studying the whole field of sex education in schools and for adults. It is hoped that better sex information, improved contraceptive instruction, new developments in contraceptive methods, and last, but not least, further development in social and family policy will reduce the need for more liberal abortion legislation.

9

Abortion in the German-Speaking
Countries of Europe

Leopold Breitenecker, M.D.
and Rudiger Breitenecker, M.D.

It is the inviolable right of every man to freely decide upon matters concerning his body. However, this right is limited in women of child-bearing age by age-old laws in all countries, when, through the union of ovum and spermatozoa, a new individual is created, with its own legal rights beginning at the moment of conception. Healthy women under normal living conditions find pregnancy no great cause of concern, while those afflicted by illness or adverse social conditions consider this biological state an unbearable burden. In the distant past, it was in the interest of the state to create laws prohibiting abortion, in order to ensure that there would be sufficient numbers of subjects to secure the military defense of the country.[1] Reports reveal abortion practices among ancient peoples, such as the Egyptians, Greeks, Romans, Chinese, Eskimos, Indians, Aztecs, Africans, Jews, and Mohammedans, as well as Christians and the peoples of European countries.[2] One can find legal provisions pro-

---

[1] Baldinger, *Preface* to 1 JOHN, LEXIKON DER KAISERLICH-KÖNIGLICHEN MEDIZINAL GESETZE at ii (1790): "only then are the Dukes mighty and invincible, if they rule over large numbers of healthy and strong subjects, who are capable of using the sword, the cannon, the loom, the plough — not to mention the pen — with brave strength. . . ." 2 FRANK, SYSTEM EINER VOLLSTÄNDIGEN MEDIZINISCHEN POLIZEY, 62-163 (3d ed. 1786) (abortion among diverse peoples and its danger to the state).

[2] MEHLAN, INTERNATIONALE ABORTSITUATION, ABORTBEKÄMPFUNG, ANTIKONZEPTION: BERICHT DER INTERNATIONALEN ARBEITSTAGUNG, Rostock 1960, 5 (1961) (introductory comment). VEB Georg Thieme, Leipzig.

hibiting abortion in the first penal code of the Holy Roman Empire.[3] There, the penalty for abortion was set forth: "The man shall be executed by the sword, the woman shall be drowned or put to death by other means. . . ."[4]

But even these drastic penalties were never a complete deterrent. The new eras of Humanism and the "Age of Reason" mellowed such harsh punishment, and the nineteenth century witnessed attempts to legalize abortion. This more lenient attitude has become even more prevalent in the twentieth century and actually became the official attitude in Communist countries of Eastern Europe. The first country to break with the traditional conservative principles was Soviet Russia, which legalized abortion in 1920.[5] However, it soon became evident that such policies were detrimental to the welfare of the states. Many of these countries repealed such liberal laws and once again placed abortions under medical and legal controls. The "indications for abortion" then had to be determined by medical specialists, and the procedure was to be performed in hospitals to safeguard the life and health of the woman.

In the move to legalize abortion, two trends can be observed: (1) the liberalization of abortion laws for social reasons, such as in Bulgaria, Czechoslovakia, Hungary, Poland, Russia, and Yugoslavia;[6] and (2) the somewhat veiled inclusion of social considerations and the broadening of the definition of "medical indication," in Denmark, Finland, India, Japan, Sweden, Switzerland, and East Germany. Other countries still recognize only the preservation of the life or health of the woman as a genuine "medical indication."[7]

The number of abortions in recent decades has reached epidemic proportions. It is interesting to note that the number of illegal abortions was found to be inversely proportional to the severity of

---

[3] CONSTITUTIO CRIMINALIS CAROLINGA (1532) [hereinafter cited as C.C.C.].

[4] C.C.C., p. 60 (Ausgabe Frankfurt am Mayn 1609); C.C.C., p. 27 (Ausgabe Mayntz 1660).

[5] MEHLAN, *op. cit. supra* note 2, at 6; Vojta, *Die Abortsituation in der CSR, Vortrag auf der Internationalen Arbeitstagung*, in MEHLAN, *op. cit. supra* note 6, at 107-13.

[6] MEHLAN, *op. cit. supra* note 2, at 6.

[7] *Ibid.*

punishment.[8]   The actual number, of course, is difficult to determine
and can only be estimated by comparing a decline in birth with the
population and number of marriages.   This comparison is not extremely meaningful, however, because the calculated birth deficit
is undoubtedly related to present-day contraception practices for
"socioeconomic" reasons.   The number of abortions in Germany,
with a population of approximately 60 million, is estimated at 1
million yearly.[9]   Similar numbers are reported in France.   In Paris,
95,000 births have been compared to a calculated 150,000 abortions.[10]   Reported figures of mortality rates for induced abortions
vary from 1 to 8 per cent.[11]

Because of unfavorable experiences, the Soviet Union had to curtail legalized abortion temporarily, but in 1955 it was again legalized.[12]   The official explanation was that "the social emancipation
of the Soviet woman has brought about the conditions, which allow
her to decide herself about the disposition of her fetus."[13]   The repeated liberalization of abortion legislation arose from a desire to
prevent damage to the health of the woman by unskilled termination of pregnancy.   All "indications" were recognized; but in order
to avoid an unlimited interruption of pregnancies, a commission
was set up to advise the patients and to explain that (1) every
such operation constitutes a danger to health, life, and future fertility, (2) the laws protecting motherhood tend to eliminate social
"indications,"[14] and (3) each abortion is damaging to the Soviet
society.[15]

----

8 *Id.* at 7.

9 *Ibid.*, citing Bumm's statistics indicating that for the years 1929 and 1930 there
were one million abortions resulting in 80,000 deaths and 200,000 to 300,000 cases of
chronic disease.

10 *Ibid.*, citing statistics by Dourlen and Rollier disclosing that for the year 1960
Paris had 150,000 abortions resulting in 20,000 deaths.   Monsaingeon's statistics reveal
that 61 per cent of these abortions had complications and 25 per cent resulted in subsequent sterility.   *Ibid.*

11 The computations by Mehlan suggest a mortality rate of 8 to 14 per cent.   Undoubtedly this figure has been lowered since the advent of sulfonamides and antibiotics.
Ibid.

12 *Ibid.*

13 *Ibid.*

14 *Ibid.*

The other Communist countries of Eastern Europe also recognized that even legalizing abortion did not solve the problem of illegal abortions, because many women avoided seeing the appointed commissions and returned to the illegal, private abortionists. Some countries now recommend "birth control" by contraception as the solution. However, some consider this to be biologically detrimental to a highly developed civilization with a comparatively lower birth rate than that of emerging nations, which are marked by an explosive increase in their populations. Since it seems inevitable that a nation with a high birth rate would eventually overwhelm one with a low rate of birth, artificial birth control would be equivalent to a type of national suicide. This discrepancy in birth rates may have played some part in the decline of ancient civilizations.

I. Legal Provisions against Abortion in Austria, Germany, and Switzerland

The pertinent laws of these three German-speaking countries will be discussed according to the age of the statutes. This will permit some insight into their legal development.

A. Austria

(1) Present Code Provisions.—In the sixteenth chapter of the Criminal Code of 1852, "About Abortion," which is still in effect in Austria, it is stated: "Every woman being with child who, with intent to procure her own miscarriage, effects such miscarriage or stillbirth, shall be guilty of a felony."[16] The punishment for attempted abortion is imprisonment from six months to one year; for achieved abortion, the punishment is incarceration from one to five years.[17]

---

15 *Ibid.*

16 KANIAK, DAS ÖSTERREICHISCHE STRAFGESETZ MIT ERLÄUTERHUNGEN § 144, at 301 (5th ed. 1960); MEHLAN, *op. cit. supra* note 2, at 243-76 (app.). The appendix deals with laws concerning abortion and pregnancy interruption in Belgium, Bulgaria, CSR, Denmark, West Germany, East Germany, Great Britain, Finland, France, Holland, Yugoslavia, Norway, Austria, Poland, Sweden, USSR, Hungary, and the United States.

17 4 KANIAK, *op. cit. supra* note 16, § 145, at 304.

Accomplices to the crime of abortion are dealt with as follows:

> An accomplice in this crime is anyone who induces the pregnant
> woman to abort herself or who aids her in doing so, even if such
> abortion is only attempted. The accomplice is to be punished
> with incarceration from 1 to 5 years. However, if he "profes-
> sionally" aids in abortions the punishment is from 2 years to 10
> years.[18]

A person who performs an abortion or attempts to perform an
abortion on a pregnant woman against her will or without her
knowledge is guilty of a felony.[19] The punishment is normally imprisonment for one to five years; but when the mother's life is endangered or her health damaged, the sentence is incarceration for
five to ten years.[20]

From these provisions it can be seen that the special condition
of the woman is taken into consideration, since her punishment[21]
is less severe than that of the accomplice.[22] The potential father
who advises abortion or supplies money, or acquaintances who steer
the woman to an abortionist, is not the only person who is considered
an accomplice; physicians who perform the operation and claim
"medical indications" also fall within this category.[23] To cover this
area, the code was amended in 1937 with an addition to the malpractice section:[24]

> A physician who induces or performs an abortion, or advises
> such action with the intent to avert a present danger to the life
> or health of a pregnant woman, but who failed to have conscien-
> tiously determined that such danger really existed, is guilty of a

---

18 *Id.* at 305.

19 The statute provides the following: "A person is guilty of a felony, who intentionally, for whatever reason, aborts or attempts to abort a mother against her will or
without her knowledge." *Id.* at 307.

20 The following statutory language provides the punishment: "Such a criminal
shall be incarcerated from 1 to 5 years; and when the mother's life is endangered or her
health damaged, from 5 to 10 years." *Id.* at 307.

21 See text accompanying note 17 *supra.*

22 See text accompanying note 18 *supra.*

23 1 ALTMANN & JACOB, KOMMENTAR ZUM ÖSTERREICHISCHEN STRAFRECHT §§
144-48, at 375-80 (1928); 2 RITTLER, LEHRBUCH DES ÖSTERREICHISCHEN STRAF-
RECHTS (BESONDERER TEIL) 16 (1962).

24 4 KANIAK, *op. cit. supra* note 16, at 635 (medical intervention in pregnancy).

misdemeanor. If such danger did not exist in reality, the afore-mentioned will be imprisoned from 1 to 6 months for the first offense, but will lose his license temporarily or permanently for repeated offenses.[25]

Thus, the physician who performs an abortion does not commit a felony, but rather a misdemeanor. His punishment is accordingly lighter, although under certain conditions he may lose his license to practice medicine.

(2) Proposals for Reform.—At the present time, a new criminal code is being written. In it, the proposed section entitled "Abortion by the Pregnant Woman" will read: "A woman who aborts her fetus or permits abortion by another party will be pun-ished with up to 3 years detention."[26] Thus, "felony" or "incarcera-tion" are not mentioned, and the punishment is considerably less severe.

"Abortion by other persons" is defined in Section 100 of the proposed code as follows:

> (1) Whoever, with consent of a pregnant woman, performs an abortion or renders advice or aid, shall be imprisoned from 6 months to 5 years. If the perpetrator is a professional abortion-ist or performed the action resulting in the death of the pregnant woman, the punishment is from 1 to 10 years.
> (2) Whoever aborts a pregnant woman without her consent shall be imprisoned from 1 to 10 years.[27]

Thus, the punishment for the accomplice is not reduced in the new code. The amended code is particularly directed against the pro-fessional abortionist who performs this action for "social" reasons while extracting considerable sums of money from economically needy women.

The proposed code further provides that an abortion is not illegal if it is performed to avert present danger to life or prolonged damage to health which cannot otherwise be averted. The judg-

---

[25] *Ibid.*

[26] BUNDESMINISTERIUM FÜR JUSTIZ, ENTWURF EINES STRAFGESETZBUCHES (BE-SONDERER TEIL) §§ 99-103 (1964); see also pertinent comments, *id.* at 13-20 [here-inafter proposed code sections are cited 1964 E.S. §].

[27] 1964 E.S. Proposed § 100, and comments at 15.

ment as to the existence of these conditions is to be based upon a
consideration of the woman's living conditions and her physical and
emotional state.[28] This illustrates that not only pathological conditions are decisive, as in the old criminal code, but psychological
and social conditions must also be taken into consideration. Thus,
abortion for social reasons would be sanctioned in the new criminal
code.

The new code provides that if a physician performs an abortion
or advises the pregnant woman to obtain an abortion, based on an
insincere assumption as to the danger to her life, he is subject to
imprisonment up to one year. Anyone not a physician who performs or aids in performing an abortion will be imprisoned up to
six months, unless there was immediate danger to the life of the
woman and a physician could not be promptly summoned.[29] This
section also contains a decree against solicitation of abortion and
abortifacients: "Whoever publicly solicits abortion or advertises
means, objects, or methods thereto, will be imprisoned up to 2
years, or fined 500,000 schillings."[30]

This new criminal code has not been ratified by Parliament as
yet. However, these short excerpts are intended to demonstrate the
the tendency of modern lawmakers to reflect the attitudes of contemporary society.

---

[28] The pertinent sections of the proposed code provide as follows: "An abortion,
which averts present danger to life or prolonged damage to health, which cannot be
remedied by other means, is not punishable by § 99 and § 100. The judgment, whether
such danger has actually existed, has to take into consideration the physical and emotional state of the pregnant woman, and also the conditions under which she is compelled to live." 1964 E.S. Proposed § 101, and comments at 16.

[29] The statute, as proposed, provides:

A physician who erroneously assumes that a pregnant woman's life is endangered, as delineated in § 101, and subsequently performs an abortion, or
advises her to have the abortion performed by another person, or in any way
aids her in the perpetration of this deed, without having previously and con-
scientiously convinced himself that such danger really existed, will be punished with imprisonment of up to 1 year.

Whoever, without being a physician (previously § 344 A.C.C.), performs
or aids in an abortion, and whose action is not punishable under § 100, will
be imprisoned up to 6 months, unless he acted in an immediate emergency to
save the life of a pregnant woman, and conditions prevented prompt summon-
ing of a physician. 1964 E.S. Proposed § 102, and comment at 18.

[30] 1964 E.S. Proposed § 103, and comments at 20. This is equivalent to about
$20,000.

(3) Proving the Crime.—The proof of an abortion, according to Austrian law, involves proof of both a suitable object and suitable means.[31] The former is frequently very difficult to prove, because such a crime is often not reported and investigated until many months after its occurrence. For all practical purposes, a pregnancy leaves no traces, so that one has to depend on the testimony of the woman or of the abortionist. It is quite obvious, however, that they will often give conflicting testimony. In such cases, it is generally felt that the first statement of the woman usually comes closest to the truth; however, the relative weight ultimately given to the evidence depends upon the credibility of the testimony, the interpretation of which is up to the judge, rather than the medical expert. But the expert has to point out to the judge the incredibility of certain statements, based upon his medical knowledge.

Generally, it is also difficult to prove the second element — that suitable means had been employed. This holds true especially with internally applied or only potentially toxic substances and, to a lesser degree, with mechanical instruments. With the latter, one has to decide whether the instrument per se is suitable, and also whether it would have been effective in the particular case at hand. It is often claimed by the accused that a catheter was introduced only into the vagina, to appease a client, without actual intent to perform an abortion, or that a vaginal douche was applied only for the sake of appearance, while the abortion allegedly resulted from natural causes or subsequent intervention by another person. Particularly convincing as evidence would be the examination of recovered products of conception, but these are usually discarded and destroyed. It requires a great sense of responsibility and experience to answer a question concerning causal relation between a given procedure and abortion in such a way that the court can arrive at a just decision.

B. Germany

(1) The Code Provisions of West Germany.—The legal pro-

---

[31] For a list of pertinent legal literature, see 1 ALTMANN & JACOB, *op. cit. supra* note 23, §§ 2, 3, at 376-77; 2 RITTLER, *op. cit. supra* note 23, at 17-18; HOFMANN & HABERDA, LEHRBUCH DER GERICHTLICHEN MEDIZIN 211 (2d ed. 1927).

visions concerning abortion are set forth in the German Criminal Code of 1871.[32]   There, it is provided that any woman who performs an abortion on herself, or permits such an act, and any other person who performs an abortion on another, or is an accomplice thereto, will be imprisoned. The attempt to commit these acts is also punishable.[33] The advertisement or manufacture of objects or methods designed to produce an abortion is also proscribed activity.[34] In addition, the public offering of abortion services is punishable by imprisonment up to two years or by a fine.[35]

(2) Proposals for Reform.—This Code of 1871 is slated to be replaced by a new code.[36] Its 1959 draft states: "Impunity is granted when according to prevailing medical knowledge, only this procedure can prevent danger to the life, or severe damage to the health of the mother."[37] Also new is the acknowledgment of an "ethical indication": "Medical intervention is not punishable when pregnancy is the result of rape, when the woman consented to the procedure, and not more than 12 weeks have elapsed since impregnation, provided that rape was reported to the authorities in time."[38]

---

[32] KOHLRAUSCH & LANGE, DEUTSCHES STRAFGESETZBUCH MIT ERLÄUTERUNGEN §§ 218-20, at 483-89 (1961).

[33] The statute provides: "A woman who performs an abortion on herself, or permits such an act, will be punished with imprisonment. The attempt is also punishable. Any other person who produces an abortion or is an accomplice will be punished with imprisonment." 1964 E.S. Proposed § 218, at 483.

[34] "Whoever advertises or manufactures objects or methods which are supposed to achieve abortion or prevent pregnancy or venereal disease, shall be punished with up to 2 years in prison or a fine." *Id.* § 219, at 488.

[35] The statute states: "Whoever publicly offers his or somebody else's services to perform or aid in an abortion, shall be punished with up to 2 years in prison or a fine." *Id.* § 220, at 489.

[36] BUNDESMINISTERIUM FÜR JUSTIZ, ENTWURF EINES STRAFGESETZBUCHES §§ 140-44 (Abtreibung), 157-60 (ärztlicher Eingriff an Schwangeren), and comments (1959) [hereinafter cited as 1959 E.S. Proposed]; BUNDESMINISTERIUM FÜR JUSTIZ, ENTWURF EINES STRAFGESETZBUCHES E. §§ 140-45 (Abtreibung), 157-59 (ärztlicher Eingriff an Schwangeren), with reasoning (1962) [hereinafter cited as 1962 E.S. Proposed].

[37] 1959 E.S. Proposed § 157, at 47; 1962 E.S. Proposed § 157.

[38] 1959 E.S. Proposed § 160, at 48. The 1962 draft eliminated this section. See 1962 E.S. at 296.

According to present German law, even an attempt with unsuitable means *or* on an unsuitable subject, as well as an attempt with unsuitable means *and* an unsuitable subject, is punishable.[39] In contrast, according to the Austrian Code, an attempted abortion by unsuitable means or with an unsuitable subject is not punishable.[40]

(3) Pre-1947 East German Code Provisions.—Prior to 1947 in East Germany, the provisions of the code described above for West Germany were in force. However, in that year they were repealed.[41] In view of the prevailing poor economic conditions, a liberalization of the "indication" for abortions was decided upon. Together with the medical "indication," broadened sociomedical, ethical, and eugenic "indications" were introduced. This resulted in an increase in the legal as well as the criminal abortions and created a dangerously liberal attitude regarding abortion among women.[42] Therefore, when the economic and social conditions improved in East Germany, a law protecting mother and child was decreed in 1950. Limitation of acceptable "indications" coupled with financial aid to promote the number of marriages were supposed to increase the desire for more children. Nevertheless, the increase in the number of births of only 4.0 per cent over the number of deaths[43] hardly guarantees preservation of the present population.

(4) Current Code Provisions of East Germany.—In East Germany, the procedure is governed by a new law guaranteeing

---

[39] MAURACH, GELTENDES DEUTSCHES STRAFRECHT (BESONDERER TEIL) 52-70 (4th ed. 1964).

[40] See text accompanying note 31 *supra.*

It is interesting to note that in Germany permission by designated medical experts is required for therapeutic abortion. The procedure has to be performed in a hospital. MUELLER, GERICHTLICHE MEDIZIN 917 (1953). See Harmsen, *Die Abortsituation in der Deutschen Bundesrepublik (West-Deutschland) Referat auf der Internationalen Arbeitstagung,* in MEHLAN, *op. cit. supra* note 2, at 41-51.

[41] Mehlan, *Die Abortsituation in der Deutschen Demokratischen Republik (Ost-Deutschland) Referat auf der Internationalen Arbeitstagung,* in MEHLAN, *op. cit. supra* note 2, at 53.

[42] *Ibid.*

[43] *Id.* at 63.

the protection of mother and child.[44] The code provides that abortion will be permitted only if the pregnancy would seriously endanger the life or health of the woman, or if one parent suffers from a severe hereditary disease.[45] Even the permissible abortion can be performed only with the consent of a commission consisting of physicians, representatives of the health department, and members of the Democratic Women's League.[46]

C. Switzerland

According to Swiss law,[47] a pregnant woman may be imprisoned if she commits an abortion on herself or has such an operation performed by another.[48] The abortionist will be punished, whether or not he obtained the woman's consent before performing the operation; however, the punishment is more severe if he did not obtain her consent prior to the operation.[49]

The Swiss Code does, however, grant impunity for abortions committed under certain circumstances. Thus, an abortion may be performed by a licensed physician to obviate danger to the life and health of a pregnant woman, provided: (1) the written consent

---

[44] MEHLAN, *op. cit. supra* note 2, at 52-63, 254-57 (app.).

[45] The code provides in § 11: "In the interest of protecting the health of the woman, and in providing for the desired increase in the birth rate an artificial abortion is only permissible when pregnancy seriously endangers the life or health of the woman, or one parent is afflicted with a severe hereditary disease. Any other termination of pregnancy is prohibited, and will be punished according to the law." For a discussion of § 11 of the code, see *id.* at 245.

[46] *Ibid.*

[47] The legal provisions concerning abortion are outlined in articles 118 to 121 of the Swiss Criminal Code. GERMANN, SCHWEIZERISCHES STRAFGESETZBUCH MIT KURZEN ERLÄUTERUNGEN 178-82 (1962).

[48] Article 118 of the Swiss Criminal Code of 1942 provides the following: "If a pregnant woman commits abortion on herself or has such abortion performed, she shall be imprisoned. The statute of limitations is 2 years." *Id.* at 179.

[49] Article 119 of the Swiss Criminal Code of 1942 provides the following:
(1) Whoever aids a pregnant woman with abortion or performs the abortion with her consent, shall be punished with imprisonment up to 5 years. The statute of limitations is 2 years.
(2) Whoever performs an abortion without consent of the pregnant woman, shall be punished with imprisonment up to 10 years.
(3) Imprisonment is not to be less than 3 years: if the perpetrator is a professional abortionist, if the pregnant woman dies as the result of the abortion, and if the perpetrator could anticipate such an event. *Id.* at 179-80.

of the pregnant woman is obtained; (2) the expert opinion of a second physician has been obtained; and (3) the physician reports such a procedure within twenty-four hours to the appropriate authorities.[50] Also, punishment will be mitigated if the pregnancy is interrupted because of some other emergency.[51] If a physician fails to report an abortion under the above procedure, he can be arrested or fined.[52]

The above provisions of the Swiss Criminal Code demonstrate that a genuine social or eugenic indication *expressis verbis* is not recognized; however, the interpretation of the legal limits in the Code is very broad. For instance, the statute of limitations is only two years,[53] and the provision on mitigation of punishment where there is "some other serious emergency"[54] opens the door for possible "social" or "eugenic indications." Harsh punishment is directed particularly against professional abortionists who, devoid of social conscience, take advantage of destitute women for financial gain, although they claim social reasons as justification of their ac-

---

[50] Article 120 of the Criminal Code provides:

(1) An abortion within the meaning of the law does not exist, when the pregnancy is interrupted with written consent of the pregnant woman, performed by a licensed physician, who has obtained an expert opinion of a second physician, in order to avert otherwise unpreventable danger to the life or permanent damage to the health of the pregnant woman.

The expert opinion (see Section 1) must be rendered by a competent specialist, who is authorized by the local authorities, where the pregnant woman resides or where the operation is to be performed. If the pregnant woman is not competent to judge, written permission from her legal guardian is necessary.

(2) The regulations concerning an emergency (Art. 34, No. 2) remain extant, if an immediate, not otherwise avertable, danger to life or gross danger of permanent damage to the health of the pregnant woman exists, and the abortion is performed by a licensed physician.

In such cases, the physician has to report such a procedure within 24 hours to the appropriate authorities. *Id.* at 181-82.

[51] Article 120 of the Criminal Code concludes:

(3) In cases where the pregnancy is interrupted because of some other serious emergency, the judge can extenuate the punishment, according to his judgment. (Art. 66.)

(4) Article 32 is waived. *Id.* at 182.

[52] Article 121 of the Swiss Criminal Code states: "A physician, who fails to report an abortion, performed under Art. 120, No. 2, shall be arrested or fined." *Id.* at 182.

[53] See notes 48, 49 *supra*.

[54] See note 51 *supra*.

tions. Punishment is harsher if death, which could have been fore-seen by the operator, occurred.[55] However, proving "foreseeable death" is very difficult most of the time, if the abortionist is not a physician.

A comparison of the codes of the three countries indicates that the Swiss Criminal Code is similar to the German Criminal Code but is basically quite different from the Austrian Criminal Code.

II. ABORTION TECHNIQUES

A. Drugs and Related Substances

The scope of this article does not permit discussion of innumer-able plant extracts, drugs, hormones, and chemical substances that have been employed over the years to induce abortion. The in-gestion of chemical substances as abortifacients has given way to more effective external methods. At best, chemical methods are still used to supplement mechanical means. The desired effect of these toxic substances is to destroy the fetus or to produce conges-tion of the uterine mucosa with resulting hemorrhage at the im-plantation site of the fertilized ovum.[56] Essentially, there are no effective substances which can be taken internally and will destroy the fetus or produce labor contractions without concomitant danger to the mother. If the ingestion of such substances results in a mis-carriage, the woman may have been prone to abort spontaneously regardless of the ingested substance, or the abortion may have con-stituted only one manifestation of a generalized poisoning of the pregnant woman.

Quinine, for example, one of the commonly used abortifacients, is not, in itself, as effective as popularly claimed. If large enough doses are given to produce labor contractions, the systemic toxicity may be fatal to the mother. Experts report that if an abortion follows smaller, non-lethal doses, a condition of barely perceptible contractions pre-existed.

Suffice it to say that the notorious unreliability of ingested sub-

---

[55] See Article 119, No. 3 quoted in full at note 49 *supra*.

[56] HOFMANN & HABERDA, *op. cit. supra* note 31, at 222-39; MUELLER, *op. cit. supra* note 40, at 919-27.

stances has diminished their use as abortifacients, while mechanical means have gained in popularity.[57]

B. External Methods

The pregnant uterus is relatively well-protected against external trauma. Ordinary activities of daily life and even more strenuous pursuits, such as dancing, horseback riding, driving on bumpy roads, and lifting heavy objects have been wrongly accused of being causally related to abortion. Only if this activity is superimposed on an already existing constitutional tendency to abort spontaneously can speculation of a causal relationship have some validity.[58] Direct trauma to the abdomen is significant only if actual injury to the uterus or to placental attachment can be proven. Occasionally, more bizarre methods are employed, such as the application to the abdomen of electric shocks (frequently fatal), ultra-sonic therapy, or ultra-short wave radiation.

A great variety of poisonous substances introduced into the vagina by douche or by hand are only potential abortifacients.[59] They are only effective by penetration into the uterine cavity itself or by toxic action of the poison after its absorption through the vaginal mucosa into the circulation.

Far more effective is mechanical manipulation of the uterine cervix and the uterine cavity itself.[60] Elongated objects may be inserted by the woman herself or, more frequently, by another person. The desired uterine contractions are produced by several mechanisms: (1) laceration of the fetal membranes allowing the amniotic fluid to escape with subsequent contractions of the uterine muscle and expulsion of the fetus;[61] (2) introduction of long, thin, sharp objects into the uterus which can injure the site of implantation and cause hemorrhage which precipitates premature separation and ex-

---

[57] 8 REUTER, BIOLOGIE UND PATHOLOGIE DES WEIBES 967-1342. For a discussion on abortion, see *id.* at 1173-1235.

[58] HOFMANN & HABERDA, *op. cit. supra* note 31, at 239-58; MUELLER, *op. cit. supra* note 40, at 930-33; 8 REUTER, *op. cit. supra* note 57, at 1193-1202.

[59] MUELLER, *op. cit. supra* note 40, at 929.

[60] *Id.* at 930.

[61] *Ibid.*

pulsion of the placenta;[62] (3) direct injection into the uterus of a great variety of irritating substances, such as soapy water and various disinfectants. Beyond the potentially toxic effects of these irritating substances, air embolism is a common complication. The use of abortifacient pastes, on the other hand, may result in oil embolism. More recently, formalin or saline solutions have been injected into the uterus as a bona fide method of producing therapeutic abortion.[63]

Fatal complications of mechanical manipulation are frequently related to perforation of the uterus by the probing instrument. It is noteworthy that this is more frequently observed with physicians who perform the abortion rather than with amateurs, who prefer other methods. The most common cause of death in induced abortions, however, is a septic infection. Poor techniques, even when the instruments are properly sterilized, allow pathogenic bacteria from the vagina to gain entrance to the inner lining of the uterus. At the operative site, their growth and spread are enhanced by the damaged tissues and associated blood clots. For a more detailed discussion of the characteristic complications and causes of death, the reader is referred to appropriate medical texts.[64]

III. MEDICAL INDICATIONS FOR "THERAPEUTIC ABORTIONS"

Modern advances in therapy have greatly changed medicine's attitude toward therapeutic abortions.[65] Present knowledge shows that one must proceed cautiously in broadening the definition of a "medical indication." A number of "medical indications" of the past have proven to be erroneous, as for example when a particular disease was found to be curable by modern techniques. Today, conscientious physicians and medicolegal experts should only rarely accept a medical indication as convincing. Frequently, in disputed cases, the problem is really not a scientific one, but rather a pseudo-scientific attempt to justify abortion for personal reasons. "Eugenic

---

[62] *Id.* at 931, 934.

[63] *Id.* at 934.

[64] *Id.* at 937-39. See generally GONZALES, VANCE, HELPERN, & UMBERGER, LEGAL MEDICINE, PATHOLOGY AND TOXICOLOGY *passim* (1954).

[65] MUTH & ENGELHARDT, SCHWANGERSCHAFTSUNTERBRECHUNG UND STERILISATION IN NEUERER SICHT 34-149 (1964).

indications" must be scrutinized just as thoroughly as other medical indications, since our knowledge of the transmission of hereditary diseases is frequently quite fragmentary.

Generally speaking, termination of pregnancy may be considered in three categories: diseases resulting from pregnancy; diseases aggravated by pregnancy; and diseases of the reproductive organs.[66] The following considerations predominantly reflect the current concepts in Germany. The diseases under discussion, of course, are only representative, and it does not necessarily follow that the presented point of view is one accepted by everybody.

A. Diseases Resulting from Pregnancy

Termination of pregnancy for hyperemesis gravidarum[67] is no longer an accepted indication, while acute yellow atrophy of the liver, whether or not related to pregnancy, is a definite one. Pyelonephritis[68] of pregnancy should only rarely demand an interruption. As with other kidney diseases, abortion is indicated only if the symptoms become progressively worse, in spite of therapy. Therapeutic abortion in the case of postpuerperal[69] recurrent depression may be an acceptable indication, according to psychiatric consultants.

B. Diseases Aggravated by Pregnancy

Skin diseases should justify an induced abortion only in extreme cases. The same holds true for bronchial asthma, chronic emphysema,[70] and most heart diseases. Even myocardial infarction[71] is not an acceptable indication, since the operation itself may be more dangerous than an uninterrupted pregnancy. Pulmonary tuberculosis was long considered as being unfavorably influenced by pregnancy; but today experts deny that the influence is signifi-

---

66 *Id.* at 34-53.

67 Pernicious vomiting in pregnancy. See *id.* at 35, 37.

68 Interstitial inflammation of one or both kidneys. See *id.* at 42-44.

69 After pregnancy. See *id.* at 49-51.

70 A condition in which there is overdistention of the air spaces in the lungs or in which there is abnormal presence of air or gas in the body tissues. See *id.* at 44, 75-81.

71 A kind of heart attack. See *id.* at 84.

cant.[72] Since the progressive course of blood-dyscrasias[73] and lymphomas[74] is not altered by termination of the pregnancy, this group of diseases, too, does not constitute a bona fide "indication." Other conditions which are generally unacceptable are Grave's disease,[75] tetany,[76] manic-depressive psychoses, and suicidal threats. The latter are frequently used to obtain permission for abortion by putting the psychiatrist under duress.

Other neurological or psychiatric diseases should only constitute an "indication" when the concurrence of pregnancy and aggravated symptomatology are evident. Thus, epilepsy should only be considered an "indication" when the seizures during pregnancy become so frequent that a status epilepticus[77] can be anticipated. However, diseases such as severe Korsakow-psychosis[78] or schizophrenia are commonly accepted as an "indication." Abortion in the case of diabetes mellitus,[79] cirrhosis of the liver, and ulcerative colitis[80] is only justified if the symptoms are severe, progressive, and therapy-resistant.[81]

C. Diseases of the Reproductive Organs

As to diseases of the uterus itself, a therapeutic abortion for uterine leiomyomata[82] is generally denied. On the other hand,

---

[72] Id. at 65.

[73] An abnormality of the blood condition. See id. at 69.

[74] A group of malignant or premalignant conditions of lymphoid tissue. See id. at 102.

[75] A disease caused chiefly by overproduction of the thyroid hormone, characterized by goiter, etc. See id. at 104.

[76] A disease characterized by intermittent bilateral, painful tonic spasms of the muscles, in children and young adults. See id. at 105.

[77] A condition in which epileptic attacks occur in rapid succession, the patient not regaining consciousness during the interval.

[78] Polyneuritis with loss of memory, a retrograde amnesia. See id. at 130.

[79] A disease in which the metabolism (body utilization) of sugars is greatly impaired, due to the faulty secretion of insulin by the pancreas.

[80] An inflamation of the colon (the large bowel) characterized by ulceration of its lining membrane.

[81] Id. at 137.

[82] A benign tumor consisting largely of smooth muscle cells; these tumors are usually multiple when in the uterus. See id. at 53-65.

there is little controversy if a fetus has to be sacrificed subsequent to surgery for a malignant tumor, discovered during the early stages of pregnancy.[83] At a later stage, radical surgery can be preceded by a Caesarean section.

IV. CONCLUSION

In the German-speaking countries, one basic attitude toward therapeutic abortion may be discerned. Only if the patient's condition deteriorates and she is resistant to therapy should the termination of the pregnancy be allowed, and then only as a last effort to change the course of the patient's disease. Never should this form of treatment mark the beginning of therapeutic efforts, but rather it should constitute a means of last resort. A physician who does not follow this rule becomes subject to punishment. As a matter of course, there are always exceptions to the rule. But if an exception is to be made, it must have justification. It should be emphasized that no medicolegal expert will condemn an honest opinion by a conscientious physician. Such cases rarely come before a tribunal. The instances where typical cases of abortion by physicians are tried in court are those in which pseudo-scientific facts are employed to justify "medical indications" for an unethical procedure.

---

[83] *Id.* at 59.

10

Commentary

Robert E. Hall, M.D.

A few years ago "abortion" was a dirty word. Everyone knew it existed, but almost no one wanted to talk about it. Today it is the most popular of subjects. It is frequently discussed on television and radio, in magazines and newspapers. Whole books are devoted to it.

Why the change? There is no reason to believe that abortion is more widely practiced now than before. Now, however, it is recognized as the universal problem it always has been. Needless to say, this recognition is not an isolated event in social history; rather, it is a small but essential part of the recent broad trend toward the enhancement of individual human dignity. Civil rights, divorce, birth control, homosexuality, police brutality, drug addiction, and baby battering are among the other areas of moral, legal, and social conflict that are now being recognized, scrutinized, and re-evaluated.

In the United States every year there are about four million births, one million spontaneous abortions, and one million induced abortions. Of the million induced abortions, only ten thousand, or 1 per cent, are done in hospitals. The rest, 99 per cent, occur outside of the hospital and therefore outside of the law. Of the ten thousand done within the walls of respectable hospitals, by reputable physicians, probably 90 per cent are not in strict accordance with the law. Surely this situation will be regarded as untenable by the Alaskan as well as the New Yorker, the rich as well as the poor, the Negro and the white man, the Catholic, the Protestant, and the Jew.

224

So there is an abortion problem, and it is finally being reviewed. This book attests to the fact. Of the half dozen recent books on abortion this one is unique in that it presents not the consistent view of a single author but the different views of eleven individual experts. Through this approach the book gains in breadth of perspective and weight of authority. But through this approach it also imputes disproportionate importance to various views and deals with some aspects of abortion more than once and with other significant aspects not at all. Though my following comments are sometimes critical, the absence of comment should also be viewed as praise — or, at least, concurrence. In this introduction I have not hesitated to be frank, nor to express my own opinions and to make personal judgments.

In the first essay in this book, B. James George, Jr., professor of law at the University of Michigan, reviews the current state laws governing abortion. This is a scholarly, comprehensive piece. As a lawyer he points out that although these laws vary greatly, basically in forty-five states they permit abortion to preserve maternal life, and in five states and the District of Columbia they permit abortion to preserve maternal health. None of the laws permits abortion for rape, incest, or the risk of fetal deformity. As a doctor I would point out that all of these laws are so completely incompatible with the practice of modern medicine that they are virtually ignored by most American physicians. In their place the doctors have substituted a code of their own. Because doctors also vary in their views toward abortion (and in their fear of the law), this code is not uniform, but over the years it has assumed a certain recognizable shape.

To begin with, since doctors are dedicated to the protection of health as well as the preservation of life, they *do* perform abortions for health in all fifty states. Such abortions can of course be rationalized by arguing that health and life are inseparable. Ironically, in New Mexico, one of the five states where abortion is permitted for threat to health alone, almost no abortions are done because of the prevailing Catholic influence.

And since doctors try to prevent as well as to alleviate human suffering, they *do* perform abortions when there is a significant risk of fetal deformity, despite the absence of legal sanction in such cases. During the German measles epidemic of 1964, 329 abortions were performed for this reason in New York City hospitals alone. Yet in other, more conservative communities, abortions are denied to women with German measles — and the hospitals which allow them to "their own" patients do not allow them to women from out of town. To illustrate how ludicrous this situation has become: in California, revocation-of-license proceedings, resulting from the concern of prominent Catholic physicians, have been instituted against doctors for having *done* abortions for German measles; whereas, in New Jersey, lawsuits brought by the parents of a child deformed during pregnancy by the German measles virus have been instituted against doctors for *not* having done an abortion.

This medicolegal farce is the result of the impossibility of applying nineteenth-century law to twentieth-century medicine. The dangers of German measles in pregnancy were not known when the abortion laws were passed. Nor were the teachings of Freud or the science of genetics. In fact, the science of medicine was so comparatively primitive in the nineteenth century that the mortality from Caesarean section was over 50 per cent and many abortions were performed then in order to avoid a Caesarean six months later.

In addition to documenting the legal status of abortion, George examines the various alternatives to the status quo and courageously takes his stand among those who would remedy this untenable situation by law. I trust that it is already apparent that I bring a similar bias to this Commentary.

Proposals to liberalize the abortion law are expected to be brought again this year to the New York and California legislatures. Movements are afoot in many other states to do the same. Growing numbers of prestigious professional and lay groups are rising to support such reform. In New York alone the County and State Medical Societies, the Obstetrical Society, the Academy of Medicine, and the Bar Association are among these groups — not to mention the *New York Times*. In California an equally impressive array of reformers has been opposed by elements within the Roman Catholic Church, and the Beilenson bill has been openly attacked from

Catholic pulpits. It is inevitable that these and other similar bills will pass, however, for common sense and secular justice must eventually prevail.

The California and New York bills are nearly identical in that both would permit abortion when pregnancy imposes a risk to the mother's mental or physical health, when pregnancy is complicated by a condition that entails a significant risk of fetal deformity, and when pregnancy is a result of rape or incest (all three stipulations were recommended by the American Law Institute in 1959). Having thus broadened the grounds for abortion, the bills would circumscribe these grounds by requiring that two physicians request the abortion and a five-member medical board pass upon each request, that the abortion be performed in a licensed hospital and reported to a governmental agency, and that cases of rape and incest be reviewed by the district attorney and, if necessary, by a judge.

In my opinion these bills should stop with their definition of permissible abortions. It does not seem proper to me for the law to dictate to the medical profession how to police itself. Most hospitals have already established therapeutic abortion boards for this purpose. Needless to say, they serve to curtail the number of abortions permitted, for, like other committees, these boards tend to be impersonal and dissentient. Nor does it seem proper to me that the district attorney pass upon cases of rape and incest. I would doubt that he is better qualified than the physician to render this judgment, and I would lament the loss of both time and face incurred by the patient in this pursuit. But these are merely my own personal opinions; certainly the new bills are a vast improvement over the old.

Following the one legal essay by George there are three medical essays, by Niswander, Ryan, and Rosen. That the doctors differ somewhat in their proffered prescriptions for curing the abortion ill is understandable and, indeed, these differences will provide the principal source of interest for the reader of these papers; but it goes without saying that three lawyers would differ as widely. It is the physician who is most intimately and most often concerned with abortion in his professional life, however, and for this reason his word should perhaps carry a bit more weight.

Niswander leads off with a straightforward, factual dissertation on the medical aspects of abortion, based largely upon a study of abortion in two Buffalo hospitals conducted by Klein, Randall, and himself. In this study the Buffalo hospitals were pridefully shown to have condoned more abortions than most other institutions reported doing, and this discrepancy was with equal pride ascribed in part to the absence of therapeutic abortion boards in the Buffalo hospitals.

I would quarrel with Niswander on only one point, namely, his perpetuation of Taussig's thirty-year-old claim that five thousand to ten thousand American women die every year as the result of criminal abortions. Whether this statistic was valid in 1936 I do not know, but it certainly is not now. There are in fact fewer than fifteen hundred total pregnancy deaths in this country per annum, very few others could go undetected, and of these fifteen hundred probably no more than a third are the result of abortion. Even the "unskilled" abortionist is evidently more skillful and/or more careful these days. Although criminal abortion is of course to be decried, the demand for its abolition cannot reasonably be based upon thirty-year-old mortality statistics.

In their as-yet-unpublished Buffalo paper, Niswander and his co-authors come out forcefully for abortion law reform. ". . . Changes are occurring in the attitudes of doctors and . . . of society at large toward therapeutic abortion," they write. "The law has not reflected these changes as yet. If good law represents the opinion of the majority, the time for reconsideration of the laws governing therapeutic abortion has arrived." If Niswander alone is less forceful here, nevertheless he implies that his view is unchanged.

Ryan calls clearly for a law permitting abortion "when pregnancy constitutes a grave threat to the life or health of the mother," but he hedges somewhat when rape, incest, illegitimacy, and fetal deformity are involved. Here he would, rightfully, individualize the medical disposition, but he fails specifically to call for a change in the law which would allow this individualization. He is troubled, as we all are, by the fact that fetal risk is rarely certain, but this merely supports the contention made by many of us that the law should let the properly informed patient make this decision herself.

Ryan concedes that a 60 per cent risk of fetal deformity may be unbearable to most parents, but what if the risk is 20 per cent, as it more commonly is in these cases? Forewarned that the risk of bearing a severely deformed infant during this complicated pregnancy is 20 per cent and that during the next, uncomplicated, pregnancy the risk will be 2 per cent, should not the patient be permitted to decide for or against abortion without further interference from medicine or the law?

I would like to correct one small error in the first sentence of Ryan's paper. Contrary to his view, widely held by others, all accredited hospitals do not have therapeutic abortion committees. To cite just one illustrious exception, The Johns Hopkins, should suffice; there are many others. I make this quibbling correction only because, as I have already intimated, with others I question the necessity for these boards and I certainly would not like to see them required by law in the mistaken belief that they are required by medicine.

Rosen is a veteran in the campaign for improved abortion legislation. His classic book on the subject was published twelve years ago. I trust that he is pleased by the progress made since then, at least in the enlightenment phase which must precede the actual legislation. Like most of the others who have dealt with abortion daily, wrestled with its complexities, reached an independent conclusion, and had the courage to voice it, Rosen says, "Mature women, as mature human beings with all the respect and dignity to be accorded mature human beings, should have the right to decide whether or not they wish to carry a specific pregnancy to term. The responsibility for the decision, right or wrong, is already theirs. The extra-legal abortion rate shows that they have already illegally assumed it. It should be theirs *legally*." With equal clarity he concedes, however, that "this is for the future. Our hypocritical attitudes, conscious or unconscious as they are, will not allow of this today. The recommendations of the American Law Institute, if adopted, will help take at least some of the hypocrisy out of our present medical and legal approach to the problem."

I reproduce these words, despite their appearance elsewhere in this book, because they represent not only my conviction but also,

I believe, that of the vast majority of intelligent Americans who have thought through to the core of the matter.

Father Drinan has revealed the classic Catholic position, rarely seen in print. The first and last sentences of his article summarize this position. I would agree with the first and paraphrase it thus: the difference between the Catholic and the non-Catholic view of abortion rests upon their divergent evaluations of the embryo or fetus. I cannot of course agree with the modern Catholic definition of abortion as it is set forth in Drinan's last sentence: "the destruction of [any] innocent human being carried out by other human beings for their own benefit." In the intervening text his arguments are predicated upon the assumption that the fetus is a human being, an assumption with which no non-Catholic scientist can agree. A *potential* human being, yes. A human being if allowed to incubate sufficiently long. But certainly not a human being at the time of abortion, three months after conception, when it is still far from capable of independent survival.

In pursuing this assumption, Drinan asks, "If medical science makes it possible for a fetus to be viable at a time much earlier than the present moment of viability, will the advocates of the abortion of the defective fetus eliminate the distinction that only the nonviable fetus may be aborted?" Projecting this thought forward in the course of human development, he then equates the abortion of "a defective nonviable fetus" with "the taking of life of an innocent but unwanted and troublesome person." This sort of fanciful supposition does not serve to strengthen my confidence in the priest's reasonableness. To be fair, however, I would level the same criticism at Rosen's analogy between abortion and appendectomy. The fetus is no more an appendix than it is an innocent but unwanted and troublesome person.

In trying to establish the "non-issues" between Catholics and non-Catholics, Drinan claims that rape is a non-issue because Catholic canon law permits physicians to take "appropriate medical measures following a rape to prevent the possibility of pregnancy." In fact, of course, no such measures exist.

Drinan labels as "unfortunate" the tendency in abortion-law debates "to polarize the disputants into those who desire to make

America's abortion laws more 'humane' on the one side and Roman Catholics on the other." I regard this as unfortunate too, but not for the reasons of Father Drinan. I regard it as unfortunate because the Catholic in opposing reform would impose his minority will upon the entire public, whereas the non-Catholic in advocating reform would merely make hospital abortion slightly more available to those who voluntarily request it.

In attempting to explain the difference between the Catholic and non-Catholic stands on abortion, Drinan avers that the Catholic Church has "retained, more than the teaching of most other religious denominations, the traditional, and until recently, unchallenged view" that feticide is equivalent to homicide. I would challenge his interpretation of history. Until 1869 most religious denominations, including Catholicism, sanctioned early abortion. (It is true, as Rabbi Jakobovits writes in the next chapter, that all abortions were equated with murder by Pope Sixtus V in 1588, but this edict was rescinded three years later by Pope Gregory XIV and not reinstated until 1869, by Pope Pius IX.) It would seem to me, then, that it is the *other* religious denominations which have retained the traditional view by consistently maintaining that early abortion is *not* murder.

Father Drinan does not provide a precise statement of the Catholic view of abortion or of its historical origin. Fortunately this void is filled in the ensuing chapter by Rabbi Jakobovits. The Rabbi succinctly sets forth the Orthodox Jewish position that "the only indication considered for abortion is a hazard to the mother's life, that otherwise the destruction of an unborn child is a grave offense, although not murder," and that "Jewish law would consider a grave psychological hazard to the mother as no less weighty a reason for abortion than a physical threat." The dichotomy between Catholic and Jewish dogma on abortion is traced, incredibly, to their different interpretations of a five-word phrase in the book of Exodus, the Catholic interpretation having originated, according to the Rabbi, in Tertullian's ignorance of the Hebrew language. Since the unique Catholic position on contraception is widely thought to be based upon an erroneous interpretation of another brief passage in the Bible (the story of Onan), I cannot but marvel at this Church's tenacity in applying the ambiguities of antiquity to the clear-cut issues of today. Not that Catholicism stands alone in its rigidity: according to Jakobovits, Jewish law still "debars children born [as bastards] from marriage with anyone except their like"!

The Orthodox Jewish faith would, then, sanction abortion for the same reasons now permitted by forty-five of our states' laws. Absent from this book is the view of the Reform and Conservative Jews, who vastly outnumber their Orthodox brethren in this country and who regard abortion far more liberally. A recent nation-wide survey shows that abortions for maternal health, rape, and fetal risk would be approved by about 50 per cent of Roman Catholics (!), 60 per cent of Protestants, and 90 per cent of Jews. And most Jews would go much further than that. Rabbi Israel Margolies of New York, an eloquent spokesman for the non-Orthodox, asks, "Is it not time . . . that we matured sufficiently as a people to assert once and for all that the sexual purposes of human beings and their reproductive consequences are not the business of the state, but rather free decisions to be made by husband and wife?"

The last three chapters are devoted to abortion abroad. A lawyer, a statistician, and a doctor describe the Danish system in great detail. First liberalized in 1937 in response to a petition from the working women of Denmark, their law is more liberal than ours but basically no more liberal than the American Law Institute's proposal except for the Danes' consideration of sociomedical factors. As a result about 10 per cent of their pregnant women apply for legal abortion and, after intensive screening and counseling and reviewing, about half of these applications are approved. In round numbers, one hundred thousand Danish women become pregnant every year, four thousand are legally aborted, and fifteen thousand are illegally aborted. The practice of criminal abortion is not eliminated, in other words, but the Danes at least have made a conscientious effort to provide abortion when medically and/or sociologically indicated and their four-to-one ratio of illegal to legal abortions looks fairly respectable in comparison to our ratio of one hundred-to-one. Probably this is the most to be hoped for without total legalization.

The fate of the pregnancies of the turned-down applicants is noteworthy: only 16 per cent were illegally aborted, yet among the children born under these circumstances a "considerably higher" incidence of maladjustment was encountered than among originally wanted children. This latter observation may cast some doubt upon the validity of Rabbi Jakobovits' assertion that "some children may be born unwanted, but there are no unwanted children aged five or ten years."

Leopold Breitenecker, dean of the University of Vienna Medical School, and his son, Rudiger Breitenecker, Assistant Medical Examiner of the State of Maryland, combine forces to present the abortion picture in Austria, Germany, and Switzerland. They conclude that in these "German-speaking countries, one basic attitude toward therapeutic abortion may be discerned," namely that abortion should be performed only as a last resort. Yet in actual fact the life-health-and-heredity abortion law in West Germany is strictly interpreted and vigorously enforced; a similar law in East Germany is loosely interpreted and laxly enforced; the life-and-health law of Austria is being rewritten to approve abortions for social reasons; and the life-and-health law in Switzerland is so broadly interpreted that there are about as many abortions there as births. I do not agree that this represents consistent Germanic thought or policy.

Essentially there are three types of abortion laws in the world today, although the interpretation of similar laws varies a bit from country to country. (1.) In Japan and most of the Communist countries abortion is permissible for very broadly interpreted social conditions. As a result, for all practical purposes abortion is practiced on demand of the pregnant woman. Approximately one-third to one-half of all pregnancies in these countries end in abortion. (2.) In Sweden, Norway, Finland, and Iceland the laws have been liberalized along lines similar to those described for Denmark in this book. As a result, approximately 5 per cent of pregnancies are thus terminated and the problem of illegal abortion persists. (3.) In England, Western Europe, and South America the laws remain stringent, as in the United States. Approximately 0.2 per cent of pregnancies are thus terminated, and the practice of criminal abortion is rampant. The laws of the countries in the first two groups were passed in the twentieth century; the laws of the countries in the third group were passed in the nineteenth century.

One immutable truth emerges through this confusing maze: if an individual pregnant woman is determined to get an abortion, she will do so whether it is lawful or not. And preferable as contraception is to abortion, no matter how effective and how available contraceptive measures become, there will always be unwanted pregnancies and hence abortions. In the world today there are an estimated 30 million induced abortions and 115 million live births, a ratio of one to four. Countries with legalized abortion have sanctioned unchangeable social custom. Countries with liberal abortion laws have legitimized current medical practice. Countries with stringent abortion laws have buried their heads in the sands of time.

Index